Non-Nuclear

Futures: The Case for

an Ethical Energy Strategy

Amory B Lovins
John H Price

HARPER COLOPHON BOOKS
Harper & Row, Publishers
New York, Cambridge, Hagerstown, Philadelphia, San Francisco
London, Mexico City, São Paulo, Sydney

CB/ 16348 £4.30 6.81

the text of this book is printed
on 100% recycled paper

A hardcover edition of this book is co-published by Friends of the Earth International and Ballinger Publishing Company. It is here reprinted by arrangement.

Contents

List of Tables

List of Figures

Foreword

If atomic energy could be made safe, would it provide an ethical and economic solution to the world's energy problems? This is a question two physicists have asked themselves—one an American and the other an Australian, as they worked together in the office of Friends of the Earth Ltd, in London. What Amory Lovins and John Price have to say in reply is of worldwide importance and applicability in arriving at non-nuclear energy decisions that humanity can live with. If too many human and natural resources are preempted for the wrong decision, the right decision is likely to be placed beyond our reach. It can be placed there disastrously soon if an electric panic bloodies the planning process.

Call it the environmental crisis or the energy crisis, the ingredients are the same, and nations are floundering for solutions. Finite resources have been spent as if there were no future to worry about. Suddenly the future has arrived, accompanied by shortages, inflationary pressures, and unemployment. People tend in time of trouble to forget solutions and to assess blame. Someone must be to blame for not having discovered vanished resources faster or developed the technology to use what's left more rapidly. Or the system of government and corporate management must be wrong, or the people who urge conservation and warn about the limits to growth. Hardly anyone wants to admit that we and Old Mother Hubbard have something in common.

In the United States, therefore, leaders in government, the energy industries, and in part of the labor movement collaborate in advocating a course of Strength Through Exhaustion. The US, now vulnerable to the whims of foreign suppliers, wants to solve its problem by using up energy faster still. It proposes to invest vast sums of talent and capital on this nonsolution and threatens the suppliers as well. Its concurrent nonsolution to the problem of dependence upon OPEC for oil is to deplete the last US reserves, onshore and offshore, and to construct enough supertankers, superports, and superrefineries to use up OPEC oil faster too. The third US nonsolution to the problem of fossil-fuel exhaustion is to devise assorted shortcuts toward a nuclear future, letting safety depend upon faith, hope, and charity—faith that technology can carry on where miracles leave off, hope that no one will suffer if other public needs are sidetracked, and unprecedented charity toward the overextended atomic-industrial complex. Moreover, we hide from ourselves the fact that it is the same atom, whether in a fist or a glove. Having already honored the first man to split the atom, we all race to see who will be the last. We are out to outdo King Midas. What he touched became gold; what we touch must turn to energy—inedible, unbreatheable, unwearable joules.

Then what is the US solution? The obvious one: to use less energy, and let a little sunshine back in. Everybody else does, and so did we. We can do it again, starting at the most sensible time: now. We can be confident that more people will find good things to do, and fewer machines bad things to do, when we turn off the energy that was diverted to dull labor-saving devices; it will be more demanding of human resources to put a land and cities back together than it was to take them apart in the first place.

Friends of the Earth Energy Papers are published to help persuade industry, government, labor, and the public to try. We want nations to achieve a sustainable economy, one that lives within its environmental budget. It is time to stop digging deep into environmental capital and passing the loss on to the future generations who are not here to vote no. FOE's first Energy Paper was an every-other daily reporting on reactor safety hearings held by the AEC in Bethesda, Maryland, in August 1972. Our next was a sobering book on the glaring inadequacies of the untested emergency core cooling system of those reactors. The third was a technical and sobering book about the myriad problems in the nuclear-fuel-cycle labyrinth. Then came *Cry Crisis! Rehearsal in Alaska*, exposing the evils of exponentialism in energy growth of all kinds, in language readily understood by all. *World Energy Strategies: Facts, Issues, and Options* is a major contribution by Amory Lovins, and handles a critically important technical synthesis in an enjoyable and informing way that governments ought to heed promptly. There have already been several printings of the work in Sweden.

Now, in *Non-Nuclear Futures*, Mr Lovins and Dr Price describe for the intelligent energy executive some ethical and economic matters that should no longer escape his attention. The book can help intelligent, concerned citizens correct the adamant executive's failure to take notice. We invite all readers to do some of the rate-and-magnitude exercises Mr Lovins speaks of—and note the unattainable amount of capital needed for the nuclear dream, so unattainable as to be ridiculous, yet nevertheless being sought, ridiculously, by governments and excess-energy advocates almost everywhere because they have not bothered to do their sums.

To a person who has been in the conservation business for forty years, a noneconomic fact transcends all others. If, because world leaders refuse to do their arithmetic, the reactor-building program they are forcing actually comes into being, all in the name of peaceful atomic energy, then the year 2001 would find humanity plagued with machines that would be producing each year an inventory of high-level radioactivity equivalent to what several million Hiroshima-type bombs would unleash if they exploded. Fourteen years later, with a 5 percent growth rate continuing, the world would be in trouble twice as deep. Catastrophe would ensue if even a minor part of the inventory escaped control, and economic disaster would likewise be in store if the reactors were switched off. Scare talk? What is scary is silence when an alarm needs sounding.

The environmental view, then, is that the sooner the threat of energy addiction is ended, the better. It goes without saying that there will be no energy sold or bought on a dead planet, and the nuclear experiment could kill this one. FOE welcomes help in its program to persuade people that enough is enough. Since extirpatory growth must end sometime, it ought to be stopped by people, while they and the earth still have some roots left. We are pleased with the force of the authors' demonstration that there are such strong economic and ethical arguments for a strategy that is in humanity's own self-interest.

David R Brower
President, FOE International

Introduction: Non-Nuclear Futures

In a recent speech to the European Nuclear Society, Dr Dixy Lee Ray, former Chairman of the US Atomic Energy Commission (USAEC), declared that opposition to nuclear power stems from fear. This may be correct. If nuclear power were perceived as benign and innocuous rather than threatening and dangerous, probably fewer people would argue against it on other grounds—for example, that it is unnecessary, impractical, uneconomic, or socially inappropriate. Moreover, some people's fear of nuclear power may rest, or appear to rest, on detailed assumptions that are technically unsound; proponents of nuclear power, seizing on this, may be tempted to infer that this occasional defect is universal and, conversely, that there is no sound and defensible basis for anyone to fear the technology.

It is apparently such an inference that led Dr Ray to state further that fear can be dispelled only by knowledge. Evidently the more Dr Ray learns about nuclear power, the more reassured she becomes. But many scientists, including ourselves, have found instead that the more they learn about nuclear power, the more frightened they become. Their fear rests not on ignorance but on a body of knowledge—amply buttressed by the professional literature—that has presumably not come to Dr Ray's attention or that she prefers to interpret as inconsequential. Presenting and assessing this knowledge in a way that is technically sound but is also intelligible to those of modest technical background is the purpose of the first part of this book. The second part amplifies a specific and novel policy question, namely, whether the energy benefits claimed for nuclear programs are real or illusory.

Public and governmental attitudes toward nuclear power in most industrial countries seem to be evolving in a pattern that many scientists know from their own experience. At first, one's knowledge of nuclear power is superficial—derived mainly from the non-technical public-relations materials circulated by its more zealous promoters, and from the presumption that the peaceful atom must be a good thing, or else so much money and effort would not be spent on it. Gradually, as one's knowledge of the technical and, even more important, of the social and ethical problems of nuclear power expands, one realizes that there are substantial problems, but one presumes that they are soluble by sufficiently careful engineering. This opinion prevails today among most governments, especially those which have committed much money and prestige to nuclear power and do not wish to think that they might have been wrong. Finally, though, as one becomes aware of the real gravity and difficulty of the problems, of the disturbing but promptly forgotten failures of many engineering measures taken to try to solve these problems in the past, and of the limits of engineering solutions to problems of human nature, one starts to realize that the problems might be too difficult to solve. For us this realization came only in the past few years, and for many, the same perception arrived even more recently.

Why has it taken so long for so many scientists to run this course of complacency, then qualified optimism turning to worry, and then alarm? First, because we really hoped that nuclear power would live up to the early promises made for it and justify the immense talent and effort devoted to it; second, because we were rather naïve about the intense social pressures, the resulting group behaviour, and, in some instances, the lack of good faith that can exist within institutions committed to promoting a technology; third, because public-interest science and law were still in their infancy, so we lacked independent scientists to study the problems and independent lawyers to devise and use the legal tools needed to extract suppressed information; and fourth, because the very possibility that insoluble trans-scientific problems might exist was such a new idea that it took several already-classic papers, such as that published by Hannes Alfvén in 1972, to make many of us realize that care, ingenuity, dedication, and money were no longer enough to solve all problems.

This familiar sequence of complacency, uncertainty, and disquiet or outright opposition is reflected in the evolution of public opinion today. Many people (though fewer each week) neither know nor care about these problems. Some other people are aware of at least some of the problems but they religiously share the engineer's faith that he can solve them even though they are quite different from the problems of keeping an airplane or a building or a bridge from falling down. And some other people suspect or believe, as the first part of this book argues in detail, that the engineer's faith in nuclear safety is both unfounded in principle and unattainable in practice: indeed, that no matter what low level of risk society may somehow deem "acceptable", the nuclear engineer cannot be certain of attaining it without having utterly infallible people working within a society of unprecedented homogeneity and stability through countless millenia.

A transcending thesis of this book is that the most important parts of the debate about nuclear power are not technical disputes and are the legitimate province of every citizen, whether technically trained or not. In the past, nuclear experts often said that we must trust them because these matters are too complex for laymen to understand. Such statements worried laymen who thought that wise democracies do not take decisions that laymen cannot understand. But the laymen are now discovering, to their relief, that though responsible participation in the nuclear debate may be easier with a little technical knowledge, too much expertise tends to obscure rather than illuminate the basic questions at issue, for they are questions not of nuclear engineering but of ethics, history, psychology, politics, and plain common sense, and are thus the kinds of questions that the political system is uniquely suited to address.

Accordingly, this book tries to impart not a working competence in nuclear engineering, but an adequate and closely focused knowledge of the main technical, ethical, social, economic, and policy issues that people should consider in making political decisions about nuclear power. Through a combination of highly condensed text, specialized appendices, extensive references, and notes containing miniature essays on technical points, we have tried to serve the needs both of technically oriented readers and of concerned laymen who are willing to read carefully. Whether we have succeeded in informing both kinds of readers while confusing neither is for you to judge; but our experience with several preliminary editions leads us to hope that we have struck a useful balance between the needs of our several audiences.

(Writing for both sides of the Atlantic, we compromise on orthography: spelling is British except for units of measure and the word "program", punctuation is mid–Atlantic, money is in US dollars or pounds sterling. Units are generally those of the Système International and are explained in the text where necessary, as are technical terms. The symbol *** represents ellipsis of a substantial section of the text quoted, or reversal of the original order of the excerpts quoted on either side of the symbol.)

As is explained in *World Energy Strategies: Facts, Issues, and Options*, nuclear issues cannot be considered in isolation from a complex tangle of broader issues of energy and social policy, any more than automobiles can be considered in isolation from the wider patterns and values of human settlements and mobility. To do so would be a common but serious error. The most important and difficult questions of energy policy are not primarily technical or economic but rather social and ethical, and cannot be properly framed by people whose vision is purely technical.

Which energy policy makes sense for a given society depends on what sort of society it is to be, what values are important in it, where people want to live, what they want to eat, and what they want to get out of their lives and to leave behind for their children. All these things can to a large extent be chosen through the political and economic process. But people cannot choose options that they do not perceive, and often cannot perceive options that they have not experienced. One job of the energy strategist is thus to present and assess some alternatives, as carefully and credibly as possible, with enough imagination to see how wide the range of choices really is. People suffering from a three-day week in Britain, or going without hot water in Stockholm, or deprived of their accustomed air-conditioning in sealed New York buildings, may believe (or be led to believe) that they are having a taste of life in a low-energy society; and this may be true. But it may equally be true that it would not be like that at all—that disruption and privation are instead a taste of life in a vulnerable high-energy society. The energy strategist must not only develop tools to help the political process to explore such choices; he must also encourage a fundamental reëxamination of the social role of energy, of the difference between demand and need, and of the possibility of achieving liberal social goals without rapid, or even any, growth in the rate of consumption of primary energy stocks.

Our energy choices have traditionally rested on a series of self-fulfilling prophecies—forecasts based on correlation, not causality. Our forecasters have assumed that rapid energy growth is essential for a healthy economy and full employment. Yet there is no evidence that this assumption is true; indeed, in the only country (USA) where it has been carefully studied, it appears to be untrue. So entrenched is the dogma nevertheless that most people in the countries with the grossest national products find it hard to imagine what life would be like with more efficient use of energy but with the levels of primary energy use that prevailed only a few years ago. For example, some Danish economists say that a civilization in Denmark using only half as much electricity as now would be impossible; but one existed in 1965, when Danes were at least half as civilized as now. What would 1965 have been like with greater efficiency and more equitable distribution for more rational ends? Surely it could have been more agreeable than life in Denmark today. Likewise, what would life in the United States be like at per-capita energy levels vaguely comparable to those of, say, 1910 (half the present US value, or about the same as the present UK value), but with much better distribution, with our best modern technologies of energy use, and with some important but not very energy-intensive amenities such as modern medicine and telecommunications? These are the sorts of questions we should be asking now. No energy future, least of all a future deriving from "business as usual", will be free of social change, but we have to ask what kinds of social change we want. Low-energy futures can (but need not) be normative and pluralistic, whereas high-energy futures are bound to be coercive and to offer less scope for social diversity and individual freedom.

Fundamental to any discussion of energy alternatives is a choice—usually tacit but nonetheless real—of personal values. The values that make a high-energy society work are all too apparent today. The values that could make a lower-energy society work are not new; they are in the societal attic, and could be dusted off and recycled. They include thrift, simplicity, diversity, neighbourliness, craftsmanship, and humility. They also include the clear thinking needed to avoid a prevalent confusion between growth and distribution (the "let them eat growth" theory), between movement and progress, and between costs and benefits. For example, many people today count personal mobility as a benefit even when mobility is reduced to the involuntary traffic made necessary by the existence of cars and by the settlement patterns which cars create. If, in order to live in the utopian slurbia, we work in order to buy a car without which we cannot get to work, the net benefit of the transaction may be insubstantial. Ivan Illich has calculated an illustrative number, and whether or not the number is correct, the idea is undoubtedly important: that the average American man drives about 7500 miles a year in his car, but to do this and to earn the money to finance it requires his spending about 1600 hours a year, which works out to about 4½ miles an hour, and we know another way to go 4½ miles an hour.

We are learning, increasingly and irreversibly, that many of the things we had been counting as the benefits of affluence are really remedial costs, incurred in the pursuit of unstated intangible benefits which might be obtainable in other ways without those costs. This perception seems to be gaining ground in many industrial societies where consumer ephemerals are losing their allure and more people are wishing that advertising copywriters would go back to being poets. Conspicuous consumption—including its ultimate form, war—is not our only or necessarily our best path to happiness. We need instead to have, as Herman Daly puts it, growth in things that count, rather than in things that are merely countable. Such discussion of values and goals may seem fuzzy and unscientific; but it is the beginning and end of any energy policy, and must be explicitly considered if policy is to do what is expected of it.

No matter what patterns of energy use are considered desirable, the best energy source is that energy which is spared by not being wasted on inefficiency or nonessentials. Increasing energy supply in the usual ways tends to be slow, costly, risky, and of temporary benefit, whereas decreasing demand tends to be comparatively fast, cheap, safe, and of permanent benefit (but unpopular with energy-mongers). It is hard to find a method of saving energy that does not also save money. For example, from the work of the Energy Policy Project (EPP) of the Ford Foundation it can be shown under conservative economic assumptions that the US could afford to spend, on "technical fixes" to save energy, about $200 000 million initially plus $200 million per day—and that would still cost less than increasing supply by the amount which would otherwise be projected. What is more, one would still have the fuel but not the environmental and political problems of extracting and using it. In short, saving a watt is nearly always cheaper than increasing supply by a watt.

Three simple facts from Britain suggest useful questions for all countries, and suggest too why energy shrinkage—not just energy stability—may be quite feasible. First, the energy needed to produce a unit of value in the British economy varies at least 600-fold depending on what good or service is being produced; so how much energy it takes to run the country depends very much on the shape of the economy. Second, since 1900 the gross UK energy consumption has doubled (it has grown so little because a lot of coal used to be inefficiently burned in open grates), but in those 75 years the energy at the point of end use has only gone up by half (or by a third per capita); the rest has been swallowed up by the energy industry itself and never reached the consumer. Gross energy consumption for heating houses grew rapidly, but the heat grew scarcely at all. (In the US, analogously, half the energy saved by the EPP "technical fixes" would have gone to fuel the fuel industries.) The largest energy consumer in Britain—the energy industry—could consume far less if its technologies were more appropriate. Finally, if British end-use energy is classified not by economic sector but by physical type, the very approximate result is: 55 percent low-temperature heat, 25 percent high-temperature heat, 15 percent mechanical work, and only about 5 percent requiring special forms such as electricity. These rough estimates might be 5 to 10 percent off either way, but they cannot possibly bear any sensible relation to the thermodynamics of the energy systems we are now building, where for "convenience" we use our highest-grade energy resources—often in the upgraded form of extremely high-quality electricity—to perform low-grade functions such as space heating, thus guaranteeing that most of the original primary energy will be thrown away.

Once we decide how much energy we really need, want, and can afford to have, we must consider the supply patterns that various constraints—environmental, geopolitical, sociotechnical, economic, and so on—will allow us. Instead of blindly following incremental ad-hocracy in the hope that it will lead in the right direction, we need to ask where we want to be a long time hence, and then to ask what we must avoid now in order to get there. This approach immediately eliminates many short-term policies that might otherwise seem attractive within politicians' limited time horizons. Moreover, we are now entering an era when discontinuities and instabilities probably matter more than the fragments of trend in between them; yet our forecasters still cling to extrapolation of a surprise-free world. We are therefore foreclosing certain valuable options by committing scarce money, skills, and time, which is not recyclable, to other options.

The implications of these ideas for our future energy supplies can be stated concisely: two main policy paths for the rich countries are now rapidly diverging, and we must jump for one or the other. The first is high-energy, nuclear, centralized, electric; the second is lower-energy, fission-free, decentralized, less electrified, softer-technology based on energy income. If we choose the first of these paths, we shall have to continue spending on fast breeder reactors money and skills that could instead develop all the non-nuclear energy options, especially the soft ones, to commercial usefulness, so they will not get developed. They are really an option only if we recognize them now.

It is true that the soft energy technologies take much time and money to develop and deploy. But nuclear power requires so much time and money that the softer policy path leads to the same place (or rather a nicer place) at similar or better rates and costs. The more modest scale and lesser technical complexity of the soft energy options makes them much quicker in principle to demonstrate and build than the huge high-technology devices on which we now rely:

for example, scaling up a fast breeder reactor to commercial size requires several stages, each of which is likely to take the best part of a decade and billions of dollars, whereas if the basic building-block is an assembly of selective-black solar panels perhaps the size of a house roof, the corresponding requirements are likelier to be a few months and thousands of dollars.

To illustrate the danger of not realizing how wide our range of choices really is, consider Japan, widely regarded as the industrial country most desperately short of energy and land. A line of technically sound reasoning suggests that Japan can attain an economy of energy income (as opposed to energy capital, or fuels) directly—without an intervening stage of reliance on nuclear fission—merely by devoting her resources to the former rather than the latter.

There is probably less scope for energy conservation in Japanese industry than in that of many other countries; for example, the remarkable savings made in the Japanese steel industry can only be made there once. There is, however, much scope for redeployment of Japanese economic activity towards light and service industry, with some existing and nearly all future heavy industry being exported to countries that want it. Efficiency can also be much increased in the residential, commercial, and electricity-generating sectors. Japanese policy is now moving in these directions (as well as towards hidden energy imports in the form of materials rather than overt energy imports in the form of fuels). But what of energy sources? With respect to almost all the unconventional sources, Japan is the best situated of any major industrial country—and doesn't even know it. Japan is at low latitude, and receives much energy from the sun at all seasons. Japan has exceptional on- and offshore wind resources. Japan is in an excellent geothermal (and, if these technologies prove attractive, seathermal and wave) zone. And Japanese settlement patterns are peculiarly well suited to converting domestic, agricultural, and industrial wastes to clean fuels.

It is not hard to calculate the sort of energy economy that might be constructed from a diverse mix of presently available soft technologies of these types, taking due account of land-use and other constraints and assuming that most of the present coal and hydroelectric production can be maintained. Conservative calculations of this sort, paying special attention to the thermodynamic matching of energy sources with energy uses, suggest that unconventional sources of the types now available, together with wide-ranging energy conservation, can then give Japan a sustainable energy future within a few decades. Meanwhile, of course, Japan must rely on Persian Gulf oil, Indonesian and Australian coal, Indonesian and South China Sea oil, and belt-tightening; but nuclear power could not improve this medium-term outlook significantly faster than could the program suggested here, and, as the second part of this book shows, nuclear power would probably even make it worse.

Those who believe that traditional Japanese patterns of rapid energy growth must be extrapolated decades hence, and that Japan must, in the next three to five decades, find a new long-term source of large blocks of industrial energy, may say that only nuclear power can then suffice. This, too, is incorrect. For example, at rates and costs comparable or superior to those of nuclear power, Japan could lease some of the Aleutian Islands, build there some high-velocity aero-turbines, and ship hydrogen to Japan. We are not formally advocating this idea; but it suggests that if Japan wants to stay energy-intensive in the long run, there is a way to do it (and we can think of others) that is technically feasible, that on present knowledge looks economically acceptable, and that the Japanese Government has not studied. There is a manifestly unsound alternative: installing, in a densely populated and politically volatile earthquake zone, an unforgiving technology with enormous capacity for devastating accidents and for the deliberate or inadvertent spread of nuclear weapons.

Similar calculations could be done for, say, the Scandinavian countries, where the large installed hydroelectric capacity of Norway and Sweden could meet all the region's electrical needs if there were modest conservation efforts and if heat pumps were substituted for resistive space-heating in some areas. Even in the Scandinavian climate and latitudes, diffuse solar collection by sophisticated devices already developed could supplement conventional space-heating with surprising speed and could take up nearly all the space-heating load (roughly half of total energy demand) by early in the next century. Windpower offers a significant decentralized, and probably non-electrical, resource throughout the region, particularly with the new vertical-axis designs: there has been much technical progress since the decline of the Danish wind-power economy. The many wastes from agriculture, forestry, and cities could be readily and efficiently converted to methanol and methane. Scandinavian industry, including the auto industry, provides the technical resources needed for complete self-sufficiency in designing, mass-producing, and even exporting energy hardware, including transitional technologies such as fluidized-bed combustors and gas turbines (especially those that offer neighbourhood-centred district heating) and heat pumps. Excellent research in these areas is seeping into official consciousness and will soon be reflected in policy.

Two common threads run through all these examples. The first is that by prompt redirection of national resources, the fission economy can generally be not merely superseded promptly but bypassed altogether. The second is that in order to realize in time that this is possible, one must imagine where one wants to be in fifty years or so and then work backwards to see what must be done when and what must not be done at all. This method reveals the existence of radically different policy options which would be completely invisible to anyone working forward in time: such a person could only see in hindsight, say thirty years from now, that he might have implemented certain policies if he had thought of them twenty years earlier before it was too late.

Too often the present method of energy planning consists of regretting opportunities missed, options foreclosed, necessary steps not seen soon enough to take them. This approach is not likely to yield sustainable energy systems that will fulfill our social goals. It is, however, the method implicitly relied upon by many proponents of nuclear power who follow a fallacious argument similar to that of Hans Bethe and Alvin Weinberg: that since (1) coal, fission, and solar technologies are the only obviously feasible long-term sources of large amounts of energy, but (2) the solar technologies can allegedly play no significant role during this century, therefore (3) we must now undertake a huge commitment to fission and coal. This argument ignores the obvious possibility that the more intelligent and sophisticated use of fossil fuels, particularly coal, can form a fission-free bridge well into the next century, by which time the solar technologies can be fully developed and deployed.

Modern thinking about energy strategy requires us to examine "rate-and-magnitude problems", the practical constraints on how fast we can do how much. Rate-and-magnitude arithmetic can be done (but too seldom is) on the back of an envelope. On a global scale, for example, if energy use increases 5 percent a year and if we commission one large reactor (1000 electrical megawatts) per day, starting now, then in 2000 we shall have spent approximately 10 current US GNP-years on reactors—*and we must still get most of our primary energy from fossil fuels and must burn them more than twice as fast as now.*

The same is true on a national scale: after thirty years and many billions of dollars worth of research and development, nuclear power in the US has probably just passed firewood as a national energy source, for national energy use is so prodigious that we can scarcely catch up, especially if it keeps growing. Likewise, if Danish energy use and electricity use grow by 3 percent a year and 4 percent a year respectively (both far slower than historical rates), and if a major nuclear program (one large reactor every other year) is begun now, then in 2000 nearly as much fossil fuel will be burned in power stations as is now used for this purpose, and Denmark—the Japan of the West—will still be more than 90 percent dependent on imported fuels, burned at nearly twice the present rate, for her national energy supplies.

Here is another way to look at rate-and-magnitude problems. In any industrial country (except a few unusual ones like Norway) the exponential growth of energy supply has been made up of successively added curves, each initially exponential, and each introduced as the previous one—representing the previous "new" energy source—matures or begins to falter. In such a system, each source must be capable of faster growth than the preceding one. The traditional succession of sources—wood, coal, oil, gas—permits this because of its trend towards increasing technical simplicity per unit of output, culminating in gas, whose relative simplicity at large scale has let it account for about 2/3 of US energy growth in the past few decades. What, then, is the next big source, simpler than gas and therefore capable of even faster sustained growth? It certainly isn't nuclear fission, which is far too complex. Both rate-and-magnitude constraints and the other side of that logistical coin—the net-energy constraints discussed in the second part of this book—lead one irresistibly to conclude that the comparatively simple, low-technology, decentralized, non-electrical energy technologies make the most sense.

These technologies are small-scale. What matters, though, is not aggregate or even unit energy production, but ability to meet the energy needs of people in particular circumstances. Indeed, the energy technologies that most people in the world need are those which perform basic end-uses such as heating, cooking, lighting, and pumping; and these can be done admirably by simple devices using sun, wind, and organic conversion. These are not glamorous technologies, are ideal for poor as well as rich countries, and have no military applications, so people seriously interested in developing them tend to receive every assistance short of actual help. Moreover, so long as the main industrial countries remain officially committed to the equally exciting-to-develop and far more difficult fission technologies (which are also not so useful to poor countries), many first-rate technologists will be reluctant to commit their careers to developing the soft options.

Of the criteria mentioned above for practical energy systems—small-scale, simple, low-technology (which does not mean unsophisticated), decentralized, non-electrical—the last is perhaps the most controversial and, to thoughtful analysts, the most obvious, because electricity is the costliest form of energy to make, store, or transport in bulk. Electrification of most end-uses in an industrial economy is simply too expensive for any major country outside the Persian Gulf to afford it. Building the capacity needed to deliver a unit of energy to the consumer now requires approximately twenty times as much capital investment with a typical nuclear-electric system as with, say, a North Sea oil system (including pipelines, refineries, distribution, etc), and this in turn is several times as capital–intensive as most traditional oil and coal systems.

The social implications of centralized electrification, too, are as disquieting as its capital intensity: it is the most complex and slowest kind of technology to deploy, is remotely administered by a highly bureaucratized technical elite with little personal commitment to their clients, is vulnerable to large-scale and extremely expensive technical mistakes and failures, and is entirely at the mercy of a few people. (A handful of power engineers can turn off a country, and a single rifleman can black out most cities.) Finally, very few end-uses of energy in modern societies actually require electricity, and they require little of it at that.

Some people have a remarkable facility for ignoring these obvious features of centralized electrification. Some people still think that nuclear capacity in, say, the United States will increase about 20-fold by the year 2000 and that the equivalent of the total present US generating capacity will then be built every 29 months. (The USAEC was still predicting in December 1974 that US electricity demand would increase 15-fold by 2020.) Some people think that only the most complex, costly, unforgiving, and vulnerable major energy technology known is capable of doing this. There is no accounting for what some people think.

The special environmental and social risks of fission technology need not be previewed here. These risks include not only the obvious hazards of accident and sabotage, or of failure to contain radioactive wastes, but also the hazards of nuclear violence and coercion through misuse of toxic or explosive materials in the nuclear fuel cycle. Proposed safeguards are likely to be repressive or ineffective or (probably) both. The profound and permanent social commitments and controls that adoption of nuclear power requires deserve special note: persistent nuclear materials may damage social diversity and personal freedom as much, if not for so long, as they damage the wider biological environment. Moreover, in our increasingly inter-dependent and unstable world, the mere creation of atomic-bomb materials endangers everyone. Robert Heilbroner thinks that some poor countries may resort to nuclear blackmail or "wars of redistribution"; and it is conceivable that some poor countries which have great economic needs and no other assets might be tempted to sell bomb materials or designs to other countries with great assets and military ambitions. Obviously, a decision by any one country to forego and discourage nuclear power will marginally diminish, not solve outright, a worldwide problem of this sort. Exceptionally, such a decision by the United States in the next few years could virtually eliminate the problem everywhere, while technological dependence is still great and technological metastasis small. Yet such a principled decision by even the smallest country could have a profound political impact everywhere.

Social and political innovation is unfortunately a less obvious element of energy policy than is technological innovation. But what is most often lacking in the latter is a sense of why one wants a particular technology. Is it considered a stopgap, a mainstay, or a permanent solution? Part of a diverse mix or a single panacea? Transitional or final? Something to do while we look for something better, make-work for a powerful industry, or a result of institutional momentum and political sloth? Is it capable of doing what we want, when we want it? Can we afford to pay for it? Have we hedged our bets in case it doesn't work? Is it a worthy way to invest the fossil fuels needed to build it? Does it supply energy in the forms and patterns in which people need it? These crucial questions are seldom asked.

Consider, for example, the two main classes of energy technologies (other than nuclear fission) which are generally regarded as permanent or semipermanent supply options: terrestrial nuclear fusion, and its extensively tested, remotely sited sister—solar conversion in its numerous direct and indirect forms. Terrestrial nuclear fusion has the same problems as fission except that the risks are smaller by perhaps tens or thousands of times and are somewhat different in kind. The radioactive inventories and leftovers may well be too big for fusion to be an attractive energy source, though they, like the potential fuel supply, would be more attractive than for fission. Fusion technology is probably (not certainly) feasible, is bound to be complex and costly, will place heavy demands on some scarce resources, can be used to make atomic-bomb materials, is several decades behind fission in its development, and once available could be demonstrated and deployed at similar rates. More to the point, though—and one that is often overlooked in purely technical discussions—is that fusion is probably a very ingenious way to do something that we don't really want to do, namely to find yet another slow-to-deploy, complex, costly, centralized, high-technology way to generate electricity. Directors of two national fusion programs have recently told me that if fusion turns out to be a rather dirty energy source, as they half-expect, then knowing us we'll have put all our eggs in that basket and we'll use it anyway; whereas if it turns out to be a marvellous clean source as advertised, we'll lack the discipline to use it with restraint and the resulting release of heat will change global climate unfavourably and irreversibly; so, they conclude, on a pragmatic view of the wisdom of future decisionmakers, we should forget fusion and go straight to solar technology, because we know it works *and because it limits the amount of mischief we can get into.*

These are only two of the many advantages of diverse and decentralized solar technologies. Some others are that solar technology is reliable, not easy to disrupt, sufficient for our needs, simple, low-technology, transferable, flexible with respect to cultural and settlement patterns, safe, with minimal environmental and climatic impacts, has free fuel, tends to resist commercial monopoly, has a high thermodynamic source potential ($5500°K$), is well matched to common energy end-uses, reduces international tensions arising from uneven distribution of fuels and of high technologies, is a spur to decentralization and local self-sufficiency, and helps to redress the severe energy imbalance between temperate and tropical regions. And these benefits are not impossibly remote. Technical assessments by expert panels of the US National Science Foundation/National Aeronautics and Space Administration in 1972, of the USAEC in 1973, and of the Federal Energy Administration in 1974 broadly agreed that a significant fraction of, say, US energy supply could be taken up by diverse solar technologies (including wind and organic conversion) within this century. For example, the FEA estimate, which was regarded as realistic, would have direct and indirect solar collection supplying about 5 percent of all US primary energy needs in 1990 and 31 percent in 2000 if the US followed the "Technical Fix" scenario of the Energy Policy Project; and with the EPP "Zero Energy Growth" scenario (which, despite its name, would entail about 33 percent energy growth to 2000 with steadily increasing efficiency of use as well), the solar fraction would be about 39 percent in 2000.* Starting in the 1990s, these solar supply estimates

---

*Since most of the soft energy systems would meet principal end-use energy needs directly at high efficiency, whereas roughly half the gross input to conventional energy systems is lost before it reaches the consumer, the real impact of the soft sources in meeting national energy needs would be substantially larger than these percentages suggest.

considerably exceed the USAEC's most sanguine projections of the contributions of nuclear fission: these presume 1400 thousand electrical megawatts of installed nuclear capacity in 2000, but even if the reactors sent out 70 percent of their theoretical capacity as projected instead of the 55 percent observed so far, they would produce only three-quarters as much energy as the FEA's solar projection for 2000. Indeed, the USAEC's WASH–1535 (December 1974) conceded that in 2020 new non-fission technologies could supply five times as much *electricity* as the US now uses. In short, relatively simple and small-scale solar technologies, starting decades after fission, could quickly overtake it, and within a few decades could meet virtually all our energy needs.

Whether these soft supply options are made available or not, traditional energy growth cannot continue. People in countries like the US, Japan, and the Netherlands will learn, in David Brower's phrase, to think twice as hard and waste half as much, whether they want to or not; they can only decide whether to do this by deliberate normative choice now or by frantic improvisation later in the face of imminent shortage. Alwyn Rhys says that when you have come to the edge of an abyss, the only progressive move you can make is to step backward: he might equally have said that you can turn around and then step forward. Planners whose thoughts revolve around econometric extrapolation, economies of scale, centralized electrification, and marginal mills per kilowatt-hour are not the planners who can most constructively address the problems of turning around. That process, too, will require the thoughtful intervention of concerned citizens in order to ensure that technical experts do not lose touch with more widely held social goals. How we, as citizens and as nations, meet the challenges of energy strategy is a crucial test of our ethical values, our political institutions, and even our conception of ourselves.

We can perhaps see the ethical issues more clearly if we imagine, as Hugh Nash has done, some of the questions we might ask our grandchildren about our nuclear decisions: for example, we might ask them, "As a by-product of nuclear power we may generate more radioactive waste than we actually need; would you like us to set some aside for you?" Or we might ask our grandchildren, "Isn't it a bit selfish of you to want some of our oil?" Or perhaps "How can we better show our faith in your boundless technological ingenuity than to make sure you need it?" To questions like these, I think we know what kinds of answers we would get. But in the technicalities of abstract debate about acceptable risks, economic growth, and the like, it is too easy to lose sight of such simple moral issues; too easy to forget that energy problems offer a useful integrating principle for thinking about the whole range of values and goals fundamental to the sustainable society that our descendents would be glad to inherit.

At the root of the issues we consider here is a difference in perspective about man and his works. Some people, impressed and fascinated by the glittering achievements of technology, say that if we will only have faith in human ingenuity (theirs), we shall witness the Second Coming of Prometheus, bringing us undreamed-of freedom and plenty. Other people think that we should plan on something more modest, lest we find instead undreamed-of tyrannies and perils; and that even if we had an unlimited energy source, we would lack the discipline to use it wisely. Such people are really saying, firstly, that energy is not enough to solve the ancient problems of the human spirit, and secondly, that the technologists who claim they can satisfy Alfvén's condition that "no acts of God can be permitted" are guilty of *hubris*, the human sin of divine arrogance. We have today an opportunity—perhaps our last—to exercise our responsibility to foster in our society a greater humility, one that springs from an appreciation of the essential frailty of the human design.

—ABL

Pinkham Notch, New Hampshire
1 June 1975

Part One

**Nuclear Power: Technical Bases
for Ethical Concern**

Amory B Lovins

An annotated semitechnical assessment of the impact of human fallibility and malice on some highly engineered and persistently hazardous systems; a survey of social and institutional implications; and a
brief discussion of certain policy problems and prospects.

Acknowledgements

Critical comments by many general reviewers, and particularly by Dr Warren Donnelly, are gratefully acknowledged; the manuscript also profited greatly from review in draft by a dozen specialists in nuclear science and engineering, by many others in the preliminary editions, and by David Brower and Geoffrey Gunn during production. Responsibility for all facts and opinions stated herein remains solely that of the author, whose views are not necessarily those of his various employers and clients.

Preface

As the economic and political impetus behind civilian nuclear power programs has increased in recent years, and as the prospective scale of these programs has become more obvious, so has public disagreement over whether they are wise, necessary, or capable of solving our energy problems.

At first much of this disagreement was of a technical character and was confined to scientific circles. Some experts said that we must have more nuclear power quickly and that its risks are exceedingly small; others, equally informed and responsible, said just the opposite. Even in a purely technical debate between such experts, the stakes would be high: if the advocates of nuclear power were completely right, deciding against them might mean giving up the only safe and practical method of providing enough energy for human development, whereas if the critics of nuclear power were completely right, deciding against *them* might mean adopting an irrevocably and fatally dangerous option while foreclosing others equally practical and more attractive. And the debate is not academic or apolitical: it concerns the future of a $100,000 million–plus international industry to which all major governments have committed immense resources and prestige.

Over the past few years, the nuclear debate has become part of a far wider debate about various social and ethical issues which the political process is well suited to address. Ordinary citizens and their representatives have begun to take up their responsibility to judge for themselves the merits of the more technically tinged arguments, rather than merely believing those experts who seemed most congenial or most authoritative. Under this public scrutiny, the official experts have often tended to come off rather badly. Those issues which were earlier thought to be highly technical and accessible only to experts have turned out to be simple in essence and have rightly become the province of every citizen willing to become informed about them. Now that political discussions of nuclear power are starting to mature in several countries, it is time to untangle the main threads of the controversy and to lay them out in an orderly way for everyone—layman or expert—who was previously daunted by the size and seeming complexity of the literature.

Nuclear power has three main kinds of specific advantages:

1. it avoids most of the environmental effects of extracting, transporting, and burning fossil fuels;
2. in generating electricity (but not otherwise) it largely substitutes nuclear fuels for fossil fuels, some of which are potentially subject to earlier geological or geopolitical scarcity;
3. it is claimed to produce electricity more cheaply than fossil-fuelled power stations (though the validity of this claim has been challenged and appears to depend on how the bookkeeping is done).

In contrast, critics of nuclear power adduce three kinds of concerns, some of which are also applicable to the large nonnuclear power stations which nuclear stations are supposed to replace:

1. *Environmental impacts* that arise mainly from
a. the risk of nuclear violence and coercion, either domestic or international, through misuse of toxic and explosive materials unavoidably associated with nuclear fission;
b. the risk that human fallibility or malice will cause major failures in the containment of large inventories of radioactive materials;
c. the difficulty of ensuring that geological or social contingencies will not jeopardize the isolation of long-lived radioactive wastes;
d. conventional environmental insults (heat release, land–use and aesthetic impacts, etc);
e. potential radiobiological hazards governed by inherent scientific uncertainty (low-level radiation effects, lung cancer risks from "hot particles", etc).

2. *Sociopolitical impacts* that arise because nuclear power
a. is a highly bureaucratized high technology that must be permanently run by a self-perpetuating (and probably paramilitary) technical elite, likely to be remote from much of their clientele;
b. is large scale and highly centralized, and therefore incompatible with certain cultural or settlement patterns, and vulnerable to mistakes or disruption;

c. requires social controls inconsistent with traditional civil liberties and perhaps with the imperatives of competitive markets;

d. involves insensible, exotic, or long term hazards which depart from social experience and are therefore difficult to subject to political judgment.

3. *Policy impacts* that arise because nuclear power is

a. extremely capital-intensive (so much so that no major country outside the Persian Gulf can afford the "all-electric all-nuclear economy");

b. extremely complex, hence inherently unreliable and subject to severe practical constraints in its rate of deployment;

c. subject to some net energy constraints which, like the two more obvious features just mentioned, prevent it from substituting for oil before the oil runs out;

d. poorly matched (in a thermodynamic sense) to the kinds of energy that people commonly need, thus requiring extensive infrastructure and social change to make the type and pattern of energy use conform to those of the source of supply;

e. poorly transferable to developing countries, and if transferred likely to bring with it some culture-bound values that may be inappropriate;

f. subject to resource and technological dependence and to commercial monopoly;

g. subject to technical uncertainties or surprises and to unique psychological handicaps which together make it prone to generic shutdowns in case of an accident or an unexpected type of malfunction;

h. subject to high-consequence low-probability mishaps not readily redressed by traditional mechanisms such as insurance or tort liability;

i. so demanding of scarce resources and time that it effectively forecloses all other long term options (which, more modest in scale and complexity, tend to be easier to develop and demonstrate).

The specific advantages of nuclear power have been and are now being intensively promoted in many forums, especially by powerful commercial forces. This attempt at a reasonably dispassionate account of a different perspective will, I hope, help to bring to wider public notice matters that are far too important to be left to experts.

As far as I know, this is the first attempt to tell technically minded advocates of nuclear power, in approximately their own idiom and with rigorous enough references to support further research, why the critics are worried. The two British preliminary editions of this study have already led some nuclear advocates, previously unaware of these arguments, to reevaluate their positions, and this suggests that a need in promoting responsible dialogue has been met. But I have so framed the arguments that the lay reader who is willing to read carefully will be able to understand the facts and issues with only the most rudimentary prior knowledge of nuclear power. More technical matters are relegated to footnotes, or so treated that they can be skipped without obscuring the structure of the argument. Both in technical level and in brevity, I have also borne in mind the special needs of legislators and civil servants, all of whom should have no trouble following the argument whether they are technically trained or not.

A few sentences from the Introduction to *World Energy Strategies: Facts, Issues, and Options* need to be repeated here:

> This summary of a tangled and fast-moving field cannot present a consensus where none exists, but can only suggest where the merits of a dispute may lie. . . . The aim . . . is to outline certain assessments and conclusions on which much top-level energy thinking has in recent months begun to converge, presenting such information, and no more, as is needed to convey a sound grasp of the subject. Such an authoritative statement deserves a caveat: never believe an expert. No expert can tell the whole story, nor avoid emotional entanglement with particular ideas. And never, never believe an expert who is trying to sell you something!

I have no connection with any part of the energy industry, and have tried to write about nuclear power with the same disinterested judgment with which I hope readers will read about it. I also hope that skeptics will take the trouble to verify the references cited, and will ensure that any errors of fact or logic which have escaped three stages of critical review are brought to my notice so that this exploratory manuscript, always in transition, can be further improved.

—ABL

London
15 May 1975

Chapter One

Introduction

A substantial and rapidly growing body of competent technical opinion now shares the Pugwash Conference's view [1] that "[t]he as yet unsolved problem of waste management and the possibly unsolvable (in an absolute sense) problems of catastrophic releases of radioactivity and diversion of bomb grade material combine to create grave and justified misgivings about the vast increase in the use of nuclear power that has been widely predicted. The wisdom of such an increase must at the present time be seriously questioned." The reasoning that has led many distinguished scientists to such conclusions—contrary to those of many other equally competent scientists—appears not to be well understood among advocates of civilian nuclear fission technology. This is partly because the reasoning is as much ethical as technical in substance, and hence may appear merely polemical to those who disagree with it; but partly also because it has seldom been summarized for technical persons in their own idiom. This study attempts such a summary—necessarily brief, hence incomplete and somewhat conclusory, and not always able to treat issues at a length commensurate with their relative importance. It seeks to explore broad issues [2] rather than to treat all technical details with sophistication and rigour, though references giving fuller treatments of specific points are noted throughout. Reliance mainly on US sources and examples is a result of nearly unique local circumstances—independent and active critical expertise, a tradition of adversarial technical evaluation, and the operation of the Freedom of Information Act—and does not imply that the issues here framed are necessarily different in countries where these conditions are lacking or where the style of national discussion and decision is unlike that of the USA.

Associated with fossil–fuel and other energy technologies, and indeed with many technologies of other types, are important technical and ethical issues, some of which have so far received too little public attention. In order to retain focus, this paper will not attempt to contrast such issues with those arising in fission technology, nor to explore the comparative role of nuclear power, other energy technologies, and conservation measures in achieving balance between energy need and supply. The author has attempted this in a separate and extensively annotated book [3], a few parts of which have been used without specific attribution as a basis for several sections of this study. Though both works try to clarify the grounds of disagreement over substantive issues, neither is a summary and analysis of all arguments on all sides. This study attempts instead to explain the basis of certain salient concerns which constitute an unorthodox but respectable body of technical opinion: concerns which the author believes deserve earnest consideration, but which could be obscured if presented (inevitably with less emphasis and coherence) in the midst of a comprehensive survey of all opposing views. Statements of such views are in any case available in a familiar and extensive literature.

Chapter Two

Fundamental Issues

The very large inventories of fission and activation products[†] in the nuclear fuel cycle create hazards unlike those of any other single technology. These hazards combine the geographic range of certain military pathogens, the permanence of irreversible changes in climate or in soil fertility [4], and the medical and moral significance of the most persistent synthetic mutagens, all potentially at a substantial level. Because this unique combination of inherent hazards departs so much from our experience, we must define with special care, before we choose to incur these hazards, the limits of our ability to cope with them. Thus Weinberg states [5] that

> ... the advent of nuclear energy poses issues of unprecedented magnitude and weight for mankind. The half-life of Pu-239 is 24,400 years, and nothing man can do will change this. We have created materials that man has never seen before, that remain toxic for times much longer than we have ever had experience with. We are forced, willy-nilly, to think on a time scale that exceeds Pharoah's time scale 10- or even 100-fold. This is indeed unprecedented in human history. *** When I try to visualize

---

[†]When a neutron splits the nucleus of a fissionable ("fissile") atom, two fragments called "fission products" are generally formed, each containing approximately half of the original nucleus. Among the more important fission products are strontium-90 (^{90}Sr), caesium-137 (^{137}Cs), and iodine-131 (^{131}I). But a neutron can also be absorbed by a nucleus without fissioning it, thus transmuting it into a different element or making it radioactive. Structural metals, such as those used in stainless steels, can be "activated" in this way to form radioactive "activation products", very small amounts of which may be transported by chemical corrosion into the liquid effluents of reactors. A more important type of activation product is the series of "transuranic" elements, such as plutonium (Pu: principal isotope ^{239}Pu = Pu-239), formed when nuclei of very heavy elements (such as uranium) absorb neutrons without fissioning.

matters from this very long-range point of view, I sometimes am concerned about our present course.

Most fission technologists realize that they are creating new categories and magnitudes of risk; they respond with ingenious precautions and with highly skilled and dedicated attention. But by stressing the care that they take, they avoid addressing the central question: are the safety problems of fission too difficult to solve? If they are, then (as Alfven's classic paper [6] points out) one cannot claim that they are solved by pointing to all the efforts made to solve them.

It is *impossible to prove*, save by experiment, whether or not the safety problems of widely deployed fission technology are too difficult to solve (according to some given definition of "solve"—a problem taken up in the next paragraph). On the contrary, in assessing the risks of a complex enterprise in which "no acts of God can be permitted" [6], we can only rely on analogies with other highly engineered systems whose potential risks are in principle several orders of magnitude smaller and quite different in kind. Such analogies suggest to critics of fission technology that ultimately its safety is limited not by our care, ingenuity, dedication, or wealth (as has been true of all previous technologies [7]), but by our inescapable human fallibility; limited not by our good intentions, but by gaps between intention and performance; limited not by our ability to solve problems on paper, but by our inability to translate paper solutions into real events. If this view were correct, it would follow that nuclear safety is not a mere engineering problem that can be solved by sufficient care, but rather a wholly new type of problem that can be solved only by infallible people. Infallible people are not now observable in the nuclear or any other industry.

OPPOSING PARADIGMS

It may be objected that this formulation, by failing to quantify "solving the problem", is tacitly based on an absolutist zero risk criterion rather than on some nonzero level of "acceptable risk". Yet the argument is the same *whatever* low level of "acceptable risk" is assumed; the reason is somewhat Gödelian and abstract, but is important enough to be worth setting out explicitly. If "solving the problem" (and hence assessing the problem and possible solutions to it) were purely an engineering exercise performable by divinely perfect automata, then the degree of human imperfection that would be tolerable in achieving a given level of risk could be computed with confidence. But if it is "difficult to argue . . . that any completely technological approach ... can be found and trusted in a world characterized by human error and irrationality"[8], then it must follow that risk analysis, as a "technological approach", is itself an uncertain guide; hence that *either* nuclear risk analysts *or* all other persons engaged in the nuclear enterprise must conform to the strict standard of infallibility here proposed—because if anyone else in the enterprise might make a mistake, then the risk analyst must unfailingly identify, assess, and guard against that mistake. He must overlook nothing, for the potential significance of a gap in knowledge is by definition unknown: hence the risk analyst cannot know the importance of his omissions—which would not be omissions if he knew what they were.

This argument may be restated thus: If it were asserted that present knowledge permits assessment of risks and of the efficacy of countermeasures with sufficient accuracy for policy purposes, it would then become necessary to assert in turn that risk analysts now know how to make quantitative, arbitrarily detailed, and *infallibly correct and complete* calculations not merely of engineering variables (such as the effectiveness, reliability, and relevance of safety devices), but also of human malice *and of human fallibility, including their own.* Even the most generous enthusiasts of risk analysis are not in the habit of making such a claim; yet it is logically necessary if their engineering paradigm is to be internally consistent. (This paradox inherent in the engineering paradigm is familiar to risk analysts in another form: they seek to identify significant hypothetical failure modes which, if identifiable, would *ex hypothesi* have been guarded against already. They seek, too, to discover the designers' omissions; but who is to discover their own?) From such reasoning it would appear that those who, in order to attain a specified level of computed risk, demand only partial (and presumably attainable) human infallibility must either make a technically unwarranted claim of their own analytic infallibility or else concede in some measure the merit of the opposing paradigm, according to which such matters are beyond calculation—to an extent that is itself beyond calculation [9].

Empirical evidence is relevant to risk assessment, but seems conclusive to different people in different ways. International experience of noncatastrophic errors and malfunctions at many stages of the nuclear fuel cycle demonstrates impressive human ingenuity in overcoming foolproof systems and in inventing new kinds of mistakes. Some analysts infer from this experience that describing nuclear safety problems as "amenable to engineering solution" confuses the way things are with the way we should like them to be. Yet other analysts fail to detect in the same events any evidence that careful precautions cannot prevent catastrophe—especially if aided by some luck [10]. Such persons are in general technically trained and have a "problem-solving" orientation: they tend to perceive the world primarily as a series of technical problems which must *ex hypothesi* have technical solutions. Critics of this view tend to stress "paratechnical" problems—those whose solution (or lack of it) lies in the interaction of people with technology, in the social and psychological processes on which the implementation of technical solutions must depend. Thus Kendall writes [11] that though "no purely technical obstacles to the safe implementation of nuclear power [that are] of a fundamental nature have been identified", pervasive mismanagement which he alleges in the US civilian nuclear program has raised "the possibility that controls may not be adequately developed or applied in spite of both the obvious need and a general . . . appreciation of the possible hazards."

Today a vigorous dispute persists and intensifies between those who perceive engineering problems and those who perceive people problems as the dominant element in nuclear safety. This dispute is not a technical dispute and hence cannot be resolved on its technical merits; it is instead a conflict of incompatible paradigms. Persons learned in the technical details of nuclear engineering therefore cannot justifiably claim a monopoly on informed discussion of the disputed issues: it could be claimed with equal warrant that history, biology, psychology—even untutored common sense—can offer as valuable an insight into nuclear safety as can the formal disciplines that deal with its purely technical substance. Abrahamson has so stated [12]: "To suggest that one must be a nuclear expert to understand and judge the issues involved is equivalent to saying that one has to be a hen in order to judge the quality of an egg." Weinberg, too, agrees [5] that nuclear safety "is only in part a technological problem" and that solubility of such problems ". . . is a matter of opinion, not a matter of scientific fact. In the language that I have come to savor, these questions transcend science, belong to 'transscience' [13], not science. *** We as nuclear technologists cannot, in dealing with such trans-scientific questions, trust only our own instincts, instincts perhaps colored by our aspirations." Moreover, Weinberg tells his fellow nuclear technologists [5] that "the burden of proof is upon us: it is we who . . . must bend every effort to visualize the problems in their full magnitude, so that if any appear insuperable we can seek out appropriate alternatives." It is not clear that these exhortations have been adequately heeded in the evolution of institutions charged with regulating hazardous technologies.

SOCIAL AND INSTITUTIONAL PROBLEMS

Some thoughtful advocates of fission technology, such as Weinberg [5, 14, 15], have discussed "the social mechanisms that seem to be required if we concede that we shall always be dealing with huge amounts of ^{239}Pu" [15]—for example, "a cadre that, from now on, can be counted upon to understand nuclear technology, to control it, to prevent accidents, prevent diversion *** in Uganda as well as in the USA, in Ethiopia as well as England."[15] While such discussions concede that "we probably ought to examine whether our social visions match our technological inventiveness"[15], they generally do not specify how the management goals enunciated are to be realized: the problems are presented as those of a whole society, rather than of individual technologists who work within a social context. Kneese [16] seems to focus on both social commitment and personal fallibility:

> ... Weinberg emphasized [14] that part of the Faustian bargain is that to use fission technology safely, society must exercise great vigilance and the highest levels of quality control, continuously and *indefinitely*. As the fission energy economy grows, many plants will be built and operated in countries with comparatively low levels of technological competence and a greater propensity to take risks. A much larger amount of transportation of hazardous materials will probably occur, and safety will become the province of the sea captain as well as the scientist. Moreover, even in countries with higher levels of technological competence, continued success can lead to reduced vigilance. We should recall that we managed to incinerate three astronauts in a very straightforward accident in an extremely high technology operation where the utmost precautions were allegedly being taken.

Edsall [17] suggests more directly that technologies are run by people, not by societies:

> My own judgement ... is deeply influenced by my general estimate of human nature and behavior, and by my reading of history. People have to operate nuclear power-plants, no matter how much automation we introduce. People are forgetful, often they are irresponsible, and quite a few of them suffer from deep-seated irrational tendencies to hostility and violence. *** I believe that the confident advocates of the safety of nuclear power-plants base their confidence too narrowly on the safety that is possible to achieve under the most favorable circumstances, over a limited period of time, with a corps of highly trained and dedicated personnel. If we take a larger view of human nature and history, I believe that we can

never expect such conditions to persist over centuries, much less over millenia.

The fission economy imposes both personal and societal require- ments of dedication and stability if reactor operation, waste manage- ment, safeguards, and similar enterprises are to be safely accom- plished. During their short careers, the people who design, build, operate, and maintain fission facilities must not make serious mis- takes, become inattentive or corrupt, disobey instructions, or the like [18]: their standard of personal conduct must differ greatly from historical norms for the general population. Societies which operate or have formerly operated fission facilities, on the other hand, must continuously provide the tranquil circumstances and the perennial incentives (with concomitant restrictions) under which such indivi- dual behaviour can survive and flourish. Thus such societies must not have, for example, overwhelming commercial or political pressures, nor social tensions that could give rise to fanatical lunatics or to guerrilla movements or to strikes by key personnel, nor policies or involvements abroad that could make domestic nuclear facilities or cities a target of foreign attack (for example, by clandestinely manu- factured nuclear weapons from the private or public sector). Such broad social constraints—most of which would today be difficult to satisfy anywhere—do not appear to have been explored in much detail by advocates of "technological priesthoods" [14] or of similar hypothetical mechanisms for perpetuating personal dedication and skill by "creating a continuing tradition of meticulous attention to detail" [14].

These constraints may imply, too, an unwelcome degree of homo- geneity enforced by strict social controls. Nuclear risks can manifest themselves not only directly—for example, as nuclear violence—but also indirectly—for example, as the drastic police action with which a society threatened by nuclear violence would probably try to avert it. In a thoughtful recent assessment [19] of the social and political implications of fission technology, Geesaman and Abrahamson state:

A complex and sophisticated society must bear the burdens of vulner- ability and constraint that are inherent in its technologies. *** One major reactor accident could change the economics and managerial structure of the electrical generating industry. One major incident of sabotage could lock a most basic industry into a paramilitary administration. One clandes- tine nuclear explosive could disrupt the total structure of our institutions. Because of worldwide social instability, it is realistic to anticipate such contingencies. . . . The opportunity is ever present and, now, the means are becoming available. The delicate relationship between strength and weakness is changing. *** [T]his is the ultimate dilemma of fission energy: the problem of guaranteeing the necessary social stability without being forced to engineer society itself. Nuclear energy will place absolute constraints on our society, for there are certain things that absolutely must not happen. When men talk in this way, environmental operants, and manipulative drugs, and images of paramilitary priesthood are at the edge of their awareness. . . . The alternative to the occasional devastation of a city may be a garrison state.

Indeed, Speth et al., referring to the Pugwash report [1] of "some sentiment . . . that the possibility of [nuclear theft is] . . . much smaller in socialist states", comment [20]: "We believe that sentiment to be true. It is also apparent that that is the direction in which we must move to accommodate the nuclear industry. After having spent billions of dollars for our nuclear deterrent, our civilian nuclear industry might well accomplish that which our defense system is trying to prevent." Trends consistent with this opinion include semiofficial US proposals [107] to authorize miniature private armies [21], a federal nuclear security force, extensive investigation and surveillance of private citizens [22], infiltration of potentially threatening groups, and new federal police powers infringing traditional civil liberties. A recent USAEC report [23] states:

> Various court rulings in recent years have been favorable to the protection of individual privacy and of individual right-to-work. These rulings have made it difficult to make a personnel background check. . . . The AEC has requested [and obtained] legislation which would allow background checks of individuals with access to plutonium and related material accountability records. We believe that enabling legislation such as this is necessary to the further improvement of personnel selection practices.

Abrahamson comments [12]: "Given the means which were implemented—for example no-knock entry and search—to unsuccessfully control the drug traffic, we can only speculate on what will be thought necessary to deal with the much more serious political problems of the nuclear fuels." Such sociopolitical impacts may be as profound as the environmental impacts against which they are directed.

Despite various analysts' emphasis on social institutions versus personal responsibility or on indirect sociopolitical effects versus direct environmental effects, the basic issue is the same: the impact of human fallibility or malice on highly engineered and persistently hazardous systems. It is apparently common ground that "fallibility problems" are likely, in the absence of strong compensatory mechanisms not yet identified, to become more prominent as reactors proliferate [24], salesmen outrun engineers, investment conquers caution, routine dulls commitment, boredom replaces novelty, and less skilled technicians take over (especially in countries with little technical infrastructure or tradition).

STANDARD OF CONTAINMENT REQUIRED

It is likewise common ground that reliable containment of radio-active inventories deserves the most diligent attention. By way of illustrating the magnitudes involved, Holdren calculates [8] that in a 1–GW(e)[†] light water reactor (LWR) at equilibrium, a quarter of the 72–MCi[†] ^{131}I inventory would suffice to contaminate the atmosphere over the 48 coterminous United States to an altitude of 10 km to twice the maximum permissible concentration (MPC) for that isotope, and that half of the 5.2–MCi ^{90}Sr inventory would suffice to contaminate the annual freshwater runoff of the same area to six times the MPC. Such estimates are used not to suggest that such widespread and uniform dispersion would actually occur, but to stress the exquisite care that containment of such large inventories demands.

Thus the consequences of an *uncontrolled* loss-of-coolant accident (LOCA) in a large LWR, whose fission product inventory is of order 10^{10} Ci,[†] may include [25] under unfavourable weather conditions an "area of disaster" of order 10^{11} m^2, with acute lethality at down-

---

[†] 1 GW(e) = 1000 MW(e) = 1,000,000 kW(e) = 1 million kilowatts of net electrical output, a typical size for a modern nuclear power station containing a single large reactor. 1 MCi = 0.001 GCi = 1000 kCi = 1,000,000 Ci = 1 million curies; a curie is that amount of any radioactive substance which undergoes 37,000 million disintegrations per second, equal to the activity of one gram of radium. The amount of material that equals one curie depends on how rapidly its radioactive decay occurs, that is, on its half-life (the time required for half of it to decay to another material which may or may not itself be radioactive). Thus plutonium–239 (^{239}Pu), with a half-life of 24,390 years, contains 0.0614 curies per gram; ^{238}Pu, with a half-life of only 86.4 years, contains 17.4 curies per gram; and iodine–131 (^{131}I), with a half-life of 8.05 days, contains about 124,000 curies per gram. Of course, the definition of a curie only counts the *rate* of radioactive decay, and says nothing about the type or energy of the radiation emitted (which determine its biological effects). Maximum allowed body burdens of the more dangerous radioisotopes, however, are typically measured in microcuries (μCi, millionths of a curie), nanocuries (nCi, billionths = 1/1,000,000,000s of a curie), or large numbers of picocuries (pCi, trillionths of a curie or $\mu\mu$Ci). These quantities are separated one from the next by an interval of three "orders of magnitude", or three factors of ten—that is, by a factor of 1000. Thus 10^{10} = 10 billion = 10,000 million is six orders of magnitude larger than 10^4 = 10,000.

wind ranges approaching several hundred km [26]. If the emergency core cooling systems (ECCS) in a 1–GW(e) LWR worked as intended, if the radioiodine inventory were all volatilized and half were vented to containment in accordance with the "design-basis accident", but if the containment shell then failed or were deliberately breached, then half of the radioiodine inventory in the containment (a quarter that of the core), held up for a day (4.6-fold decay), would produce under moderately stable meterological conditions a cloud–centerline dose of 300 rem to an adult thyroid (the USAEC† site limit under 10 CFR 100) at a range of 200 km [27]; the dose to a child's thyroid would be $\sim$ 5$\times$ as much [28]. Though the containment and its fission product removal systems are relied upon to attenuate such releases by about three orders of magnitude, it is widely conceded [27, 29] that containment integrity could not be maintained if the ECCS failed to work as intended and a meltdown ensued. (The integrated decay heat from a 1–GW(e) LWR core would suffice to melt down through an iron cylinder 3.3 m in diameter and over 210 m deep [27]. Meltthrough at the bottom, however, is not the only nor necessarily the main mechanism of failure, for containment would also be severely stressed, and could plausibly be breached [28, 30], by high internal temperatures, by various effects involving hydrogen and perhaps carbon dioxide, and by steam explosions; scoping calculations [27] and more detailed analyses [30] are both discouraging. Moreover, a recent containment liner failure [31] casts prima facie doubt on containment integrity under LOCA conditions. There is substantial evidence that underground siting [32] could offer improved integrity, as well as protection from some forms of sabotage, at small or zero extra cost, though the degree of improvement is speculative.)

RANDOM VERSUS DELIBERATE FAILURES

Most assessments of the hazards of nuclear technology assume that the probabilities of failure are governed by statistical processes and by random human error, not by deliberate attempts to set failure probabilities equal to one. This procedure may be the best that present quantitative knowledge permits, but it is qualitatively implausible. Abrahamson comments [12]:

---

†On 19 Jan 1975 the US Atomic Energy Commission was fissioned into the Nuclear Regulatory Commission (NRC) plus most of the Energy Research and Development Administration (ERDA).

Thousands of aircraft crashes have occurred and they have mostly oc-curred as a result of deliberate human efforts directed to that end. Over a thousand high technology aircraft were destroyed over Vietnam—more than would probably be lost due to other accident sources in hundreds of years of commercial aviation. This obvious class of hazards is generally ignored, though politically motivated international hijackings, crank or kidnap domestic hijackings, and rare insurance motivated air disasters . . . have drawn subliminal attention to the inherent frailty of a technology that puts hundreds of people in a cylinder of aluminum moving at 600 mph some seven miles up in the air. . . . Fortunately the size and nature of the population aboard a single aircraft makes destructive inter-vention politically unattractive. Nor is there substantial economic motiva-tion. These fortuitous circumstances do far more to protect against aircraft disaster, than all the luggage scanning and human surveillance combined.

As will be pointed out below in the section on safeguards, however, the incentives favouring nuclear violence can far exceed those favour-ing aeronautical violence: for example [19], "[i]f a small nuclear explosion of a kiloton is conjectured, devastation over an area of one square mile [2.6 km^2] may be expected. Population concentrations of up to 300,000 people occur on that scale in this country [USA] as well as concentrations of political and economic power that are necessary for our function." Other forms of nuclear violence and coercion [33] based on other parts of the nuclear fuel cycle can be readily envisaged and are already passing into public consciousness [34]. As Geesaman and Abrahamson note [19], "[t]he small quanti-ties of material involved simplify the technology in and management for the strict physical containment of the material flows. Conversely, the small quantities and careful localization of the materials make them uniquely vulnerable to small scale disruptive events." The same authors point out [19] that most things happen in the technological world because man wills them to happen. From neglecting deliber-ately caused failures it is but a small step to arguing that there will be no random failures either, because in a world without human inten-tion there will be no reactors in which failures might occur. "There is a technology", they conclude [12], "of disordering order. It is a low technology and it cannot be ignored. *** Reality is more inclusive than the dreams of the systems analysts."

SCOPE OF THIS STUDY

This survey of some specific "fallibility problems" will stress un-scheduled events in the nuclear fuel cycle. In contrast, most public attention, and most public relations efforts by nuclear advocates, have tended to focus on scheduled events which, though often locally important (and sometimes conveniently analogous to events in fossil fuel cycles), are seldom proper grounds on which to base a national decision about the acceptability of fission technology. Such routine events, which this paper will neglect, include heat release and associated biological and meterological problems, visual impact, transport and land use impacts, scheduled releases of noble-gas and other radioactivity from nuclear facilities [35], exposures of transient nuclear workers [36], the high incidence of lung cancer among some underground uranium miners [35, 37], and the escape of ^{226}Ra-bearing particles or daughter products into air and water from improperly managed uranium mill tailings [35]. The last three of these problems appear, at least historically, to be straightforward management problems whose resolution does not demand exotic technology, though the long term retention of ^{226}Ra in tailings raises some unsolved problems analogous to those considered below in the discussion of waste management.

This study will also neglect the low level radiation controversy [38]—probably an irresolvable one owing to the lack of statistical significance in small populations and the lack of a control group in large populations [39]. (It is worth noting, however, the invalidity of commonly used comparisons between external whole body doses [chiefly gamma] from medical X-rays, natural background, etc, and internal doses [often selectively deposited and partly alpha] from the nuclear fuel cycle.) The essence of the low level radiation dispute is that some persons say that safety has not been proved, whilst others say that harm has not been proved; both appear to be correct and one must decide for oneself which position is ethically preferable [40].

Chapter Three

Reactor Safety

The defence-in-depth philosophy is expressed as several successive types of protection, and several successive physical barriers, against accidental releases of radioactivity: for example, activity is contained by (1) fuel elements, (2) the reactor vessel, and (at least in the USA) (3) the outer containment shell, and these barriers are intended to be (1) carefully built for reliability, (2) protected by safety devices to cope with expected malfunctions, and (3) further protected by engineered safety systems to cope with failures in (2). In principle, correct operation of any one barrier or safety element should be able to prevent catastrophic releases, though there are exceptions in practice. This approach is logical and outwardly attractive, but as actually applied to systems that have received a public, independent, adversarial, and relatively detailed scrutiny—as is uniquely the case with LWRs in the USA [41]—it seems defective in several respects. (This may also be true of the many other types of reactors—generally of lower power density—that have not received such scrutiny and that therefore cannot be discussed in detail here; nobody knows, though some speculate [42].)

The sense of security which multiple backup systems afford is justified only if the links work as intended: to perform its function, each must be effective (properly designed and implemented), relevant (designed for an accident that is a sufficiently exhaustive description of the accidents that can happen), and reliable. The extensive and seldom read USAEC ECCS hearing record [41] contains statements by many of the USAEC's senior safety experts to the effect that too little is known to give reasonable assurance that LWR ECCS actually have these properties. Official statements, however, contradict these doubts. This diversity of opinion among acknowledged experts in a highly technical subject has naturally given rise to much anxiety both within and outside the technical community and has stimulated reviews [43] by the American Physical Society (APS) and other groups.

MAIN AREAS OF DISAGREEMENT

Skepticism about LWR safety—and hence, by analogy, about the safety of other types of reactors designed under similar technical and institutional arrangements—rests partly on operating experience [44] replete with component failures, operator errors, design or construction faults [45], and violations of licence requirements [46], but partly also on alleged methodological flaws. Among these is the arbitrary use of a single failure criterion[†] in systems routinely observed to exhibit multiple failures—random, causally connected, or common mode.[†] Multiple valve failures in boiling water reactor (BWR) overfeed accidents [47] (a type of failure apparently not properly treated by design criteria recently prevailing) and failure of steam generator tubes in pressurized water reactors (PWRs) [48] (an event which could easily stall reflooding [49] in a LOCA but is excluded from the design basis accident [50]) appear to be examples of events about which technically unjustifiable assumptions have been made in accident analyses. Similar examples, many of which are identified by the APS study [43], might be found in such areas of analysis as PWR steam binding, zirconium—water reactions, possible brittle fracture of fuel, flow blockage, core disruption under blowdown forces, and PWR reflooding rates. Likewise, when catastrophic failure of steel pressure vessels has been widely considered to be "incredible", and has hence been excluded from USAEC hypothetical accidents notwithstanding numerous technical uncertainties [51] about long term radiation embrittlement, thermal shock in a LOCA, etc, it is not reassuring to hear a senior AEC official state [52] that

---

[†]The single failure criterion is the assumption that only one component will fail at a time, so that in analysis of hypothetical accidents involving, say, the failure of one of two (or more) valves or diesel generators, the other(s) would be assumed to work. This assumption is rather often contradicted by experience [44]; on the other hand, the single failure criterion is only used sometimes. Simultaneous failure of two or more redundant devices owing to a common cause is called "common mode" failure; for example, redundant electrical systems may fail because of a shared design fault or a fire in a shared cable tray [173], or redundant valves may fail to close because grit from the same source has got into all of them. Common mode failures are easy to observe but hard to predict. In one reported incident [44], a sequence of 21 failures at the Oak Ridge Research Reactor disabled all seven backup devices for a type of emergency cooling, each device having three redundant channels.

such failure has not been considered because "no design was available which could withstand the consequences of pressure vessel failure, so it was decided to accept the risk."

Assertions of the effectiveness of defence-in-depth seem on occasion to rest tacitly upon a circularity: flaws alleged in any one of its three elements are sometimes shrugged off by cheerful reference both to the other two and to the alleged but unverified improbability that they will be needed—even though some types of failures in one element could *cause* failures in others [53]. Thus some persons apparently assume that though a LOCA in a LWR is likely enough to require ECCS, it is also unlikely enough that the ECCS need not necessarily be effective or reliable; for after all, is there not also a reinforced concrete containment dome to prevent or reduce any "extremely unlikely" release? Such persons further stress the extent of operating experience free of catastrophic accident [54]—and then state that lesser malfunctions within that same experience are irrelevant owing to the reactors' age, size, etc.

Much controversy has arisen from the widespread use of mathematical simulation in lieu of empirical proof of the behaviour of complex systems under unusual and often poorly understood conditions. Simulated results sometimes appear to be administratively construed as knowledge, whereas often they are things that we do not really know and that the reactors may not know either. Many eminent experts, apparently including Weinberg [55], share Kendall's view [56] that "[m]athematical models cannot be used reliably to span large gaps in engineering knowledge, owing to the very great uncertainties that accumulate in long and unverified chains of inference." In LWR ECCS analysis, these uncertainties [43]—compounded by numerous simplifying and restrictive assumptions [41, 43] and by starting data widely believed to be seriously defective (as from the FLECHT series [57])—seem to many experts [43, 58] to be comparable to or larger than the safety margins claimed. The behaviour of crucial safety systems—complete systems, not simply components—has never been tested at large or full scale [43, 55, 59] and under realistic conditions, as is routine in many technologies of lower risk and complexity: as Lapp remarks [60], "much AEC safety research is in the future tense, whereas power reactors are in operation." Often empirical knowledge of essential physics is so sketchy that the common technique of adding a safety margin to an educated guess may or may not ensure the claimed "conservatism": conservatism depends on the difference between a guess and what actually happens, not on the difference between two guesses [43]. The experimental and analytical problems involved, too, are ferociously difficult, and some appear to be "beyond the capability of engineering science"[61].

In short, as the APS review [43] concludes,

> ... no comprehensive, thoroughly *quantitative* basis now exists for evaluating ECCS performance. ... *** Despite qualitative indications of general conservatism ..., we feel that the experimental data are not adequate to demonstrate convincingly that the integrated ECC systems effects are conservatively prescribed, even if all of the individual pieces were demonstrated to be independently conservative (which they have not been). Therefore, any meaningful quantitative evaluation of system effectiveness, or the ECCS safety margin, must depend upon the adequacy of the systems analysis codes [i.e., computer simulations]. At this time, none of us has been convinced that the current generation of codes is adequate to this purpose.

In essence it is the lack of empirical verification of claimed conservatisms that underlies much anxiety about LWR safety, for without such evidence, criticisms cannot be refuted: but in many cases verification appears to be technically, economically, or politically impracticable, so no resolution of LWR safety questions is now in sight. The APS review's belief [43] that "it is important [to] ... quickly take major steps to bring about a convincing resolution of the uncertainties" is well founded but probably not feasible, as the report itself suggests [43]. Many of the same broad methodological questions that persist in LWR safety, too, have not been publicly shown to be inapplicable to other types of reactors whose detailed safety problems may be very different; so these designs may be expected to attract, and may merit, a greater measure of skeptical scrutiny than strictly technical analogy might justify.

RELIABILITY AND RISK

The many acknowledged deficiencies of quality assurance programs in the USA [62–4]—which has roughly half the world's installed nuclear capacity—do not increase confidence in LWR safety or in nuclear regulation. Neither does Cottrell's statement [65] that LWR safety rests on an "immaculate standard of manufacture and quality control and on regular in-service inspection of the most rigorous and demanding kind", nor his recommendation [65] (later acted upon [66] by the British government) that the UK choose some type of reactor "less critically dependent on human perfection". A USAEC Task Force reported [64] for 30 operating LWRs between 1 January 1972 and 31 May 1973 "... approximately 850 abnormal occurences ... [which] involved malfunctions or deficiencies associated with safety related equipment. *** Many of the incidents had broad generic applicability and potentially significant consequences. *** [This] raises a serious question regarding the current review and inspection practices both on the part of the nuclear industry and the AEC." The Task Force [64] did

> ... not believe that the overall incident record over the past several years, combined with the common mode failures that have been identified, give the required confidence level that the probability [random, excluding malicious intervention] for [a major] ... accident is 10^{-6} (one in a million) or less per reactor-year. ... [I]t is difficult at this time to assign a high degree of confidence to quantification of the level of risk associated with nuclear reactors.

The recent USAEC Reactor Safety Study [30] (RSS) on LWRs is unlikely to increase this confidence; the preliminary results of independent review suggest that the RSS draft conclusions will be placed in doubt by orders of magnitude, for reasons illustrated in Appendix I–1. Experts in the methodology used have stated [67, 167] that its results are meaningful only in comparing similar systems, not in absolute magnitude, and that in such exercises the input parameters are commonly adjusted so as to yield a desired result. Moreover, as two senior USAEC analysts have written [68] of conventional reliability analysis in nuclear safety:

> (a) There is little or no concrete evidence that the [rare] events under consideration obey the laws of probability that underlie the theory. There is no assurance that accident events are random in time or independent of each other. The intellectually satisfying idea of reliability analysis is no more than a hypothesis for these events; (b) Even if the framework of the theory were correct, the values of the parameters are largely unknown [69].
>
> The method now generally used to predict these probabilities—cascading of probabilities of the individual "failures" that make up the event—is known to be inadequate. The serious or potentially serious events that have occurred have been characterized by concurrent failures, usually interdependent or causally related. Thus the theory's assumption of independence of failures has not been borne out by experience [70].
>
> Despite these shortcomings, reliability analysis and, to a lesser extent, risk calculation techniques are used in reactor safety evaluations in the United States.

It is difficult to reconcile such statements with others in which the then chairman of the USAEC *(inter alios)* relied extensively on some

RSS results both before and after their publication in draft. The director of the Safety and Reliability Directorate of the UK Atomic Energy Authority has taken [71] perhaps a more pragmatic view of the risk of major accidents:

> ... I doubt very much whether our engineering capability can take us lower than ... 1/1,000,000 per reactor year, or indeed whether we, as yet [,] have developed the capability in our technology and organization to achieve this figure. ... In my opinion, it is hard to show a failure rate in the range 1/1,000,000 to 1/10,000,000 with reasonable confidence. We need also to take into account errors in interpreting the designer's specifications, or errors in installation or maintenance, since systems are sometimes not as good as they were originally thought to be.

Likewise, Cottrell's hope [65] that "the safety of the public ... will never be made dependent upon almost superhuman engineering and operational qualities" seems to acknowledge the importance of gaps between wish and fact.

Many estimates of future risks from nuclear power seem to respond to criticisms of current deficiencies by postulating "learning curves" whereby increasing experience inevitably leads to improved reliability. Examples of such behaviour in other technologies can be adduced. Yet the validity of the learning curve hypothesis in nuclear reliability and safety must rest on unique and well-documented causal relations, not on casual analogy. There is no evidence that strong "learning curves" will occur in such a complex and rapidly deployed technology—especially with the rapid rises in unit size that have occurred in recent years, but arguably even after diverse designs have been fully standardized. Indeed, the US incidence of "significant events", and of such specific indicators as valve failures, has increased considerably in the past few years [46]. Perhaps this is because the doubling time of reactor population has been much shorter than the doubling time of supremely competent and dedicated technicians, particularly those accustomed to the harsh discipline of naval reactor quality-control programs. Some observers believe that the degree of unstintingly meticulous care that nuclear power demands cannot in practice be attained within profit-seeking commercial enterprises, and that quasi-military (Rickoverian) stringency, together with direct government administration of the nuclear enterprise, may be the best hope of maintaining sufficient quality (unfettered by economic considerations) to achieve adequate safety and availability [72, 152]. Those who hold this view often argue that the extraordinary measures which nuclear safety requires tend to conflict both with traditional democratic mechanisms and with the imperatives of the competitive market system.

FAST-NEUTRON REACTORS

The safety problems of large liquid-metal-cooled fast breeder reactors [73–5] (LMFBRs) deserve special mention. Some promoters of this technology seem to be trying to persuade licencing authorities that severe core-disruptive accidents, whose containment apparently cannot always be assured [75, 76], are "incredible". Despite elaborate mathematical simulations, understanding of the basic physics of such accidents (especially of possible multistage reassemblies) is rather primitive and seems likely to remain so. Safety problems would be even more acute with the higher fuel rating, smaller Doppler coefficient, fewer delayed neutrons, shorter prompt-neutron lifetime, smaller channels, faster coolant flow, and more chemically reactive fuel of proposed short-doubling-time breeder reactors. There is a widespread belief in the technical community that the technical and ethical issues associated with loading a ton or more of a uniquely potent respiratory carcinogen (plutonium) into a reactor whose explosive potential is not known with confidence, and whose accident probability is equally speculative, deserve far wider public debate [74].

Chapter Four

Fuel Transport and Reprocessing

The risks of fuel transport and reprocessing, though they will not be treated here in detail, seem to have been underestimated, particularly with respect to ^{134}Cs and ^{137}Cs release [77], improper cask construction [78], special hazards associated with (for example) high temperature combustion of organic chemicals or with ammunition train or chemical explosions in railway switchyards [80], requirements for shipping short-cooled breeder fuel, and deliberate attempts to breach containment (especially in spent-fuel cooling ponds and in reprocessing plants). It would be interesting to know the ability of both transport and reprocessing facilities [81] to withstand the skilled application of sophisticated munitions [82]—either conventional or nuclear, and of either military or civilian origin. (The same question applies to reactors, which seem, even if shut down, to be strategically important targets if attacked by tactical methods [83–4].) DeNike [82], inquiring into such possibilities and exploring the politics of nuclear fear, states that "[t]he toxicity and persistence of radioactive substances has radically altered the power balance between large and small social units"—a possibility seldom considered in the open literature and therefore the subject of much speculation, little of which has served to allay apprehensions.

Geesaman and Abrahamson call attention [19] to more immediate sociopolitical effects: "Under the civilian nuclear energy program, nuclear materials will become vital elements in human commerce. They will be very special elements of commerce, and they will warp some of our existing institutions beyond recognition. This process is already incipient in existing perceptions." Even now, according to Abrahamson [12],

The concepts upon which our transportation networks are based are proving incapable of dealing with the movements of radioactive materials. The Association of American Railroads is refusing to ship radioactive wastes on the grounds that they are ultrahazardous. The Association is insisting [on] . . . special trains, with special crews, at reduced speeds, and with other restrictions. Do we need a separate railroad system to serve the nuclear industry? . . . Regulations dealing with transportation of nuclear fuels are also rapidly being made more restrictive. In its most recent change the AEC proposes several armed guards to escort shipments of fuels . . . [with], at least in some cases, orders to shoot to kill. In a time when there are relatively few shipments this may not seem . . . particularly oppressive. But . . . do we want [eventually] to create private armies that operate in the commercial transportation sector?

Chapter Five

Waste Management

Persons charged with the isolation of the relatively compact but extremely toxic wastes arising in fuel reprocessing seem confident that they will devise ways to create a perpetually closed system—something never before accomplished in the management of other hazardous substances, particularly those that can be biologically reconcentrated by orders of magnitude per trophic level once released. Such persons further state that their confidence is sufficient basis to warrant rapid expansion of nuclear power. A current technical advance which they often cite is the development of methods for prompt solidification of high-level liquid wastes. Such a practice could probably reduce risks arising from the sorts of accidents that have already led to the loss (from temporary storage [85]) of nearly two million liters of such wastes, generally of military origin. Storage, however, is not disposal. Even with solidification, ". . . none of the suggested long-term solutions to the problem of permanent disposal of high-level radioactive waste is technically or economically feasible today. . . ."[86]

The required periods of isolation vary but are of order 10^3 yr for the main long-lived fission products [87] (excepting the longer-lived ^{93}Zr, ^{93m}Cb, ^{99}Tc, ^{129}I, ^{135}Cs, etc) and of order 10^6–10^8 yr for actinides[†]: perhaps the higher value for actinides because of the ^{237}Np decay chain, whose hazard "does not decrease significantly in

---

[†]Actinides are the family of very heavy elements: actinium (Ac), thorium (Th), protactinium (Pa), uranium (U), neptunium (Np), plutonium (Pu), americium (Am), curium (Cm), berkelium (Bk), californium (Cf), and five more that are even rarer. In general, all but the first four are man made by successive additions of neutrons. All actinides are radioactive, most emit alpha radiation, most have (in their commoner forms) relatively long half-lives, and all are very toxic, particularly if daughter products are taken into account (see Appendix I–2).

more than 10 million years"[88]. (See Appendix I-2, "Transuranic Decay Chains".) There is no evidence that solidified wastes will remain monolithic, insoluble, or inert over periods much shorter than these [88].

Recent proposals [89] to try to develop means for thorough separation [90] of actinides from fission products, so that the former can be recycled and fissioned [90] in reactors, may have advantages if feasible: most fission products, as noted above, need be isolated for shorter periods than most actinides (though still for a very long time) if their actinide content is truly negligible. But this approach is generally considered, not as the terminal stage of cleanup after abandonment of fission technology, but rather as part of a commitment [14] to maintain reactor operation and its associated large actinide inventories for periods long compared with the 24,390 year half-life of the dominant isotope, ^{239}Pu [91]. In such steady-state recycling there is also a fundamental practical problem, for actinides that are to be fissioned must be recycled repeatedly—probably 10-20 times—through a reactor, producing new wastes (including contaminated reagents and cladding hulls and various other dilute alpha wastes) each time, and it is not clear that this process will significantly reduce the long term hazards arising from the quantity [94] and entropy of all the actinides [90].

The central problem of disposal, especially of actinides, is that the degree of permanence required subjects any terrestrial disposal scheme to geological requirements [92] of which we have no experience and for which no responsible geologist can offer a guarantee: the time scale is less the realm of geology than of theology. Terrestrial disposal must therefore be "retrievable" in case of geological contingencies [92]; and if it is "retrievable" to one sort of person it may be "retrievable" to others too, entailing "surveillance" on a time scale far exceeding the observed life span of human cultures. The wide array of technical disposal options proposed [93] does not appear to meet this requirement of social longevity [15] nor to take sufficiently into account its unique moral implications. So far, the only options actually available [93] are for interim management until a safe method of disposal, if one exists, can be devised.

It appears that medium and low level waste management, like the decommissioning of nuclear facilities (few of which are designed to facilitate it), has received too little attention. The accumulation, over the next few decades, of tons of highly dilute and persistent hard alpha emitters (e.g., protactinium) seems to give particular grounds for concern, despite the USAEC's long overdue 11 September 1974 proposal [94] to eliminate the current practice of commercial soil burial of some transuranic wastes.

Chapter Six

Plutonium Toxicity

The risks posed by the 10^2–10^3-kg ^{239}Pu inventory of every modern power reactor and by large inventories elsewhere deserve special note. Despite much study [95], chiefly in animals, human plutonium toxicity is still not well understood. Liver, not bone, may be the critical organ for soluble Pu, and the distribution of the radiation dose from an inhaled insoluble Pu particle with long pulmonary residence time is not now known. Aerosols of very many such particles can result from fires (plutonium metal and some compounds can ignite spontaneously), industrial or LMFBR accidents, weathering of plutonium-contaminated wastes or soil, or deliberate dispersal. Competent critics [96], relying on detailed lung modelling [97] by the Pu expert Geesaman, have argued that current ambient Pu standards for most such aerosols are about five orders of magnitude too high; the critics might have gone further, but their calculations as they stand imply that inhalation doses whose annual radiation would be capable of inducing lung cancer in 3.9×10^9 people could probably be contained in a piece of ^{239}Pu less than one cm in diameter [98] (rather than approximately 50 cm as current standards imply). No persuasive evidence against this general thesis—which rests on a straightforward geometric argument and on a histopathological hypothesis consistent with all clinical evidence—appears so far to have been presented, despite several lengthy reviews [99]. It is hard to imagine a definitive refutation that does not present a detailed cytochemical mechanism of radiation carcinogenesis; and no critic of the hot particle hypothesis seems eager to demonstrate such a mechanism.

Dispersion of Pu may be essentially permanent: aerosols fall out eventually, but data on their later resuspension vary over 11 orders of magnitude, leaving much room for conjecture. Escaped Pu can also be biologically reconcentrated in ways which, owing to its very complex chemistry, are poorly understood and probably still not all discovered [94]. As Rose remarks [100], "If the Tamplin and Cochran risk estimates turn out to be correct, nuclear fission power will need to be rethought, because the consequences of even a single large accident become disastrous." The same could be said for non-fission applications of actinides (e.g., of ^{238}Pu, with its very high specific activity, as a heat source). Acceptance of the hot particle theory would appear to heighten perceived risks from radiological terrorism [82, 101], from reduction of refractory fast reactor fuel by hot sodium after clad failure, from commonly observed industrial exposures [102], from aerosols of transuranic elements other than plutonium, and from Pu releases other than in reactor accidents (e.g., from the Pawling [102] and Rocky Flats [103] accidents or from the 1974 ^{238}Pu release from the Miamisburg weapons facility). More stringent Pu exposure standards would also lack operational meaning and be unenforceable because the air concentrations and lung burdens involved would be all but undetectable [98]. Whether the nuclear industry could operate under such standards would depend on whether the burden were on the industry to prove compliance (which would be impossible) or on others to prove noncompliance (which would be presumptive but debatable). Since neither position could be strictly proved, the outcome would depend in detail on the language and construction of the relevant regulations.

Chapter Seven

Safeguards

Many experts believe that the most critical problem of civilian nuclear power is likely to be that of safeguarding inventories of strategic materials [104] against theft [105] and subsequent illicit manufacture into crude but convincing nuclear weapons [101, 106-8]. The design and construction of such weapons by one or more enterprising and technically minded but still essentially amateur fanatics from a few kg of strategic materials, plus data and materials readily available to anyone, is far easier than is commonly believed [101, 106]. This is true even of nonmetallic chemical forms, such as oxide powder [109], or of fissile Pu heavily contaminated with isotopes of high spontaneous fission rate such as ^{240}Pu [110-112]. Though the resulting weapons would probably be relatively inefficient and of unpredictable yield, far more sophisticated weapons could be built by national or subnational groups with greater expertise, perhaps aided by any of the growing thousands of persons (of "varying psychological attitudes" [107]) formerly engaged in governmental weapons programs.

Dispersal of actinides could result from deliberate acts, or from incompetent attempts at theft or fabrication, or from a low yield explosion (which could release prodigious amounts of prompt radiation over km ranges [101, 106, 108]). Terrorists not desiring the trouble and risk of actually making a bomb or a far simpler Pu dispersion device could merely make instead a credible but perhaps anonymous threat of having done so—a threat which strategic reprisals, which apply only to attributable threats, would not deter. Blackmail based on threats of nuclear violence has already been attempted in several countries; the reputable journalist Burnham has claimed [106] that in 1973-4 seven plutonium bomb threats, several of which are "still under investigation", were made to the US govern-ment. The existence of analogous potential for antisocial abuse of chemical and microbiological preparations does not make the more spectacular nuclear risks (perhaps attractive to an *ex hypothesi* irra-tional terrorist) more acceptable; nor does the possibility that mili-tary weapons might be stolen (e.g., from US bases overseas, where the security arrangements have been much criticized [18]) make protection of raw strategic materials less important.

Extensive, mainly secret, and clearly inadequate [101, 106–8, 113] measures are now taken to prevent theft of strategic materials in the USA: the position in other countries is less clear and often more disquieting [114]. The extensive literature of this subject shows that continual small thefts from fuel facilities can be made in principle undetectable, that it may take weeks or months to detect large single thefts (whereas theft can take minutes or hours, and making a bomb days or weeks [107]), that physical security and detection devices can impede but not prevent undetected thefts, that precision of inventory assay (now nearly 1 percent [107]) will re-main inadequate to detect losses equivalent to a large number of reflected critical masses, and that complex materials accountancy methods can be readily misled [115]. Since safeguards techniques concentrate on where strategic material is supposed to be rather than on where it is supposed not to be, they cannot tell where it has gone; recovery is likely to present great difficulties, especially after theft from the vulnerable transport network [108, 116]. Unannounced diversion of civilian fuels or by-products to military purposes by sovereign governments, or by factions of governments [172], can be effectively beyond the reach both of international controls and, if competently done, of detection.

Possible nuclear thieves, or instigators of theft by agents, include terrorist groups, nonnuclear states [117], lunatics, criminal syndi-cates, and speculators—a diverse range with some strong transnational connections and with a history of impressive persistence and sophisti-cation in some past enterprises. Safeguards far more costly and thorough than those now applied to fissionable isotopes have failed over long periods to halt aircraft hijackings, bank robberies, and the black market in heroin (whose black market price is comparable to the open market price of ^{239}Pu: nobody knows, one hopes, what ^{239}Pu might cost in a demand-stimulated black market [118]). As with heroin, too, strong domestic safeguards are useless if safeguards anywhere abroad are lax—perhaps the most discouraging aspect of the problem [119]. Such analogies suggest, and the technical litera-ture tends to confirm, that it is impossible to prevent the theft of strategic materials by sufficiently determined groups whose motives "are subversive or economic"[108].

Many analysts believe that nuclear theft can and must be made far harder than it now appears to be. This view may not be heeded until the potential for violence unavoidably latent in civilian nuclear fuel cycles (and much aggravated by proposed Pu recycle [20, 120] and by fast reactor fuel cycles) has actually been exploited somewhere [121]. It appears from authoritative surveys [101, 106–8, 113] that present safeguards and the improvements in them now contemplated would perhaps deter the casually curious or the incompetent, but do little else save to make strategic shipments more conspicuous to the seriously interested. As has been noted earlier, however, more effective measures would often have a serious impact on personal freedom [20, 23, 101, 107] through added police powers, surveillance, infiltration, personal investigations, etc, and may ultimately require "very strict police control of the entire world. . . . This will be difficult to achieve and does not lead us to a very attractive future society."[122]

Chapter Eight

Nuclear Power and Public Policy

The foregoing discussion of technical and ethical issues—dealing largely with the assessment of risks and benefits and with their distribution in time and space—has bypassed several basic policy issues of a more subjective character: among them, Can nuclear power solve our energy problems? Do we need it? Who should decide? How?

PRACTICAL CONSTRAINTS ON EXPANSION

The ability of fission technology to be deployed with a sustained doubling time of a few years has classically been taken for granted, but is now being reassessed [63] as the problems of implementing and managing such rapid expansion are more clearly perceived. The rate and magnitude problems [3, 123–4] of deploying such a complex and unforgiving technology so quickly—far more quickly than technically simpler technologies have ever been deployed before on such a scale—now appear formidable. Even if one neglects such practical constraints as shortages of materials and of skilled labour, it is evident that fission cannot obviate heavy dependence on fossil fuels in this century nor soon thereafter, i.e., during the remainder of the oil-and-gas era. For example, if total world energy conversion increases by 5 percent annually and if a 1–GW(e) reactor is commissioned every day, then in 2000 most of our gross primary energy will still have to come from fossil fuels, which we shall have to burn more than *twice as fast as now*—at a time when oil and gas, especially in the USA and EEC, will already have become relatively scarce [3]. Even on a national scale, shifting energy dependence from fossil to fissile takes many decades to do—long enough to make it worth examining very closely *what else might be done instead over the same period (infra).*

The extreme capital intensity of large power stations in general and nuclear ones in particular—aggravated by large interest charges resulting from long lead times—poses special problems for prospective reactor purchasers who have increasing difficulty selling utility debt in traditional markets [125–6]. It even seems likely that the rate at which total capital for all sectors can be generated or diverted will soon become a constraint on projected growth of the energy (especially the electrical) sector in many countries. Distribution among competing sectors is already constrained both politically and economically, and the constraints are becoming more important. If investment in the electric power sector were restricted to some substantial fraction—say about a fourth, as in the USA—of gross fixed capital formation, some planned nuclear programs could not continue for long; but without such a restriction, too little capital would be left over to finance the nonenergy growth that was to require the new electricity. Meanwhile, as electrical utilities try to generate their own capital, perhaps more attention should be paid to the following positive feedback loop, already obvious in several countries: large capital programs → unfavourable cash flow → higher consumer prices for electricity → reduced demand → lower revenues, idle capacity, and increasing debt-to-equity ratio → higher prices for electricity, etc.

NET ENERGY CONSIDERATIONS

Nuclear energy has traditionally been represented as an abundant and independent source of energy that can promptly take over the dominant role of fossil fuels, especially oil, as their economic or geologic availability declines. Some persons who have superficially considered the energy inputs and outputs of nuclear power have supported this view. A more careful analysis by Price [127], however, based partly on a pioneering calculation by Chapman and Mortimer [128], has cast doubt on the ability of nuclear power to perform such a function. This study will not try to duplicate Price's lucid treatment [127] of principles and particulars, but a précis of some of his conclusions may be useful.

The "static" net energy yield of a nuclear power station—i.e., the total net energy yield for a *single* station, taking *all* its inputs and outputs into account—has been estimated by various practitioners of the new science of energy analysis [129] and by others less familiar with its difficulties and conventions. All the estimates are unsatisfactory in varying degrees. Chapman and Mortimer, though their preliminary analysis [128] is the most complete available, are obliged by a paucity of data to omit some significant terms (nearly all of them energy inputs) and to estimate others from aggregated national statistics; more detailed studies cited by Price [127] tend to support these estimates. Lem *et al.* [130] use different rules and do not show the detailed derivations. Various nuclear agencies [131] consider only the direct process inputs to the fuel cycle, thus excluding indirect process inputs (such as the energy required to make materials), investment inputs (such as the energy required to make capital plant), and inputs other than to the fuel cycle (such as the reactor itself)—a choice of system boundary so narrow as to be useless for policy. The author, whose informal estimates [132] have sometimes been rather inaccurately quoted, must (like Chapman and Mortimer [128]) estimate imprecisely known terms and omit others whose values may never be determinable [133]. Terms of the former type are to be evaluated more precisely over the next year or two by workers in several countries.

The Chapman–Mortimer estimate [128] of static net energy yield suggests that a single thermal reactor fuelled with uranium from high-grade ores can produce, over its lifetime, a maximum of about $10-15\times$ as much energy as it consumes, depending on its type. (With ores of very low grade, these energy output-to-input ratios would range from less than four to about eight.) These preliminary values are said to be a "maximum" because the underlying assumptions contain numerous conservatisms [127]. A more sophisticated or realistic analysis would yield significantly less favourable (lower) energy ratios than these upper limits [127].

Energy analysis of a single reactor is only the first step in the "dynamic" calculation of the inputs and outputs of a multireactor *program* as a function of time. Price [127] presents many important features of this dynamic analysis in general terms, then uses the Chapman–Mortimer data [128] to explore dynamic results for officially proposed nuclear power programs. (He also discusses why energy analysis and economic analysis do not always agree.) His main conclusions about nuclear programs can be outlined thus:

1. The net energy yield from each reactor alone must be not merely favourable but overwhelmingly so in the dynamic case, because at any given time some of the energy being produced by operating reactors is required to build and fuel the new reactors that are being built to increase capacity or to replace decommissioned reactors. Calculation shows that in the more aggressive national nuclear programs, the energy required for investment in new reactors continuously exceeds, sometimes by a large factor, the energy being produced by operating reactors.

2. Thus in an exponentially growing nuclear program intended to

double the number of reactors every two years or so (early projections for France and Japan), input to the program is at least 3X output and probably a good deal more; with a doubling time of about two and one-half years (recent USA), input is virtually certain to exceed output; with the exceptionally. long projected doubling time of about 4.3 years (UK) or about five years (currently projected USA to $\sim$ 2000), the energy needed for investment is at least half the program's output and perhaps more. Chapman [134] summarizes:

> Most nuclear programmes are designed on the assumption that each additional unit of capacity will be available to meet future increases in consumer demand and hence reduce fossil fuel requirements. The dynamic energy analysis shows that this is *never* the case. Under the worst conditions the nuclear programme could either increase fossil fuel requirements or decrease the fuels available to consumers. Under better conditions only a fraction of the installed capacity will be available to meet consumer demands; the rest will be absorbed by the nuclear industry itself.

If the net output of the program—i.e., the output available for general social purposes rather than for nuclear construction—is much less than the gross output, more reactors than expected will be needed to produce a unit of net output, and this could be considered a cost overrun for the program. With relatively slow growth (e.g., 4.3 year doubling time), so that the program is producing *some* net energy rather than requiring an ever-increasing fossil fuel subsidy, this cost overrun is likely to be 2–4X or more. Some countries, however, project such rapid growth that their programs would incur an increasing energy deficit.

3. The above analysis considers only the *transient* problem of nuclear power *during a growth phase.* The reactors are of course built in the expectation that after paying off their energy investments they will yield abundant energy "payback" that can provide a strategic substitute for dwindling oil supplies—though in fact it can only stretch oil reserves, not substitute wholly for them. Price [127] points out, however, three difficulties with this thesis. First, if nuclear power is to substitute enough for oil to provide a substantial fraction of a national energy budget before the oil runs out, the growth cannot be slow or brief, so the net energy deficit will be large and prolonged. A sustained and energy-intensive crash program of nuclear growth must be mounted at a time when energy supply is already limited; but the resulting cumulative energy deficit cannot be recovered until the growth abates, if then (under some circumstances it can never be recovered). Conversely, if this position is to be

avoided, nuclear growth *must be far too slow to achieve the significant and timely oil substitution expected of it.* Second, the problem cannot be evaded by substituting fast breeder reactors for present thermal reactors; for even if (which is doubtful) the net energetics of the former were far more favourable, rapid and sustained growth in thermal reactors, plus a very long period of simultaneous operation of fast and thermal reactors, would be required to produce plutonium quickly enough to fuel the new fast breeders. Third, slowing or stopping rapid nuclear growth, especially after it has gone on for some time, creates embarrassing recurrent transients in the supply of and demand for energy (and money, skills, materials, etc) that would cause substantial social and economic dislocation for many decades thereafter; and the quicker the initial growth—in order to obtain large "energy paybacks" as soon as possible—the less tractable these transients are.

Proposed rapid growth in nuclear power may therefore create more energy problems than it solves. Indeed, there is probably *no* large scale, high technology new energy source that can yield net energy while substituting rapidly for oil *unless* demand is meanwhile stabilized or reduced. More detailed analyses of static and dynamic energy balances, and of the transient problems of abating rapid growth, are needed and are now beginning, but they are likely to produce conclusions even less favourable to nuclear power than the conservative estimates presented here [127-8]. Similar estimates are of course needed for other energy technologies too—as shown by the recent and belated realization that some much-touted marginal fossil-fuel technologies may be net consumers of energy even in the static case—but are probably not very relevant to nuclear policy, since there is little doubt that many commonplace fossil-fuel technologies [128] and many decentralized "unconventional" energy technologies have much more favourable energetic properties than nuclear power.

ENERGY, TECHNOLOGY, AND SOCIETY

Whether nuclear power is necessary to meet the very different needs and aspirations of diverse peoples round the world is a complex question depending closely on social goals and on demand projections (and the credibility assigned to them). Classical high-growth projections—showing, for example, that the USA in 2000 will duplicate its total present electrical generating capacity every 29 months—would in most countries be difficult or impossible to achieve with conventional sources. But it now appears doubtful, for many cogent reasons [3, 123-4, 135] unrelated to the questions raised in this paper, whether it is either possible or desirable to make such projections come true by any means whatever (let alone whether the projections are rational in the light of the emerging importance [165] of price elasticity of electricity demand).

In the few countries where the matter has been seriously studied, chiefly the USA, it appears [135] that even modest efforts at energy conservation—those that are economically worthwhile, use existing technology, and have no significant impact on lifestyles—would make nuclear power unnecessary; and even in the short term, conservation would certainly "provide breathing room so that we can gain a better understanding of nuclear power problems, and reach some better judgments before major new expansions of nuclear power are made."[135] (The purely economic incentives favouring such conservation efforts are overwhelming [3, 135].) Indeed, on present knowledge [3] it is not clear that there is *any* country that cannot by such means, augmented in many cases by a wide range of non-nuclear energy technologies [3], fulfil liberal economic and social goals [136] without further recourse to fission [137]. But few countries have had much incentive to explore alternatives—including energy supply that is more decentralized [138], nonelectrical, and based on sources of energy income [3]. Most such supply and conservation options [3] are technically and socially simpler than fission technology; many seem to be cheaper; none has had even a hundredth of the R&D support accorded to fission, and it is thus not surprising that most are now less fully developed, whatever their technical merits may be [122]. Until all alternatives to fission have been explored far more thoroughly, the argument for fission as a last resort (rather than as a first resort) seems premature. The basic question should be: if we devote our time, skill and money not to fission but to energy conservation and "soft" energy supply technologies, starting now, can we use fossil fuels wisely as a bridge to help us construct over the next few decades an economy of energy income, without an intervening stage of reliance on fission?

The powerful and continuing R&D stress on fission—especially on fast reactors—raises important questions of public policy. In the USA, for example, official assessments suggest [73] that the proposed LMFBR budget would suffice to develop to commercial usefulness *all* major new nonnuclear energy technologies. The wisdom of effectively foreclosing these options by diverting scarce R&D resources (both fiscal and human) and nonrecyclable *time* to LMFBRs is widely questioned within the independent scientific community and, increasingly, within the US government. Reservations have increased since recent analyses [73, 139-43] have cast such doubt on the viability of LMFBR economics and on the validity of claims that LMFBRs must be deployed early and quickly. The US LMFBR program is accordingly under review in various quarters, and its continued high level of funding is in doubt [144]. Similar programs in other countries have not yet been subjected to public review.

NUCLEAR DECISIONMAKING

Present methods of balancing the public risks and benefits of fission technology (as of many other technologies) have so far made poor use of the mechanisms of representative government—it is rare to find a country whose fission program is ever subjected to broad legislative scrutiny and debate—and seem grossly unsatisfactory to all parties. The US system of licencing hearings, for example, seems to some observers [146] to be more a pro forma system of hearings to licence than a responsive forum of open decisionmaking. It appears that national decisionmaking mechanisms relevant to fission technology would profit from prompt and independent review for fairness, scope, autonomy of funding, breadth of public access and participation, advance availability of full public information, scope of administrative and judicial review of abuses, and—most important—balance of human and fiscal resources available to competing interests to ensure that the adversarial process yields greater public good. It is idle to offer unaided private citizens a theoretical right to intervene if, as Lapp estimates [60], "perhaps $500,000 is the sum needed to fund an adequate intervention" and if experts at, for example, National Laboratories and federal research contractors are not available as consultants to intervenors.

Informed policy decisions about fission are hampered by the absence of value-free nuclear economic analyses. The nuclear industry has benefited from many publicly financed "incentives" (which, as Lilienthal has noted [147], cost the same as subsidies but sound nicer). Yet no published audit reflects the military subventions, R&D subsidies, low notional interest rates, antitrust concessions, limited liability [148], and other unpublicized advantages that commercial fission power continues to enjoy. Skepticism about the economic advantages claimed for fission can be laid largely to this lack of objective accountancy, which goes considerably further than the omission of externalities (an equally common practice in fossil fuel technologies). This is not to argue that a new energy technology should never receive R&D support or other subsidies; only that they should appear properly in the accounts.

Objective analyses of nuclear economics should also take account of divergence between predicted and observed performance. Nuclear power stations have often been bought on the assumption, and even sold on the warranty, that capacity factors [171] of 75 percent or 80 percent can be maintained [149] for long periods, but actual capacity factors are often much lower. USAEC forecasts [150] assume that the capacity factor will be 40 percent in the first year of operation, 65 percent in the next two, 75 percent in the fourth through fifteenth years, and then linearly declining by 2 percent/year to 25 percent in the last year (year 40), yielding a lifetime average capacity factor of 57.375 percent. Recently released USAEC operating statistics [151] suggest, however, that even these figures are too sanguine, owing both to deratings from original design power and to unexpected unreliability. Analysis of the frequency and cause of outages suggests [152] that hard-to-repair [153] aging problems (metal fatigue, wear, corrosion, accumulation of dirt, etc) actually set in much sooner than expected, only a few years after initial "teething troubles" have been resolved; that the hoped-for 12 year plateau of 75 percent capacity factor is therefore unlikely to occur; and that the engineering lifetime may be less than the predicted 40 years. The observed cumulative average capacity factor of all US LWRs in commercial operation to date appears to be no more than about 55 percent [151–2]. How this compares with the performance of fossil-fuelled stations is in dispute and depends in detail on the manner of computation [152], but there is substantial evidence [152] that the nuclear performance is inferior. It must be borne in mind that reactor materials are subject not only to the thermal, mechanical, and chemical stresses shared by materials in fossil-fuelled power stations, but also to intense radiation, yet must allow certain components to move with great reliability and precision. Maintaining this performance over several decades, despite the special hazards of nuclear maintenance [153], presents difficulties which are only now beginning to be properly appreciated.

If actual capacity factor is lower than expected, the cost of providing a unit of output is higher than expected—a hidden form of cost overrun [152]. But the uniquely rapid direct escalation of nuclear capital costs is already a serious problem. An important recent analysis [154] of the sources of this escalation interprets most of it as "the economic result of a fundamental debate on . . . the social acceptability of nuclear power", and concludes that so long as controversy persists, escalation is likely to continue—and, in another decade or two, could make US nuclear power uncompetitive with coal. Bupp et al. [154] argue, then, that when special legislation suppresses the usual market signals (such as insurance premiums and tort liability) which discourage activities publicly perceived as hazardous [148], the market will find other ways of reflecting political perceptions of high social cost by making such activities cost more.

Capital costs for nuclear power today are exceptionally high even before poor availability [72, 151-2], uniquely rapid anticipated escalation of capital costs [154], and low net energy yields [127] are taken into account. These factors can only aggravate the grave difficulties (alluded to earlier) of finding capital for nuclear investment. The sums and rates involved are so large as to demand major changes in the ways in which societies generate and allocate capital, and to increase greatly the pressures on other sectors that must compete for the scarce capital. Several further problems of capital formation and allocation were noted above (p 42). No solution to any of these problems is now in sight.

Amidst allegations [73, 139, 145] of abuse of cost-benefit economics in nuclear policy exercises, such a distinguished practitioner of the discipline as Kneese [16] has cast doubt on its applicability in this sphere:

It is my belief that benefit-cost analysis cannot answer the most important policy questions associated with the desirability of developing a large-scale, fission-based economy. To expect it to do so is to ask it to bear a burden it cannot sustain. This is so because these questions are of a deep *ethical* character. Benefit-cost analysis certainly cannot solve such questions and may well obscure them. *** Unfortunately, the advantages of fission are much more readily quantified in the format of a benefit-cost analysis than are the associated hazards. Therefore, there exists the danger that the benefits may seem more real. Furthermore, the conceptual basis of benefit-cost analysis requires that the redistributional effects of the action be, for one or another reason, inconsequential. Here we are speaking of hazards that may affect humanity many generations hence and equity questions that can neither be neglected as inconsequential nor evaluated on any known theoretical or empirical basis. This means that technical people, be they physicists or economists, cannot legitimately make the decision to generate such hazards. Our society confronts a moral decision of a great profundity; in my opinion, it is one of the most consequential that has ever faced mankind.

The strong ethical character of fission decisions places a special burden on governments, on the composition of regulatory bodies, and on the professional responsibility [155] and individual conscience of fission technologists. Moral acceptability can perhaps be judged in a social sense from decisions taken openly in political forums—though other considerations may take precedence in practice—but cannot be judged from the marketplace, where choices are narrowly limited and imperatives can be wholly opposed to those of unfettered ethical choice. Persons who argue that widespread commercial acceptance of fission technologies proves their safety should recall that at one time the sales of Thalidomide, too, were rapidly increasing.

PUBLIC PARTICIPATION

In Sweden, Norway, Denmark, the Netherlands, France, the Federal Republic of Germany, Switzerland, Japan, Spain, the USA, and other countries, public acceptance of new technologies—especially fission—is an important policy problem. Not merely in the scientific community, but also in the public mind, confidence in the value of nuclear power, once widespread, is now rapidly eroding. It would seem appropriate in countries with a democratic tradition to subject to public scrutiny the issues underlying acceptance or rejection. Yet there seem to be four main obstacles to informed public discussion of the "Faustian bargain"[14] before the irreversible de facto commitment to it which is now only a decade or two away—less in some countries.

The first obstacle is the apparent unwillingness of most national authorities to foster such discussion of a topic which they consider either (1) too complex and technical for laymen to consider intelligently, or (2) more appropriate as a subject for a public relations program to allay public anxiety over issues which, in the view of some dirigiste governments, are technically resolved beyond doubt. (Laymen may consider it unwise, however, for a democracy to take major decisions that ordinary citizens cannot understand, and will in any case challenge the theses that nuclear decisions are really in this category or turn only on settled questions.)

The second obstacle is the lack of full public information [156], much of which is nonexistent, suppressed, alleged (with varying persuasiveness) to be proprietary, or not conveniently available. The third obstacle is the lack of adversarial expertise, especially outside the USA; this is partly a result of monopoly employment in countries with more limited numbers of nuclear experts. The fourth obstacle is the internal pressure within committed institutions [157]. When many talented people have devoted their careers to a difficult and exciting technology which they naturally think worthwhile [158], they tend both overtly and tacitly to discourage colleagues from bringing bad tidings, and in this effort they may do things as a group that they would never dream of doing individually. Members of such institutions often share, too, paradigms that may have little technical basis—for example, the belief that high and rapidly rising levels of energy conversion are essential for social welfare and full employment—a belief that in the USA, at least, does not withstand careful examination [135, 159]. Rational discussion in good faith between advocates and critics of fission technology is often impeded, too, by many advocates' unfamiliarity with recent technical literature on energy conservation and on alternative energy sources. Such unfamiliarity may lead otherwise competent persons to persist in views that are technically without merit.

STRATEGIC OPTIONS AND CONTINGENCIES

Advocates of fission technology would be well advised to acquaint themselves more thoroughly with the policy suggestions of their critics—especially those dealing with a *combination* of sophisticated coal technologies, decentralized and nonelectrical technologies of energy income, and energy conservation (the potential for which in rich countries is far greater than is commonly realized [135, 160]). If taken together rather than piecemeal, such an approach [3, 137] probably offers most countries a technically sound and socioeconomically attractive set of alternatives to conventional fission-based energy futures. Such alternatives may be easier to implement than fission but would be no less exciting to develop—and far more useful to the majority of the world's people, whose needs are often incompatible with large scale, high technology, highly centralized sources. The full R&D resources of the nuclear industry would be essential in developing the "soft" energy options and would certainly not lie idle. Nuclear power would still flourish—but remotely sited, about 150 million km away.

Institutions committed to fission would be prudent to hedge against the risk that fission might become politically unacceptable. This might happen in at least the following nine ways. Intensifying public debate (such as is now occurring, in various forms, in the USA, UK, Netherlands, New Zealand, Japan, France and Scandinavia [161]) could lead surprisingly soon to moratoria, with political and moral significance far out of proportion to their direct influence on, for example, international safeguards problems. Some reactor programs, especially LWRs and LMFBRs in the USA, appear to run a substantial risk of judicial interdict owing to apparent inconsistencies between promotional tendencies and statutory duties of care on the part of regulatory authorities. A major reactor accident in the next decade or two could shut down the industry [71], even in countries remote from the accident. A dramatic safeguards failure could do the same: India's 1974 nuclear test and the proposal to deploy power reactors in the Middle East have heightened public awareness of the dangers of proliferation. A decision by any country to forego fission technology or a particular type of reactor could have profound political influence abroad—even direct technical repercussions if major suppliers of nuclear fuel and technology decided to terminate exports. Successful sabotage or military action against a nuclear facility could spur reassessment of vulnerability: before mid-1975, a reactor (nearing completion in Argentina) had been seized by a mob, another (nearing completion in New York) severely damaged by arson, a third (operating in Tennessee) threatened with an aircraft crash by hijackers [162], a fourth (operating in Illinois) apparently sabotaged in minor respects, a fifth (nearing completion in Vermont) entered by an intruder who escaped after wounding the night watchman, nuclear equipment at a sixth (nearing completion in Alsace) damaged by bombs [84], fresh natural uranium fuel stolen from a seventh (operating in England), operating UK and US reactors and a US fuel fabrication facility threatened with explosions by terrorists, a Nike–Hercules base twice entered by persons unknown in a manner suggestive of reconnaissance by potential nuclear thieves [163], a French atomic bomb hastily detonated in the Sahara test area before it could be seized by dissident French generals [172], a Chinese nuclear base apparently threatened with seizure during the Cultural Revolution [172], and tons of unclassified metal stolen from a UK nuclear submarine base [163]. Further accidents in support facilities or in military nuclear facilities could suggest adverse inferences about civilian nuclear safety—even nuclear submarine collisions have some psychological effect. Spectacular mishaps in nonnuclear enterprises (like the 1974 Flixborough explosion [65] or the 1975 Moorgate underground train crash) could reduce public confidence in all expert reassurances of safety. Finally, further research on, for example, hot particle risks (p 35) could increase perceived dangers of fission accidents [100].

Alfvén [122] writes: "It is . . . a mistake to concentrate energy policy on a line which initially seems attractive, but which in the near future may be considered obsolete and dangerous." A more cautious, deliberate approach is clearly prudent in the case of any long term commitment involving extremely large sums of sunk capital: how much more necessary it is, then, where the social commitment is permanent even if the technological decision is reversed after only a few decades. Alfvén concludes [122] that the need for such caution must be more widely recognized:

> Because final acceptability of fission energy cannot be taken for granted, a warning should be issued that large scale application of fission technology may not be a realistic solution to the world's energy problem. It is unwise to spend more work and money on the development and deployment of fission reactors, especially breeders, before the acceptability problem is clarified. A nuclear moratorium [164–5] may be advisable in order to allow more time for a detailed analysis of this question.

In short, decisionmakers would be rash to commit themselves irretrievably to fission. On the contrary, they would be wise to explore alternatives to it while commitments of nuclear capital and generating capacity are still modest enough to permit a change of course without major discontinuities. Such exploration would facilitate a prompt response if, through growing public debate or through some singular event, the political, ethical, economic, and technical validity of fission should come to appear in a different light than it does today. As Weinberg [15] remarks: "It may turn out, after seriously studying the question, that one will conclude that Alfvén is right—man cannot in the very long run live with fission. What options will then be open . . . ?" The options which will then be open—and which many competent persons believe are already more attractive than fission [166]—will be those whose serious development we begin *now*.

Those options are certain to be needed eventually, for in the long run even the fission breeder economy cannot escape resource constraints. Faced with a choice between starting a transition to an economy of energy income now, when we have the fossil fuels to subsidize the transition, or later, when we shall not, we should do well to bear in mind the irreversibility of a commitment to nuclear power, a property unique in the evolving biological world that Geesaman and Abrahamson eloquently describe [19]:

> Man has lived until now by the chemical sublimation of the energies of sunlight. His ancient evolution has been a biochemical process. Life is mediated by collective stabilities in a space dominated by chemical energies. Persistence stems from a biochemical wisdom that is far more pervasive than conscious thought.
>
> Nuclear energy on Earth is a result of human intelligence. Human intelligence is a meaning in itself, a violent life effort to transcend the old evolution and squeeze history down into a scrap of time. Man's efforts at science and politics are a tentative and insecure facet of that evolution. "Brighter than 10,000 suns" was a prophetic description of the Trinity

event [,] for the Sun's primeval fire had burned briefly on the surface of the Earth, and the former stabilities of life, sorted out by the ages in a chemical world, suddenly seemed inadequate.

We have lived consciously with nuclear energy for a generation. In that time, we have pondered it cautiously as if it were a sleeping giant. In our wars, we have been careful to leave it undisturbed. Now, when our society is fragmented and alienated, when it is threatened by a diminished stability and a fading sense of self-duplication, is it the proper time to try our hand at nuclear energy? In this enterprise, the old reserves of evolutionary stability may be useless; and we must persist "as on a darkling plain" by the working of infallible intelligence alone.

Appendices—Part One

Some Preliminary Comments on the USAEC Reactor Safety Study (RSS)

Though severe constraints of time and money inhibit review of RSS in the depth that is urgently needed, several competent groups have undertaken independent assessments. A modest review effort is included in the American Physical Society's (APS) reactor safety inquiry [43], published 28 April 1975. A more detailed and largely complementary review by a joint technical working group of the Union of Concerned Scientists and the Sierra Club is continuing; but in view of the premature and extensive publicity being given to the draft RSS report [30], the UCS/SC review group thought it necessary to publish on 24 November 1974 a preliminary report [167] of those findings which are expected only to be strengthened by later analysis. Fuller conclusions will be published when the analysis is complete. The main preliminary conclusions of the UCS/SC group are [167]:

1. As noted by Bryan [67] and broadly supported by the General Accounting Office [67] (and by the APS study [43], which was unable to undertake a detailed review), the RSS methodology can yield results deserving of confidence only when *comparing* two similar systems, not when predicting *absolute* failure rates for any *one* complex system. Its use for the latter purpose was abandoned in the US aerospace program over ten years ago because it grossly underestimated actual failure rates [67]. For example, very similar methodologies, applied to the fourth stage Apollo engine (a system much simpler than a modern power reactor), predicted a failure rate of one in 10,000 missions, but the observed failure rate was about four in 100; and similarly in hundreds of other instances. Somewhat more reliable ways of predicting absolute failure rates have been developed in the past decade by the aerospace industry, but are not mentioned or used in RSS.

2. One reason that the RSS methodology consistently underestimates failure rates is that it cannot identify all the ways in which a complex system can and does actually fail. For example, "approximately 20 percent of the Apollo ground test failures and over 35 percent of the in-flight malfunctions and failures" were of types not identified as "credible" by intensive prior analyses similar to RSS. Analogously, many "near misses" of types previously believed to be "incredible" have occurred in the nuclear industry [44]; these unforeseen incidents, mainly involving multiple failures of safety devices [46], were particularly disturbing to the AEC team whose 1964-5 study of reactor accidents was neither published by the AEC nor mentioned by RSS. RSS uses a narrow data base that excludes most unusual multiple failures of this type. Moreover, RSS vastly simplifies and truncates its analysis in order to render it tractable, and then assumes, without technical justification, that the thousands of unanalyzed but allegedly "insignificant" terms are *collectively* insignificant.

3. Another reason that RSS-style studies consistently underestimate the failure rates of complex systems is that such studies cannot take account of currently unknown design errors—such as those which caused a large percentage of the test failures in the Atlas missile program, about half of the safety recalls of seven million US cars in 1973, and a significant fraction of the US reactor malfunctions in the past few years. In the special and controversial case of the ECCS [41], RSS assumes that one in 100 is a "conservative", i.e., overly safe, estimate of the probability that design faults render the systems ineffective; much expert opinion [41, 43] would consider only a value of one in one to be "conservative".

4. A mistake in the RSS methodology leads to the conclusion that "common mode failures" (where several redundant and supposedly independent components or systems are simultaneously disabled by some common cause [68]) are generally insignificant contributors to the total failure rate, whereas reactor experience shows them to be important or even dominant contributors compared to independent and random sequential failures. This RSS error strongly affects the results, both generally and through specific cases.

5. The data available for assessing how often components and people will randomly fail are sparse, and have generally been construed by RSS in an optimistic way inconsistent with much empirical evidence. One special and important case is the RSS assumption that, contrary to some expert opinion [51] (though perhaps not that of the APS review [43]), catastrophic failure of reactor pressure vessels is extremely unlikely.

6. RSS has generally not considered "secondary failures"—those caused by exposing a component to conditions for which it was not designed—but experience shows this to be an important mode of failure in actual reactor accidents.

7. For the above and other reasons, the RSS data and methodology yield absurd results when used to predict the likelihood of major multiple failures *which have actually occurred.* For example, in the case of a typical example of a certain class of multiple failures in boiling water reactors, RSS calculations would yield a *predicted* rate of 2.5 per billion billion (10^{18}) reactor-years (for the major causal events only) or even of 2.4 per hundred billion billion billion billion (10^{38}) reactor-years (for all the abnormal events reported to have occurred); *yet at least 15 such accidents have already occurred* in the USA. RSS makes no attempt to compare the frequency of such multiple failures with its own predictions, though this is clearly a crucial step in trying to verify the RSS conclusions and is urged by the APS review [13].

8. RSS neglects all deliberate acts of noncompliance with procedures and regulations: for example, sabotage from within or without, or mismanagement induced by substantial economic incentives (as when the managers of the Palisades reactor failed to notify the AEC that their holdup system for gaseous radioactive emissions was not working). The RSS conclusion that the consequences of sabotage could "of course" not exceed those of a major accident is demonstrably incorrect.

9. RSS assumes in general that the sorts of serious inadvertent errors in construction and operation that have recently been observed will not continue to occur.

10. RSS postulates, without support, a "learning curve" that will allegedly improve future safety, and extrapolates from the two model reactors analyzed to about 100 very different reactors to be on-line by about 1980. (About a thousand are proposed in the USA by 2000.)

11. RSS assumes that failure rates do not increase with time, either for a given reactor as it ages or for the entire industry as its rapid growth places increasing pressure on workers' dedication and competence.

12. RSS underestimates by at least a factor of four, and probably much more, the health effects of radioactive releases in reactor accidents [168]. Many errors or questionable assumptions affect this factor: for example, the dose to the large lower intestine is assumed to be 2–100× lower than that used by the ICRP and, in 1965, by the AEC, but without technical justification for the change; the latent

cancer estimates are inconsistent with the cited BEIR Report [38] in both size and uncertainty; the population and generational terms for genetic damage calculations are, by BEIR standards, mishandled; the dose response model chosen for juvenile thyroid is inconsistent with clinical evidence; the inhalation model underestimates by a large factor the radioiodine doses to children; some significant health effects (nonjuvenile thyroid pathology, nonspecific illness from whole body doses, nonthyroid latent cancers [43] from inhalation and selective deposition, and foetal effects) are wholly omitted; and in general, through treatment inconsistent with the BEIR Report, USEPA reports, and the ICRP−based 1965 AEC WASH−740 update, health effects in almost every category are understated by a significant factor. The USEPA comments [168] on RSS conclude that deaths and injuries could be ten times higher than RSS suggests, a view reportedly shared by the USAEC Regulatory Staff; combining the RSS radiological error of at least 4× with other obvious errors in computing accident consequences (e.g., [13], [14] below) yields, according to the UCS/SC group, an underestimate of consequences by at least 16× and possibly about 260×. The APS review [43] suggests a $\sim$50× error in the particular case studied [168], owing largely to RSS's "extremely important omission" of long term doses from ^{137}Cs ground contamination. As Kendall cogently points out in his review [43] of the APS study, the often-reproduced graph from WASH−1400 (DRAFT) comparing risks of fatality from nuclear and other sources appears to include only prompt, not latent, deaths from reactor accidents. If latent deaths, corrected by the APS factor of $\sim$50, are included, the resulting data point for the RSS "Reference Accident" is $\sim$6 orders of magnitude above the RSS curve, and, as Kendall shows, probably falls above the curve shown for total risk from all sources.

13. "The amount of radioactivity released in a given core melting accident appears to have been understated by as much as a factor of two."

14. "RSS relies on prompt and effective evacuation and on shielding of exposed persons to achieve a significant reduction of health effects. We have found RSS assumptions in this area to be inadequately supported and the extent of the reductions overstated. Indeed, the evacuation model and shielding assumptions contradict one another." Thus [167]:

On the one hand, there is evacuation so effective that large numbers of people surely must be moving with the precision and velocity of Patton advancing toward the Ruhr. Forty-five percent of the persons at risk actually reach "safety" in the RSS scenario 2 hours after warning; a population presumed to be accomplishing this feat with no prior practice and little chance to prepare. Moreover, only 5 percent of them are in vehicles at any given time. However, at the time the population caught under the airborne plume from the damaged reactor is being exposed to radioactivity, 90 percent must be assumed to be huddled in their cellars conservatively reducing their radiation exposure by a factor of 3. . . . It is a confused picture. One has a vision of two subcommittees of the RSS—one taxed to extract diligently all the benefit of shielding and another to get maximum mileage from evacuation. By happenstance the subcommittees never met.

15. The RSS conclusion that the probability of a core melt accident is one in 17,000 per reactor-year is at variance with an established AEC policy on which 20 years of safety analysis and design have rested: that though meltdowns have very serious consequences, they are extremely unlikely—as WASH–1250 put it in July 1973, "so unlikely as to verge on the impossible". RSS now says that the likelihood is "somewhat" (i.e., 60–600×) higher than previously believed but that, for previously unperceived reasons, the consequences of a meltdown are fairly innocuous. This overturning of traditional beliefs has some specific implications for policy, e.g., that offshore nuclear plants present an unacceptable hazard; but it also implies that if RSS is right, then all previous AEC and industry safety analysis throughout the world has been founded on a basic error, is now inoperative, and must be considered incompetent. The same conclusion is suggested by some other new RSS findings, e.g., that the pipe breaks most to be feared are not the large ones on which nearly all ECCS analysis and design is based, but the small ones that have received relatively little study [169]; indeed, RSS says that the small pipe breaks are so much more important as contributors to total risk that it does not make much difference in the end whether ECCS will work or not. If this is correct, the thrust of a decade or more of official safety regulation in all countries has been misdirected owing to an erroneous identification of the main source of risk. RSS and previous AEC safety analyses cannot both be right.

16. RSS does not adequately explain the serious discrepancies between its calculations of accident sequences and those of earlier AEC studies such as BMI–1910 and WASH–740. The most puzzling divergences are with a more sophisticated study, the 1964–5 WASH–740 update, which RSS does not mention at all. In this unpublished exercise, senior AEC experts anxious to discover any possible ways to mitigate the disturbing conclusions of WASH–740 (1957) were unsuccessful in their quest; they managed only to verify that a major accident in a large modern reactor could yield worst-

case consequences some 40× worse than those described, for a 1957 vintage reactor of 500 MW(t), in WASH-740. (See the AEC internal memoranda quoted in note 167 at p 108 and Appendix C.) It is thus of special interest to learn why the RSS consequence estimates for a 500-MW(t) reactor are one or two orders of magnitude lower than those of WASH-740.

Numerous individual reviewers have also submitted to the AEC their personal comments on WASH-1400 (DRAFT) [30]. The author's comments [170] are perhaps typical; the main points raised include the following in addition to most of those listed above:

1. RSS claims to have obtained a narrow (generally 3×) error spread in its final risk assessments. These are calculated from very many cascaded terms, each of which has an inherent uncertainty often of one or more orders of magnitude. Ordinarily these cumulative uncertainties would be expected to multiply. RSS has obtained a narrow final error spread, however, by applying certain elaborate statistical techniques, not only to genuine random variables whose variation arises from effectively stochastic (random) processes, such as the weather, but also to engineering and biophysical variables whose great uncertainty arises mainly from *lack of scientific knowledge*. Thus the assumed error bands may "cover" technical uncertainty, but the assumed statistical distribution within those bands *covers it up*, introducing spurious precision into a system whose fundamental problem is lack of accuracy. That a number is unknown does not make it random nor make it a fit subject for statistical treatment. Imposing any sort of statistical error distribution on a range of mainly technical, mainly nonstochastic uncertainty introduces information or knowledge which *ex hypothesi* does not exist. Confidence in the accuracy of such results is unfounded.

2. The RSS report omits a wide-ranging and multivariate sensitivity analysis for many engineering variables far more basic than the few demographic, meterological, and health physics variables that are considered. Values have been assigned to these engineering variables through the extensive exercise of subjective judgment and of simplifying assumptions, owing to the lack of physical understanding and experimental data relevant to many important phenomena (e.g., pressure vessel rupture under thermal shock, containment failure modes and pressures, core distortion and flow blockage, destructive steam explosions, hydrogen generation/mixing/deflagration/detonation, etc). For example, the APS review [43] tersely concludes at pp V-38-9: "The mechanisms of steam explosions are not well understood and the likelihood of steam explosions involving even a small part of the core is unknown."

3. Comparison between failure rates assumed or predicted by RSS and those actually observed is sparse and difficult to interpret, particularly where *calculated* failure rates are given to two significant figures whilst *observed* failure rates are "rounded to the nearest order of magnitude to help cover averaging effects and uncertainties in data" [30].

4. RSS assumes that land and structures contaminated with radioactivity can be rapidly and efficiently decontaminated both by human effort and by natural processes. These assumptions seem unjustified [43], are reported by the APS review [43] at pp AII–52 and AII–59 not to be supported by the unpublished reference which RSS cites, and should be analyzed for specific isotopes, not for all isotopes aggregated together as in RSS. Moreover, the effect of limiting the health physics calculations to 45 isotopes and the effect of possible ground water contamination [43] should be assessed. (Migration rates of ~ 1 km in 8 yr have been observed for ^{90}Sr injected into an Idaho aquifer [43]; RSS assumes an average reactor is sited only ~ 460m from a large body of water.)

5. The RSS evacuation assumptions are based on unpublished plans whose implementation is doubtful [43]. A short warning time is also assumed. RSS analogies to nonnuclear evacuations seem psychologically invalid, especially in view of widespread public panic in response to the Scandinavian radio spoof of 13 November 1973.

6. The RSS core meltdown model, like other computer exercises on which RSS results rely heavily, is elaborate but unverified; it is doubtful whether it is technically adequate to support the vast computational edifice built on it.

7. The maturity of the engineering judgment brought to bear by RSS in assigning values to highly uncertain physical variables should be judged in the light of past divergences between claimed and empirically validated degrees of conservatism.

8. All principal investigators and their respective contributions to RSS should be identified; the degree of detail in the various sections of the RSS report should be made commensurate with the importance of the subjects treated; numerous missing assumptions and intermediate steps should be supplied; all RSS working papers and memoranda should be promptly published.

9. The RSS Summary Report (given wide public distribution) should reflect uncertainties stated in the main report. Both should reflect uncertainties and reservations expressed by the authors of appended engineering studies. As the UCS/SC review group comment [167],

As one moves from the very technical material (mostly in the RSS Appendices), to the assembly and explication of the study's results (in the report itself), to the report summary, and then to the AEC's interpretation of the report results, the cautionary notes, the uncertainties, the sense that there may be limitations to the results—all these successively drop away. What replaces these dwindling and vanishing cautions is increasingly forceful declarations that nuclear technology is benign and that this conclusion is, at last, overwhelmingly confirmed.

10. All comments on RSS received by the AEC should be appended to the final draft report; quasi-adversarial review should be sought from ad hoc groups to be convened by the National Academy of Sciences and by a suitable consultant such as RAND; and existing independent reviews should be given time and funds to achieve the degree of detailed scrutiny that RSS deserves. The UCS/SC review group [167], like the author [170], comments on AEC procedures so far:

> Normally the release of a major technical report alleging the resolution of a national controversy of considerable importance would follow . . . two . . . exhaustive reviews: the first by the authors and internal agency advisors to the program and a second by outside reviewers following a limited release of a draft version of the report. Careful review procedures such as these can much reduce the possibility of grave error being widely disseminated as truth and can diminish the possible need for significant retraction or major controversy over the study's conclusions with attendant embarrassment. The AEC chose to bypass prudent reviews before widespread public release of the results . . . [which began] some seven months *before* the draft version of RSS was released. . . . *** The AEC's premature use of the results to confirm the safety, and thus the public acceptability, of nuclear power, with no mention of the limitations expressed in the report itself, or of the even more acute defects that we have found, . . . is *improper and wrong.*

Appendix I-2

Transuranic Decay Chains

The biological significance of transuranic isotopes depends not only on their chemistry, half-lives, and characteristic radiations, but also on the corresponding properties of the daughter isotopes resulting from their decay. For this reason, ^{239}Pu and its daughters may be less important for very long term storage than ^{237}Np and its daughters. (Some ^{237}Np is produced by alpha decay of ^{241}Am, itself a beta daughter of ^{241}Pu, but the main source of ^{237}Np is the reaction ^{238}U$(n,2n)$ ^{237}U(β^-) ^{237}Np. Further neutron capture by ^{237}Np produces ^{238}Pu.)

Actinides are classified into four groups according to whether their atomic mass is an even multiple of four—the so-called $4n$ group—or is expressible as $4n + 1$, $4n + 2$, or $4n + 3$. The commonest transuranic nuclides are classified in Table A; there are of course others, which in practical reactor systems tend to be much less plentiful. In general the higher actinides are produced more profusely in high than in low burnup fuel (e.g., more in LWRs and HTGRs than in Magnox reactors). Claiborne calculates [90] that the actinides beyond ^{244}Cm, though omitted from Table A because of their small physical quantities, increase the total biological hazard of LWR wastes by a factor which varies with time and has a maximum value of about 2.5 at 10^4 yr.

Table A also shows the approximate mass (kg) and activity (kCi) of the main transuranic nuclides present in the waste stream typically derived from reprocessing 1000 metric tons of PWR fuel, roughly the lifetime discharge of a single large PWR. (We assume that the fuel is irradiated to the standard PWR burnup of 33 GW(t)–days per metric ton (T) of uranium at a specific power of about 37.5 MW(t)/T, then cooled for 0.3 yr, then reprocessed to produce a waste stream from

Table A.　Concentrations and Projected Annual Production of Principal Transuranic Nuclides

Class	Nuclide	Approximate amount in waste stream from 1000 T PWR fuel (33 GW(t)–d/T U, 99.5% U,Pu recovery, .3y decay)		Approximate amount in annual waste stream from 1500 GW(e) LWRs + 1500 GW(e) LMFBRs† (99.5% U,Pu recovery, ~.3y decay)	
		$kg^{[87]}$	kCi	T	MCi
4n + 1	Np–237	482.	0.34	35.	0.025
4n + 2	Pu–238	0.82	14.1	0.15	3.
4n + 3	Pu–239	26.4	1.6	15.	0.9
4n	Pu–240	10.6	2.4	6.	1.2
4n + 1	Pu–241	5.	514.	1.5	150.
4n + 1	Am–241	49.	159.	27.	90.
4n + 2	Pu–242	1.8	0.007	0.9	0.003
4n + 3	Am–243	91.	18.	15.	3.
4n	Cm–244	30.	2400.	3.	210.

†Based on OECD–ENEA projections ("Radioactive Waste Management Practices in Western Europe", Paris, 1972) which omit [237]Np; the estimate for this isotope is very uncertain. Among the more plentiful isotopes not shown in the table are [236]U (see Table B, 4n series) and [242]Cm (a 163 day alpha emitter yielding [238]Pu); for these two isotopes the respective entries in the third and fourth columns would be 22.6 kg (0.0014 kCi) and 5.13 kg (17,000 kCi). See also Blomeke et al. [87] and Pigford [94].

which 99.5 percent of the fissile isotopes ^{239}Pu and ^{241}Pu, of the other Pu isotopes, and of all the U isotopes have been removed. Present recovery is seldom so thorough. The transuranic concentrations in a waste stream from LMFBR fuel would generally be larger than those for a PWR by up to an order of magnitude.) For orientation, the table also gives very rough projections (in metric tons and megacuries) of the annual production of each isotope by an installed capacity of about 3,000 GW(e), assumed to be half LWRs and half LMFBRs; many official sources project such a world nuclear capacity for the year 2000 or shortly thereafter.

Note that the activity shown for each isotope excludes the activity of daughters, which may at its maximum for each parent (when the short-lived isotopes are most abundant) be one to three orders of magnitude larger than for the parent alone (ORNL–TM–3548, 1971, Table 8). (Indeed, the sum of all activity for all the parents shown and their numerous daughters, *integrated over all time*, is of order 10^{22} Ci/10^3 T LWR wastes, owing mainly to the high specific activity of polonium isotopes: fortunately, very much less activity than that is present at any one time.) Clearly the actinide activity depends on the decay time allowed: WASH–1250 (1973), Table 4–3 shows that in a 1100–MW(e) PWR the actinide activity is 3450 MCi at shutdown, 1330 MCi after one day, 9.35 MCi after 30 days, 5.90 MCi after 120 days, 5.17 MCi after one year, and 3.27 MCi after ten years.

The complete decay chains for the principal transuranics are shown in Table B, based on the US Public Health Service *Radiological Health Handbook* (USGPO, 1970). Half-lives are given in years (y), days (d), hours (h), minutes (m), or seconds (s); spontaneous fission, gamma emissions, secondary (e.g., α–n) reactions, and the energy of alpha (α) and beta (β) emissions are not shown, though all are important. In order to emphasize the rate-limiting steps, decays with half-lives exceeding 1000 years have been underlined once, and decays with half-lives exceeding 10,000 years have been underlined twice. Only the principal decay modes are shown: an asterisk indicates a decay mode to which a less probable alternative exists, yielding a different product whose daughter is identical to the daughter of the product shown (i.e., each branch from the main decay chain returns to it after one variant step).

Study of these decay schemes reveals that once a nuclide has passed the initial rate-limiting steps, it undergoes many alpha and beta decays (many of which are also significant gamma emitters) relatively quickly, producing the sort of potential for internal radiological hazard that is so familiar for the ^{226}Ra daughters. Obviously

Table B. Principal Transuranic Decay Chains

4n + 1 series: ^{237}Np$(2.14 \times 10^6\,\text{y}\,\alpha)\,^{233}Pa(27\text{d}\,\beta)\,^{233}U(1.62 \times 10^5\,\text{y}\,\alpha)\,^{229}Th(7340\text{y}\,\alpha)\,^{225}Ra(14.8\text{d}\,\beta)$
^{225}Ac$(10\text{d}\,\alpha)\,^{221}Fr(4.8\text{m}\,\alpha)\,^{217}At(0.032\text{s}\,\alpha)\,^{213}Bi(47\text{m}\,\beta*)\,^{213}Po(4.2\mu\text{s}\,\alpha)\,^{209}Pb(3.3\text{h}\,\beta)\,^{209}$Bi.

4n + 2 series: ^{238}Pu$(86.4\text{y}\,\alpha)\,^{234}U(2.47 \times 10^5\,\text{y}\,\alpha)\,^{230}Th(78,000\text{y}\,\alpha)\,^{226}Ra(1602\text{y}\,\alpha)\,^{222}Rn(3.8\text{d}\,\alpha)\,^{218}$Po
$(3.1\text{m}\,\alpha*)\,^{214}Pb(26.8\text{m}\,\beta)\,^{214}Bi(19.7\text{m}\,\beta*)\,^{214}Po(164\mu\text{s}\,\alpha)\,^{210}Pb(21\text{y}\,\beta)\,^{210}Bi(5\text{d}\,\beta*)\,^{210}$Po
$(138\text{d}\,\alpha)\,^{206}$Pb.

4n + 3 series: ^{239}Pu$(24,390\text{y}\,\alpha)\,^{235}U(7.1 \times 10^8\,\text{y}\,\alpha)\,^{231}Th(25.5\text{h}\,\beta)\,^{231}Pa(32,500\text{y}\,\alpha)\,^{227}Ac(21.6\text{y}\,\beta*)\,^{227}$Th
$(18.2\text{d}\,\alpha)\,^{223}Ra(11.4\text{d}\,\alpha)\,^{219}Rn(4\text{s}\,\alpha)\,^{215}Po(0.0018\text{s}\,\alpha*)\,^{211}Pb(36.1\text{m}\,\beta)\,^{211}Bi(2.15\text{m}\,\alpha*)$
^{207}Tl$(4.79\text{m}\,\beta)\,^{207}$Pb.

4n series: ^{240}Pu$(6600\text{y}\,\alpha)\,^{236}U(2.42 \times 10^7\,\text{y}\,\alpha)\,^{232}Th(1.41 \times 10^{10}\,\text{y}\,\alpha)\,^{228}Ra(6.7\text{y}\,\beta)\,^{228}Ac(6.13\text{h}\,\beta)\,^{228}$Th
$(1.91\text{y}\,\alpha)\,^{224}Ra(3.64\text{d}\,\alpha)\,^{220}Rn(55\text{s}\,\alpha)\,^{216}Po(0.15\text{s}\,\alpha)\,^{212}Pb(10.6\text{h}\,\beta)\,^{212}Bi(60.6\text{m}\,\beta*)\,^{212}$Po
$(0.3\mu\text{s}\,\alpha)\,^{208}$Pb.

The principal higher transuranics enter these decay chains as follows:

4n + 1 series: ^{241}Pu$(13.2\text{y}\,\beta*)\,^{241}Am(458\text{y}\,\alpha)\,^{237}$Np etc.

4n + 2 series: ^{242}Pu$(3.9 \times 10^5\,\text{y}\,\alpha)\,^{238}U(4.51 \times 10^9\,\text{y}\,\alpha)\,^{234}Th(24.1\text{d}\,\beta)\,^{234m}Pa(1.17\text{m}\,\beta*)\,^{234}$U etc.

4n + 3 series: ^{243}Am$(7370\text{y}\,\alpha)\,^{239}Np(2.35\text{d}\,\beta)\,^{239}$Pu etc.

4n series: ^{244}Cm$(18.1\text{y}\,\alpha)\,^{240}$Pu etc.

nuclides which do reach the region of rapid decay can be biologically significant out of proportion to their abundance if they happen at that time to be inside an organism. For this reason, even if a rate-limiting step has an extremely long half-life and lets very few nuclides through in a given period, those few can be biologically important: for example, naturally occurring ^{226}Ra is a substantial hazard to uranium miners [37] and others [35] notwithstanding that it is derived from the successive decay of ^{238}U (half-life 4.51×10^9 y), ^{234}Th (24.1 d), ^{234m}Pa (1.17 m), ^{234}U (2.47×10^5 y), and ^{230}Th (7.8×10^4 y). The only effect of these long half-lives is to make the crustal abundance of ^{226}Ra some $3 \times 10^6 \times$ less than that of ^{238}U, not to make it biologically insignificant.

Fortunately, the man made actinides are less plentiful than ^{238}U, but the dynamics of their decay are broadly similar. Thus the juxtaposition of two rate-limiting steps makes the initial decay of ^{239}Pu more important (in periods less than $\sim 10^8$ y) than the decay of its daughters. For the same reason, only the initial decay of ^{240}Pu is particularly important in periods of biological interest. But a rate-limiting step with half-life of 10^7 years or more does *not* occur at the start of the $4n + 1$ or the $4n + 2$ series, so that for decay periods of order 10^6 years these series can become more important than the others. For example, after 10^6 years virtually all of the 26.4 kg of ^{239}Pu in the waste stream from 1000 T of PWR fuel (we ignore for the present the ^{239}Pu elsewhere in the fuel cycle, but there is $200 \times$ as much of it) will have decayed to ^{235}U, but only about 10^{-3} of that will have decayed further—to products which, though biologically hazardous, are at least not plentiful. In contract, essentially all of the initial 54 kg of ^{241}Am and ^{241}Pu will have supplemented the initial 482 kg (or, according to WASH–1250, 760 kg) of ^{237}Np, of which 28 percent will have decayed to ^{233}Pa, of which virtually all will have decayed to ^{233}U, of which a small fraction will have decayed to ^{229}Th, etc. Hence the $4n + 1$ series will have yielded, over the first 10^6 years, nearly $5\times$ as much alpha and beta radiation as the $4n + 3$ series. In the long run the ^{237}Np series may be the dominant hazard and may require isolation for periods of order 10^8 years [88], roughly two to two and one-half orders of magnitude longer than for the ^{239}Pu decay chain.

Notes—Part One

1. Statement from the Continuing Committee (*cf.* Report of Working Group 5), 23d Pugwash Conference (Aulanko, Finland): *Pugwash Newsletter 11*:1+2 (July and Oct 1973). These misgivings were confirmed by a majority at the 24th Pugwash Conference (28 Aug–2 Sept 1974, Baden, Austria), where "A strong majority held that universality of the Non–Proliferation Treaty *must be* achieved if fission power is to be further deployed." (Statement from the Continuing Committee, 24th Pugwash Conference.) For a contrary view, see Bethe, H *et al.*, *Wkly Energy Rpt* special issue, 16 Jan 1975 and *Bull Atom Scient 31*, 3, 4 (1975). For general background, see Patterson, W C, *Nuclear Power* (Pelican, ~ Jan 1976).

2. This study will not address issues that seem more rhetorical than substantive: *e.g.* whether nuclear reactors are "environmentally superior" to fossil-fuelled boilers. Such a case could easily be made, and often is, by defining "environmental superiority" so as to embrace nuclear power's specific environmental advantages whilst excluding its equally specific environmental disadvantages. Opponents of nuclear power, using (from their point of view) similar semantics, could perhaps argue that cyanide is a more healthful food than candy because it does not promote tooth decay. This sort of wordplay offers scant insight into major issues and will therefore be ignored here.

3. Lovins, A B, *World Energy Strategies: Facts, Issues, and Options*, Ballinger (17 Dunster St, Cambridge, Massachusetts 02138) and Friends of the Earth International (c/o FOE Inc, 529 Commercial St, San Francisco, California 94111), 1975; previous edition reprinted in *Bull Atom Scient 30*, 5, 14–32 (May 1974) and *30*, 6, 38–50 (June 1974); conclusions summarized in part in *Ambio 3*:123 (1974) and in remarks to the Conference on Growth and Technology, Ministry of Science and Technology/International Society for Technology Assessment (Ottawa, 5 Feb 1975).

4. Or—it could well be argued—of depletion of high grade fossil fuel resources; though nuclear power, as Abrahamson has remarked (see note 12), "does not, in any meaningful way, avoid the resource constraints imposed by the finite nature of the world's fuel reserves."

5. Weinberg, A M, *Nucl News 14*, 12, 33 (1971).

6. Alfvén, H, *Bull Atom Scient 28*, 5, 5 (1972).

7. Save perhaps manned space flight. In *The New Yorker*, 11 and 18 Nov 1972, and in *Thirteen: The Flight That Failed*, Dial (New York, 1973), H S F Cooper Jnr gives a fine account of the impact of human fallibility on Apollo 13. Such analogies with nuclear systems are often illuminating.

8. Holdren, J P, "Radioactive Pollution of the Environment by the Nuclear Fuel Cycle", Paper XXIII–2, 23d Pugwash Conference (Aulanko, Finland, 30 Aug–4 Sept 1973); revised and reprinted in *Bull Atom Scient 30*, 8, 14 (1974).

9. Engineers who find these two paragraphs troublesome might pretend they are Professor Rasmussen (see note 30) and ask themselves, "What are the errors and omissions in my risk analysis, and how do I know?" The only answer can be, "I have tried to avoid errors and omissions, but within the rules of my engineering paradigm I can never prove that I succeeded, nor state the probability that I failed." Once one admits the possibility that the risk analyst might be wrong, one must take seriously the nonengineering paradigm's view that human fallibility can be an important element of risk—an element that we do not know how to quantify. The "fallibility" paradigm is all the more persuasive because the engineering judgment which the nuclear industry (especially in the USA) applies to risk analyses is not yet mature, as demonstrated by the numerous changes made in technical approaches and assumptions (*e.g.* in design and analysis of many engineered safety systems) as new knowledge has come to light in recent years.

10. USAEC, *Reactor Operating Experiences* 69–9 (1969) states: "In the recent past, there have been a number of occurrences at reactors where human error resulted in undesirable situations. None of these situations represented a threat to the health and safety of the public. The absence of more serious effects is largely the result of good luck." See also the citations in note 44, all basic reading.

11. Kendall, H W, "Nuclear Power: A Review of Its Problems", The New Zealand Energy Conference 1974, University of Auckland, New Zealand, 23–5 May 1974. Similarly, the APS review (see note 43) concludes at p I–3 that "unless diligence is maintained, quality assurance and human error may well represent a limiting factor in maintaining safe operation."

12. Abrahamson, D E, "Nuclear Power: Its Hazards and Social Implications", Centre Party/School for Adult Education Symposium on Energy, Development, and Future (Stockholm, 25–6 Nov 1974).

13. Weinberg, A M, *Science 177*:211 (1972). In his 23 Apr 1975 address to the European Nuclear Society in Paris, USNRC Commissioner Mason agrees that "World-wide public skepticism about [nuclear] . . . energy has grown over the past several years to where a discussion of only technical issues fails to address completely the realities of the situation. *** [W]e would be remiss if we did not recognize that serious problems presently impede the total public acceptance of nuclear energy. *** [T]he real decision . . . will be made, as Albert Einstein predicted years ago, in the village square."

14. Weinberg, A M, *Science 177*:27 (1972).

15. Weinberg, A M, "Can Man Live With Fission—A Prospectus", Project on Sustainable Growth, Woodrow Wilson International Center for Scholars, Washington, DC, 18 June 1973.

16. Kneese, A V, "The Faustian Bargain", *Resources 44*:1 (Sept 1973), Resources for the Future Inc (1755 Massachusetts Avenue NW, Washington, DC 20036). A similar version was published in *Not Man Apart 3*, 5, 16 (May 1973), Friends of the Earth Inc (*supra* note 3).

17. Edsall, J T, *Envir Conserv I*, 1, 32 (1974).

18. The difficulty of enforcing such stringent conditions may perhaps be illustrated by the failure of a former top security officer of the USAEC to repay more than $170,000 out of $239,000 borrowed from fellow employees: he had used substantial sums, unknown to his superiors, for racetrack wagers. (He was sentenced to three years' probation in Feb 1973.) Analogously, press reports based on congressional testimony say that thousands of persons responsible for handling US nuclear weapons have been relieved of their duties in recent years owing to their use of illegal drugs or the like, and that every year about 3 percent of the ~ 120 000 people working with US nuclear weapons are discovered to be security risks (*e.g.* AP, *Observer* [London], p 1, 27 Jan 1974; UPI, *Intl Her Trib* [Paris and London], p 3, 14–15 Dec 1974; *Los Angeles Times*, 27 Jan 1974). The Rosenbaum Report (see note 107) envisages that up to three "insiders", who might include "anyone up to the higher levels of management", could credibly take part in a conspiracy to steal strategic materials—a prudent conclusion in view of the apparent theft of a large amount of confiscated heroin from the vaults of the New York City Police Department. The Japanese laboratory closure (see note 115) and the recent indictment of seven people for extortion in connection with construction of the Calvert Cliffs station suggest that the nuclear industry is not immune to dishonesty. In an institutional rather than personal context, "Notes and Comment" in *The New Yorker*, 22 July 1974, calls attention to two other recent failures of arrangements that were presumably subject to the most rigorous controls: the alleged failure of the proper NATO authorities to find out about the Oct 1973 US strategic alert for several hours, and the 40 minute delay in countermanding the accidental Feb 1971 announcement by the US National Emergency Warning Center that a nuclear war was beginning. Likewise, mustard gas and a Sidewinder missile have been stolen from US bases in Europe, and "US Army exercises have shown that nuclear-weapon stores can be penetrated without detection, in spite of armed guards, fences, and the most modern electronic barriers" (Barnaby, F, *New Scient 66*:494 (29 May 1975), and reported in *The Times* [London], p 7, 13 June 1975).

19. Geesaman, D P and Abrahamson, D E, *Bull Atom Scient 30*, 9, 37 (1974).

20. Speth, J G *et al.*, *Bull Atom Scient 30*, 9, 15 (1974). A forthcoming comment, "Policing Plutonium: The Civil Liberties Fallout" (*Harv Civ Rights— Civ Lib L Rev*, 1975), amplifies Speth's political concerns. In hearings before the Subcommittee on Energy and Environment, Committee on Interior and Insular Affairs, US House of Representatives (2 May 1975), Speth discusses several recent instances of coercion, including the firing or transfer of Kerr McGee employees who refused to take a wide-ranging polygraph test.

21. The USAEC is ordering utilities to arm their guards: *N Y Times*, 1 May 1974; *Nucleon Wk*, 17 Oct 1974.

22. According to a *N Y Times* report of 11 Aug 1974, Texas state police have been maintaining dossiers on opponents of nuclear power, and Business and Professional People for the Public Interest was apparently under surveillance by Chicago police (*Chicago Tribune* editorial, 29 Mar 1975, and *Chicago Daily News*, 25 Mar 1975). Recent experience suggests a potential for abuse. In April 1975, the Virginia House of Delegates passed a bill giving Virginia Electric Power Co access to criminal records for employee background investigations; Vepco had unsuccessfully sought powers to investigate other persons and to make arrests anywhere in Virginia (*Not Man Apart 5*, 9, 9 [May 1975], FOE Inc [*supra* note 3]).

23. WASH–1237 (USAEC, Aug 1974). *Cf.* Casimir, H B G, interview in *Milieudefensie 3*, 5/6, 3 (1974).

24. Approximately 150 civilian power reactors are now operable in about 19 countries; over 350 are planned for about two dozen countries in 1980, and about 3000 by the turn of the century, with rapid growth projected to continue thereafter. Many dozens of countries have civilian nuclear R&D programs. World inventories of long-lived fission products and of waste actinides are projected to be $\sim 4 \times 10^{10}$ Ci and $\sim 2 \times 10^9$ Ci respectively about the year 2000 (when annual ^{239}Pu throughput is projected to exceed 5×10^5 kg), with continued rapid increase for some decades thereafter. J A Lane *et al.* of IAEA ("The Role of Nuclear Power in the Future Energy Supply of the World", 1 Oct 1974) envisage an accelerated nuclear program with world installed capacity of 316 GW(e) in 1980, 1900 GW(e) in 1990, and 5330 GW(e)—about 5000 large reactors—in 2000. The corresponding stocks of plutonium would be respectively 150, 1300, and 5500 metric tons. Perhaps a third of the ^{239}Pu would be produced in countries now lacking nuclear weapons.

25. USAEC, internal memorandum from A P Kenneke, Minutes of Steering Committee on Revision of WASH–740, 28 Jan 1965 (USAEC Public Document Room, 1973).

26. Estimated from data in Courts, A J *et al.*, "Exposure Potentials and Criteria for Estimating the Costs of Major Reactor Accidents", USAEC internal working paper, 1965 (USAEC Public Document Room, 1973).

27. Morrison, D L *et al.*, "An Evaluation of the Applicability of Existing Data to the Analytical Description of a Nuclear-Reactor Accident—Core Meltdown Evaluation", BMI–1910, USAEC, July 1971.

28. US Environmental Protection Agency (EPA), "Environmental Analysis of the Uranium Fuel Cycle, Part II—Nuclear Power Reactors", EPA–520/9–73–003–C (Nov 1973). According to reference 38, a 1500–rem dose to a child's thyroid corresponds to a probability of thyroid cancer of the order of 15 percent. See also Pigford, T H, *IEEE Trans Nucl Sci NS–19*:15 (Feb 1972).

29. Ergen, W K *et al.*, "Emergency Core Cooling (Report of Advisory Task Force on Emergency Core Cooling)", TID–24226, USAEC, 1967; see also note 30 and Appendix I–1.

30. Reactor Safety Study (N Rasmussen, director), *An Assessment of Accident Risks in US Commercial Nuclear Power Plants*, WASH–1400 (DRAFT),

USAEC, Aug 1974: Summary Report, Main Report, and Appendices I–X. Summarized in part by Gillette, R, *Science 185*:838 (1974).

31. On 13 Nov 1973, an 18 inch secondary steam pipe in the Indian Point 2 reactor (an 873–MW(e) PWR ∿38 km from New York City) sustained a spontaneous 180° fracture. The jet of steam, impinging on the steel liner of the containment dome, buckled it over a 12 m span (Burnham, D, *N Y Times*, 12 Dec 1973). Such structures are normally tested at or above the design pressure but at ambient temperature.

32. Blake, A *et al.*, UCRL–51408, Lawrence Livermore Laboratory, May 1973; Watson, M D *et al.*, EQL Report 6, Environmental Quality Laboratory, CalTech (Pasadena), Sept 1972; Smernoff, B J, HI–1686/2–P, Hudson Institute (Croton-on-Hudson, NY), 12 Sept 1972; United Engineers and Constructors Inc, UEC–UNP–710701, July 1971; Olds, F C, *Pwr Eng*, pp 34–9, Oct 1971; Rogers, F C, *Bull Atom Scient 27*, 8, 38 (1971); Jamne, P, IAEA–A/CONF 49/P/290 (UN Geneva Conference, Sept 1971); ORNL SD–71–66(R)–5872, Oak Ridge National Laboratory, Aug 1966. Many nuclear explosions have been conducted underground, and most of them have been contained. In Europe, three research reactors and one power reactor have been sited underground—a felicitous choice in view of the Lucens accident.

33. Recent examples range from the April 1974 contamination of the Vienna–Rome express train with ^{131}I to a US incident in which a radiopharmaceuticals worker deliberately added radioiodine to a fellow worker's drink (E R Squibb & Sons Inc, New Brunswick, NJ: letter to Division of Compliance, USAEC, 24 Nov 1971, USAEC Public Document Room). Numerous losses and some thefts of radioisotopes, usually in small quantities, are reported each year—at least 15 in the USA in 1972, for example—and some of the losses are rather surprising. A university, for example, was recently discovered to have inadvertently sold a radioactive source for scrap; it was recovered intact from the scrapheap three years later (USAEC *News Releases 5*, 44, 8 [30 Oct 1974], *5*, 47, 1 [20 Nov 1974]). In Oct 1974, according to wire service reports, the Italian defence minister told a defence committee of the chamber of deputies that a planned right wing coup (foiled when the former head of the Secret Service, a senior general, and others were arrested) was to have sown panic by polluting aqueducts with radioactive material that was to have been stolen from an Italian research centre.

34. During 1974, at least three popular "thrillers" screened on British television dealt with blackmail by illicitly acquired nuclear weapons.

35. Ford, D F *et al.*, *The Nuclear Fuel Cycle*, Union of Concerned Scientists (1208 Massachusetts Avenue, Cambridge, Massachusetts 02138), Oct 1973; reprinted 1974 by FOE Inc (*supra* note 3); enlarged edition to be published by MIT Press.

36. Gillette, R, *Science 186*:125 (1974). As reactors age and "crud" accumulates, radiation fields in repair areas often intensify: exposure (person-rem) per US reactor more than trebled between 1969 and 1973. Providing sufficient maintenance manpower for an expanding nuclear industry without exceeding the 5 or 12 rem/yr personal limit clearly presents difficulties (see note 153). In 1971, for example, Nuclear Fuel Services had 162 full-time employees with

average exposure 7.15 rem—only 32 received < 5 rem—and 1000 temporary employees.

37. Morgan, K Z, "Adequacy of Present Radiation Standards", at p 105 in TID–25857, June 1972; Lundin, F E *et al.*, "Radon Daughter Exposure and Respiratory Cancer: Quantitative and Temporal Aspects", Joint Monograph 1 (1971), Epidemiological Study of US Uranium Miners, Public Health Service (US Department of Health, Education, and Welfare).

38. Advisory Committee on the Biological Effects of Ionizing Radiations (BEIR Committee), "The Effects on Populations of Exposures to Low Levels of Ionizing Radiation", Division of Medical Sciences, National Academy of Sciences and National Research Council (Washington, DC), Nov 1972. Unfortunately, studies of low level long term effects of emissions associated with fossil fuel technologies are at least as fraught with uncertainty.

39. Weinberg states (*supra* note 14) that "if one assumes a linear dose-response for genetic effects, then to find, with 95 percent confidence, the predicted 0.5 percent increase in genetic effect in mice at a dose of, say, 150 mrem would require 8 billion animals."

40. Holdren (*supra* note 8) and others also question whether current secondary standards take proper account of biological reconcentration, multiple exposure pathways, and effects on organisms other than man. Of course, such issues are not unique to radioactive releases: releases of certain biologically active chemicals, for example, arouse similar concerns (Lovins, A B, "Long-Term Constraints on Human Activity", pp 1251–67 in Part 2, *Growth and Its Implications for the Future*, Serial 93–28, Subcommittee on Fisheries and Wildlife Conservation and the Environment, Committee on Merchant Marine and Fisheries, US House of Representatives, May 1974 [USGPO, 1974]). Whether exposure is chemical or radiological, so little is known about the phenomenology of damage on the molecular and cytochemical level that it would be premature to conclude, as is often done, that linear extrapolation of dose response curves to very low doses is *necessarily* a conservative practice.

41. The transcript and exhibits of the 1972–3 Bethesda ECCS rulemaking hearings are contained in USAEC Docket RM–50–1 and total over 60,000 pages. An annotated review appears in Lovins, A B and Patterson, W C, Appendix 1 (pp 145–78), Appendices to the Minutes of Evidence, 73–vii, "The Choice of a Reactor System", Select Committee on Science and Technology, House of Commons (HMSO, London), 1974. A more technical review, summarized in part in *Environment 14*, 7, 2 (1972), is the detailed Concluding Statement by the Union of Concerned Scientists, reprinted in 1974 by FOE Inc (*supra* note 3). Further reviews include Cottrell, W B, *Nucl Safety 15*, 1, 30 (1974); Finlayson, F, "Emergency Core Cooling Systems for Light Water Reactors", Environmental Quality Laboratory, CalTech (Pasadena), forthcoming; and Primack, J and von Hippel, F, *Bull Atom Scient 30*, 8, 5 (1974).

42. For example, in his 21 May 1974 memorandum to the Nuclear Working Group, Energy R&D Advisory Council, Electric Power Research Institute ("Review of 'The Liquid Metal Fast Breeder Reactor' by Thomas B Cochran", revised 7/3/74), Chauncey Starr remarks that "the HTGR [high temperature gas cooled reactor], while a very good reactor, also has some very basic safety

problems as yet unresolved"—and that the gas cooled fast breeder reactor "may . . . have problems that are so fundamental that from a safety and operable point of view it may never be acceptable."

43. Lewis, H L *et al*, "Report to the American Physical Society by the Study Group on Light-Water Reactor Safety", 28 Apr 1975 (summarized by Brand, D, *Wall St J*, 29 Apr 1975): only 200 copies were printed, but the report will be reprinted in *Revs Mod Phys* (July 1975). (The excellent text of the report supports both generally and in detail, and even resembles in tone in many places, the allegations of the Union of Concerned Scientists [UCS] about LWR safety [see note 41]. Curiously, the summary conclusions of the APS report are hard to reconcile with the text. H W Kendall of UCS has prepared a review of the APS report including the conclusions which he believes can properly be drawn from its text: "Nuclear Power Risks: A Review of the Report of the American Physical Society's Study Group on Light-Water Reactor Safety," 18 June 1975.) Other and less technical reviews include those by the RAND Corporation (Doctor, R D *et al.*, R–1116–NSF/CSA, Sept 1972); the Advisory Committee on Science and Technology of the California State Assembly (May 1973); the Council of the Federation of American Scientists (*FAS Newsletter*, Feb 1973); and, in a more general UK context, the joint Working Party of the Committee for Environmental Conservation, Royal Society of Arts, and Institute of Fuel (Lord Nathan *et al.*, "Energy and the Environment", July 1974). So far as the author is aware, every independent review has come to substantially the same conclusions as these groups. For some lay reaction, see *N Y Times* leaders of 31 Jan, 8 Apr, 30 May, 30 Oct, 3 Dec 1973, and 8 Apr 1975; Senator Ribicoff's *N Y Times* essay (p 47, 5 Dec 1974); *Newsweek*, p 23, 24 Feb 1975; and *Economist*, p 84, 10 May 1975.

44. See the USAEC series *Reactor Operating Experiences*; pre–1972 issues are collected in ORNL–NSIC–17, –64, and –103, Nuclear Safety Information Center, Oak Ridge National Laboratory. See also the NSIC abstract series of *Safety-Related Occurrences*, ORNL–NSIC–69, –87, –91, –106, –109, –114, and E P Eppler's astonishing Oak Ridge report (footnote, p 24) in *Nucl Safety 11*, 4, 322 (1970). A review of selected malfunctions is being compiled by Comey, D D *et al.* for 1975 publication by FOE Inc (*supra* note 3). The 861 abnormal occurrences reported to have occurred in US LWRs during 1973 are abstracted in OOE–OS–001 (Office of Operations Evaluation, USAEC, May 1974). A similar review of over 1400 incidents in 1974 is to be published. A further selection of incidents appears in Appendix A of the study cited in note 167.

45. USAEC Task Force (Report to the Director of Regulation), "Study of Quality Verification and Budget Impact", USAEC, Jan 1974, Enclosure 2. Some failures of quality assurance are concentrated in particular "lemons" such as the Palisades reactor, whose owner is suing the vendor for $300 million, but other failures are more widespread, such as the 1974–5 spate of BWR pipe cracks. In Sept 1974, cracks were found in four inch recirculation bypass lines in three BWRs; all 21 US BWRs were ordered shut down for inspection (Burnham, D, *N Y Times*, p 1, 22 Sept 1974). No further cracks were found, but on 13 Dec 1974, new cracks were discovered in four inch bypass lines in one of the original three BWRs (USAEC News Release T–614, 16 Dec 1974), and later in five

others. Both sets of cracks—though not those found at Fukushima—have been traced to a particular batch of steel; the pipes concerned are reportedly manufactured to the same standards as the primary coolant pipes whose failure is assumed to initiate a design basis LOCA. A defective batch of steel, however, apparently cannot account for five circumferential cracks in ten inch ECCS pipes near the pressure vessel of the Dresden 2 BWR; these cracks, revealed by wet insulation on 28 Jan 1975, are reportedly similar to cracks observed at the Peach Bottom 3 and Fukushima BWRs. A new (Jan–Feb 1975) shutdown of all 23 US BWRs (USNRC *News Releases 1*, 2, 2 (31 Jan 1975)) showed one more crack at Dresden 2 but none elsewhere (*ibid. 1*, 7, 4 (14 Mar 1975)), though some were found at Tsuruga. These unexpected generic shutdowns seem an unfortunate characteristic for a prospective major power source.

46. Morris, P A and Engelken, R H, "Safety experience in the operation of nuclear power plants", IAEA–SM–169/47, at pp 429–46 in *Principles and Standards of Reactor Safety* (IAEA, Vienna), 1973: proceedings of an IAEA Symposium in Jülich, 5–9 Feb 1973. The paper states: "A large number of violations of license requirements and AEC regulations have been identified. . . . Approximately 75 violations have been identified in only seven . . . appraisals [although] . . . a deliberate effort was not made to look for violations. . . . *** At three of the seven facilities reactor protection system actuation levels exceeded authorized levels." Likewise, the USAEC has recently proposed assessing civil penalties against several utilities because licenced reactor operators left operating reactors unattended while fetching a cup of coffee and the like—a violation "considered to be of major significance". In the Spring 1975 *BPI Newsletter* (Business and Professional People For the Public Interest, Suite 1001, 109 N Dearborn, Chicago, Illinois 60602), D D Comey reports: "Commonwealth Edison states that it has spent $102,000 training each of its nuclear plant operators, a sum equivalent to the cost of attending Harvard for 14 years. Yet . . . after Zion Station had been operating for approximately 6 months, the AEC gave the plant operators requalification examinations; 72% of the operators failed the exam, and even after two months of intensive further training, 46% failed the second round of examinations." The US General Accounting Office report B–164105 (18 Aug 1972) gives further insight into problems of nuclear regulation and compliance; see also Burnham, D, *N Y Times*, p 1, 25 Aug 1974, describing how USAEC inspections revealed violations (very seldom punished) in more than a third of cases, and *Wkly Energy Rpt 3*, 10, 12 (10 Mar 1975).

47. Morris and Engelken (*supra* note 46) analyse eight accidents involving loss of primary coolant into the containment of five US BWRs between 5 June 1970 and 4 May 1972. The accidents, most of which involved multiple valve failures (whose incidence is high and apparently increasing [see note 46]), occurred at a rate of 0.5 per reactor year. In four of the eight accidents, the reactor staff violated clearly prescribed operating procedures. See also Appendix A of the study cited in note 167 and the USAEC report "Evaluation of Incidents of Primary Coolant Release from Boiling Water Reactors", 30 Oct 1972.

48. USAEC, *Reactor Operating Experiences* 73–8 (1973); Ikenaga, V, *Japan Times*, 8–10 Mar 1975; Institution of Professional Civil Servants (London), "Nuclear Reactor Policy in the United Kingdom", 21 Jan 1974, ¶ 22. On 26 Feb

1975, a steam generator tube at Point Beach instantaneously ruptured, causing a 120 gal/min leak. Serious wall thinning was found in many other tubes—95–99 percent of the wall thickness was gone in 10 tubes, and over 80 percent in a further 37.

49. USAEC, RM–50–1, Exh 715, p 6. According to Brockett, G F *et al.*, "Loss of Coolant: Control of Consequences by Emergency Core Cooling" (1972 International Conference on Nuclear Solutions to World Energy Problems, American Nuclear Society/Atomic Industrial Forum, Washington, DC, 1973, at p 320), rupture of a single one of the thousands of steam generator tubes in a PWR reflooding at 1.5 inch/sec would reduce the reflooding rate by 17 percent. (The rupture area assumed—2.8 cm^2—is $\sim 6 \times 10^{-8}$ of the total tube area in a 1–GW(e) PWR.) Rupture and wall thinning of many tens of such tubes has been routinely observed in normal operation of modern PWRs (see note 48). Westinghouse calculations recently released by the Advisory Committee on Reactor Safeguards confirm that rupture of ≥ 6 tubes will stall reflooding, and that wall thinning exceeding 50 percent in a given tube (see note 48) will probably lead to its rupture under the transient conditions of a LOCA. The APS review (*supra* note 43) concludes at p V–17 that "it appears that steam generator tube failure during the LOCA is an event of significant probability. Failure to consider steam injected from the PWR secondary into the primary reactor coolant loop is potentially a very serious weakness in the overall conservatism of . . . the [ECCS] Acceptance Criteria." At p AI–C–18, the APS review states that "it was the consensus of the group that steam generator tube failure during a LOCA could occur frequently. Moreover, it appears that rupture of a few tubes (on the order of one to ten) . . . could . . . induce essentially uncoolable conditions in the course of a LOCA, for PWRs with ECCS of current design." At p V–31, the APS review notes that though PWR reflood rates were originally intended to be ≥ 6 in/sec, the actual rate "estimated for current designs" is a "marginally effective 1 to 2 in/sec," and these "hazardously low values" (p AI–C–26) would exacerbate the effects of any reduction in the rate.

50. The RM–50–1 Hearing Board at Bethesda ruled that steam generator tube failure during a LOCA need not be considered in determining ECCS acceptance criteria—apparently because to do so would violate the arbitrary single failure criterion. Discussion and cross-examination on this topic were therefore excluded from the record. The APS review (*supra* note 43), in more general terms, expresses "reservations about the present almost exclusive emphasis in the licensing process on the 'design basis accident' concept in which certain highly stylized accidents are used as the yardstick against which the performance of various systems is evaluated. . . . [O]ther types of possible accidents may consequently receive insufficient attention. . . ."

51. See *e.g.* Wechsler, M S, "The Radiation-Embrittlement of Pressure Vessel Steels and the Safety of Nuclear Reactor Pressure Vessels", ORNL internal report, Mar 1970, which cites extensive UK and West German data that show large pressure vessel rates of catastrophic failure of $\sim 2 \times 10^{-5}$ /vessel yr, excluding failures whose causes are irrelevant to nuclear applications; Farmer, F R, IAEA–SM–169/43, Jülich, 5 Feb 1973 (and associated discussion); Cottrell, A, "Fracture of Steel Pressure Vessels", memorandum to Select Committee on

Science and Technology, House of Commons (reprinted at pp 122–4 in 73–i–vii, Report, Minutes of Evidence and Appendices, "The Choice of a Reactor System" (HMSO, London, 1974)); Lovins, A B and Patterson, W C, note 41, ¶ 54; Holt, A B, paper to Second International Conference on Structural Mechanics in Reactor Technology (Berlin, 10–14 Sept 1973), *Nucl Eng Intl 18*:965 (1973). (Technical uncertainties associated with pressure tube reactors appear to be very different.) Some observers doubt the relevance of failure tests using pressure vessels into which flaws have been deliberately machined: stresses tending to encourage propagation will obviously be different in such vessels than in those in which flaws have developed spontaneously during operation. Even the Jan 1974 ACRS assessment of pressure vessel integrity (WASH–1238) is somewhat clouded: see note 167, pp 64–6 and Appendices B1–B3. (The ACRS still considers thermal shock failure an unresolved issue: *Nucleon Wk 16*, 16, 6 [17 Apr 1975].) The APS conclusion (*supra* note 43) that catastrophic pressure vessel rupture is probably not an important source of risk provided that the highest standards of quality control are maintained should be interpreted in the light of the failure of ultrasonic tests (used for this purpose) to detect two out of five leaking cracks observed in Dresden ECCS pipes (see note 45): see Kendall, H W, testimony to Subcommittee on Energy and Environment, Committee on Interior and Insular Affairs, US House of Representatives (29 Apr 1975), at p 27, and *Nucleon Wk 16*, 17, 2 (24 Apr 1975).

52. Discussion by Dr Peter Morris, Director of Operations Evaluation, USAEC, in IAEA Jülich Symposium, 9 Feb 1974 (see IAEA, *supra* note 46, p 616).

53. Thus, for example, each of a wide array of mechanisms studied in BMI–1910 (*supra* note 27) appears to be capable of causing gross rupture of both primary and secondary containment after ECCS failure; these analyses are largely supported by WASH–1400 (DRAFT) (*supra* note 30). Likewise, pressure vessel rupture can melt the fuel *and* breach the containment shell.

54. Lovins, A B and Patterson, W C *supra* note 41, ¶ 30 and Annexes A and C. There is infinite room for disagreement over what is a "proven" technology, but large LWRs of high power density are not one according to any normal engineering usage. Moreover, according to Starr (*supra* note 42) they are "still approaching a commercial basis" and have "no commercial fuel cycles".

55. Weinberg, A M, letter to chairman, USAEC, 9 Feb 1972 (RM–50–1, Exh 1027); quoted in Ford, D F and Kendall, H W, Concluding Statement (*supra* note 41) and in Lovins, A B and Patterson, W C, *supra* note 41, ¶ 47.

56. *Cf.* the similar views of USAEC experts quoted by Ford and Kendall and by Lovins and Patterson (*supra* note 41), and the resignation letter of Carl Hocevar (author of the THETA code widely used in LWR ECCS analysis), who left the AEC's Idaho safety facility on 22 Sept 1974 to work with the Union of Concerned Scientists: Burnham, D, *supra* note 45.

57. Pungent memoranda by the supervisors of the FLECHT tests were incorporated into Exh 1153 of RM–50–1. Some of the defects in the tests are analyzed by Kendall and Ford in their original technical submission (Exh 1041) to RM–50–1: "An Evaluation of Nuclear Reactor Safety", Union of Concerned Scientists (*supra* note 35), Mar 1972. Other defects were criticized at Bethesda

by a vast array of AEC, ANC, Oak Ridge, Battelle, and other non–UCS witnesses. The FLECHT tests, among the technical bases of present ECCS design criteria, are apparently to be redone: Salisbury, D C, *Techn Rev*, p 6, Mar/Apr 1974. See also APS, *supra* note 43, p V–22.

58. Representative opinions are quoted by Ford and Kendall and by Lovins and Patterson (*supra* note 41): see *e.g.* ¶¶42–51 in the latter.

59. The LOFT tests scheduled for the mid-to-late 1970s will be at 1/60 scale relative to a modern LWR of slightly over 1000 MW(e). Previous semiscale tests at ~ 1/1000 scale are described thus by the APS review (*supra* note 43) at p V–27: "To date, correlations of calculations and experimental results for the "Standard Problems" have been poor. They have not provided the anticipated—and sought for—demonstration of the general adequacy of LOCA/ECCS numerical methods." Large discrepancies between predictions and semiscale test results "are not encouraging, and tend to indicate that the physical processes are not well modelled" (p AI–C–38). Even the LOFT tests are "unlikely . . . [to] lead to an assured quantitative demonstration of the ECCS safety margin" (p V–29): e.g. they are to use unpressurized fuel (p VI–62) and cannot properly simulate steam binding (p VI–63). The APS review expresses doubt that the US safety research program now contemplated is capable in principle of resolving major uncertainties.

60. Lapp, R E, Direct Testimony in the Bethesda ECCS Rulemaking Hearing, USAEC RM–50–1, 23 Mar 1972.

61. USAEC, RM–50–1, Exh 1033, III 4.4–1. The list of unresolved generic safety issues identified by the USAEC's Advisory Committee on Reactor Safeguards (ACRS), *e.g.* in its letter of 13 Feb 1974, updated in Apr 1975 (*Nucleon Wk 16*, 16, 6 (17 Apr 1975)), has been steadily expanding in recent years.

62. See note 44: recent examples include *ROE* 71–22, 72–7, 72–13, 72–14, 73–1, 73–4, 73–5, 73–6, 73–10, 73–12. Reference 46 also contains several detailed analyses.

63. Myers, R, "FEA Blueprint Writes Off Nuclear", *Wkly Energy Rpt 2*, 43, 1 (28 Oct 1974); also "Nuclear fission is an exotic energy source; 10 years away: Rogers Morton", *Ibid.*, p 4, and Clark, T R *et al.*, "Nuclear Fuel Cycle: A Report by the Fuel Cycle Task Force," ERDA–33 (14 May 1975).

64. Gossick, L V; Ernst, M L *et al.* (USAEC Task Force), "Study of the Reactor Licensing Process" (Report to the Director of Regulation), Oct 1973 (original, not expurgated, Jan 1974 draft): particularly the examples on pp 5–2 through 5–9.

65. Cottrell, A, *Fin Times* (London), p 2, 7 June 1974; reprinted in Appendix B3 of the study cited in note 167. The occasion partly contributing to this letter—the 1 June 1974 Flixborough explosion at a caprolactam plant—produced insurance claims for £66 million, Britain's largest peacetime disaster, though its explosive force was equivalent to only 20–30 tons of TNT (followed by a fire). (A court of inquiry reported on 12 May 1975 that the blast was caused by an unlikely sequence of unforeseen failures arising from an improper modification of piping.) In a contemporary letter to *The Times* (London), Brigadier Allen, speaking from decades of experience with storing and transporting munitions, concurs with "the totalitarian law of physics, which says: 'Anything which is not

forbidden is compulsory.' " Nuclear accidents which "could make Flixborough look like a birthday party" are, he concludes, inevitable because they are not theoretically impossible. Numerous historical examples of "incredible" engineering failures suggest themselves—including a 1919 US incident (*Boston Eve Globe*, 12 Aug 1971) when 21 people died in a tidal wave of molasses from a ruptured 8.3 million liter tank.

66. Secretary of State for Energy, White Paper of 10 July 1974 (HMSO, London).

67. Bryan, W, Testimony before the Subcommittee on State Energy Policy, Committee on Planning, Land Use, and Energy, California State Assembly, 1 Feb 1974; reprinted in *Not Man Apart 4*, 5, 1 (mid–May 1974), FOE Inc (*supra* note 3). Bryan's views are supported by Comptroller General of the US, "Review of Reliability Data on Weapon and Space Systems", 120 *Congr Rec* S20775–6 (9 Dec 1974).

68. Hanauer, S H and Morris, P A, A/CONF 49/P/040 at Fourth International Conference on the Peaceful Uses of Atomic Energy, Geneva, 6–16 Sept 1971; in *Proceedings*, Vol III, pp 202–16, UN (NY) / IAEA (Vienna), 1972.

69. Most AEC and vendor estimates published before mid–1974 seem inconsistent with the incidence of reported failures in identical or similar elements of operating reactors: Lovins and Patterson, *supra* note 41, ¶¶ 37–8. Weinberg, A M, "Nuclear Energy—18 Years After" (address to American Public Power Association, San Francisco, 27 June 1972) states that the LOCA-initiating pipe break in LWRs "is deemed by some to be incredible: to others, the probability is conceded to be very low, but not zero. I think there is really no way to quantify such an estimate (I call such an estimate *trans-scientific*, since I know of no scientific basis for making it). In any case, it is extremely small."

70. Thompson, T J and Beckerley, J G, eds, *The Technology of Nuclear Reactor Safety*, MIT Press (Cambridge, Mass., 1964–70), vol I, p 5: ". . . the dependence may be subtle. . . . A structure as complex as a reactor and involving as many phenomena is likely to have relatively few completely independent components." The Rasmussen study (see note 30) tries to take account of possible common mode failures; but see Appendix I–1.

71. Farmer, F R, "Development of Adequate Risk Standards", IAEA–SM–169/43, Jülich, 5 Feb 1973 (see note 46).

72. Ehrich, T, "Atomic Lemons", *Wall St J*, p 1, 3 May 1973: "their unreliability is becoming one of their most dependable features." *Cf.* McWethy, J, *US News & World Rep 76*, 23, 43 (10 June 1974).

73. Cochran, T B, *The Liquid-Metal Fast Breeder Reactor: An Economic and Environmental Critique*, Resources for the Future and Johns Hopkins University Press (Baltimore, Maryland, 1974); Natural Resources Defense Council, Comments on USAEC Draft Environmental Impact Statement for LMFBR Program (WASH–1535), NRDC (917 15th St NW, Washington, DC 20005), reprinted in "proposed final" draft of USAEC WASH–1535, Dec 1974; Cochran, T B *et al.*, "Bypassing the Breeder" (with Appendix), NRDC, Mar 1975 (reprinted in *Environment*, May/June 1975).

74. Lovins, A B, *New Scient 61*:693 (14 Mar 1974). Some similar points are made by Teller, E, *Nucl News*, p 21, Aug 1967.

75. Kelber, C N *et al.*, ANL–7657, Argonne National Laboratory (Feb 1970).

76. Jackson, J and Boudreau, J E, "Postburst Analysis (Preliminary Report)", internal document, Argonne National Laboratory, Dec 1972; Boudreau, J E, "Autocatalysis During Fast Reactor Disassembly" (PhD dissertation, University of California [Los Angeles], Feb 1972), summarized by Boudreau, J E and Erdmann, R C, *Nucl Sci Eng 51*:206 (1973); Board, S J *et al.*, *Nature 254*:319 (1975).

77. Ross, M, "The Possibility of Release of Cesium in a Spent-Fuel Transportation Accident", Physics Dept, University of Michigan (Ann Arbor), Jan 1974. In current practice, a single shipping cask generally contains a fission product inventory in the MCi range.

78. Comptroller General of the US, B–164105, US General Accounting Office, 31 July 1973.

79. Anderson, M, "Fallout on the Freeway: The Hazards of Transporting Radioactive Wastes in Michigan", Public Interest Research Group in Michigan, 18 Jan 1974.

80. Railway shipments spend a good deal of time sitting in switchyards, which in the USA have been the scene of several spectacular explosions of ammunition trains in the past few years. An unexpected recent explosion of a chemical tank car being shunted in the state of Washington is said to have dug a crater 21 m across by 15 m deep, destroyed a nearby factory, and caused $7 million worth of damage. Maritime shipments are not immune from trouble: a *New Scientist* report (p 185, 18 Oct 1973) cites a *Lloyd's List* report (p 4, 5 Oct 1973) that two trips after a ship had left behind a shipment of radioactive waste because an insurance premium could not be agreed upon, the same ship on the same route collided with a submarine "and No. 2 hold was ripped open to the sea; it was this hold that underwriters had been told was safest for the nuclear cargo!"

81. Holdren (*supra* note 8) calculates that 10^{-4} of the projected US ^{90}Sr inventory in 2000 would suffice to contaminate the annual freshwater runoff from the 48 states to twice the MPC—another illustration of the impressive degree of control required. In testimony before the Nuclear Study Committee of the South Carolina Legislature, J W Gofman has pointed out ("Some Important Unexamined Questions Concerning the Barnwell Nuclear Fuel Reprocessing Plant", 7 Jan 1972) some implications of releases from the extremely large inventories in such facilities. He calculates, for example, that the malicious release of 1 percent of the Barnwell inventory of high-level waste could seriously contaminate a minimum of $\sim$373,000 km^2 ($\sim$144,000 mi^2) of farmland: the inventory itself is equivalent to $\sim$15 $\times$ the total fission product activity produced by all US and Soviet atmospheric tests, and includes at five year equilibrium $\sim$5 GCi of hard gamma emitters and $\sim$0.8 GCi ^{90}Sr. Gofman's thesis is that if the consequences of a release are large, the probability of its occurrence must be closely examined. (As pointed out recently by the US General Accounting Office, analogous numbers could perhaps be derived for reactors' spent-fuel cooling ponds, which will apparently—at least in the USA—become highly congested: Gillette, R, *Science 185*:770 (1974); ERDA–25 (Mar 1975); *cf. Nucleon Wk 16*, 17, 5 (27 Apr 1975).) *Cf.* USAEC, WASH–1539 (DRAFT), Sept 1974,

p 3.1–33: "It is recognized that there is a possibility an act of sabotage [to a Retrievable Surface Storage Facility] could release more radioactive material than would the maximum credible accident. . . . Studies are now under way to evaluate both the probability and the consequences of various acts of sabotage, and additional design or operating precautions will be taken as indicated to be desirable by these studies. Results of these studies will be discussed in the final environmental statement to the extent that this can be done without jeopardizing the security of the project. . . . Retrievable surface storage facilities will not be designed for continued waste confinement following the direct impact of massive or explosive missiles, such as large meteorites or aircraft. Such events are of such low probability of occurrence that they are considered to be incredible." Detonation of terrorists' nuclear weapons near fission facilities of any kind is also apparently considered "incredible": see *e.g.* WASH–1535 (Dec 1974) at p 7.4–24.

82. DeNike, L D, *Bull Atom Scient 30*, 2, 16 (1974); *30*, 8, 48 (1974); and *31*, 2, 3 (1975); WASH–1535 (Dec 1974) at pp V.12–2–15; Krieger, M, *Bull Atom Scient 31*, 6, 28 (1975); Jenkins, B M, "High Technology Terrorism and Surrogate War: The Impact of Technology on Low-Level Violence", *The RAND Paper Series*, RAND Corp (Santa Monica, CA), 1975. At the 1974 ANS Annual Meeting, W C Bartels of the USAEC reported (*Nucl News 17*, 10, 46 [1974]) more than 400 incidents of international terrorism by small groups in the past six years, causing more than 200 fatalities. Kriegsman (*infra* note 121) states that "the number of terrorist incidents has quadrupled over the past five years". Dr Michael Flood (7 Edward St, Bath BA2 4DU, England) has prepared an annotated chronology of nuclear and related thefts, threats, sabotage, etc.

83. Schleimer, J D, *Bull Atom Scient 30*, 8, 24 (1974): the article appears to have some technical gaps, but is nonetheless instructive. *Cf.* Eschwege, H, B–164105, US General Accounting Office, 16 Oct 1974 (*Nucleon Wk*, p 2, 29 Oct 1974); *Environment 16*, 5, 24 (1974); and the APS report (*supra* note 43). Eschwege states: "Licensee and AEC officials agreed that a security system at a licensed nuclear powerplant could not prevent a takeover for sabotage by a small number—as small, perhaps, as two or three—of armed individuals." Potential saboteurs have available, of course, not only details of plant layout and design, but also the WASH–1400 (DRAFT) event trees, permitting action more effective than contemplated by Turner, S E *et al.*, *Nucl Safety 11*, 2, 107 (1970). The resources that modern terrorists can probably command include wire-guided rockets, plastic explosives, thermite, helicopters, mortars, frogmen, nerve gases, bazookas and other shaped charges, recoilless rifles, demolition mines, and infrared aiming devices for rifles. Large sabotage hazards are also associated with other energy technologies, such as oil supertankers and LNG facilities (*supra* note 3)—an argument for controlling these hazards too. According to the British defence minister (*Fin Times*, 12 Feb 1975), one such hazard is now appreciated: five special ships are to be built and four aircraft modified to protect North Sea oil rigs against terrorist attacks (*cf.* Blundy, D and Dawe, T, *Sunday Times* [London], p 3, 11 May 1975).

84. Edsall, J T, *Science 178*:933 (1972) suggests that nuclear facilities, often sited near cities or major military targets, "will be enormously attractive objects

for sabotage and blackmail". The latter is perhaps a more serious possibility since $1 million was demanded of the Bonneville Power Administration (serving 3/4 million people in Oregon via $\sim$20,000 km of transmission line) by a person (later imprisoned) who, between 26 Sept and 20 Oct 1974, dynamited 14 transmission line towers and demolished six. Similar sabotage occurred near Spokane in 1974; power facilities were bombed near San Francisco in 1968 and 1970, in San Jose in 1975 (*Intl Her Trib* [Paris and London], p 3, 28 Mar 1975), and in Scotland in 1974–5 (*Guardian* [London], 4 and 7 Feb 1975), and others in Alabama were sabotaged by striking power workers in 1966. According to *The Times* (London), p 4, 5 May 1975, two bombs damaged equipment awaiting assembly inside the reactor building at Fessenheim on 3 May 1975, seven months before the scheduled core loading. Flood (*supra* note 82) lists many other incidents of sabotage of power facilities, and in a press release on 24 Feb 1975, the US Federal Bureau of Investigation reports that of 2041 bombing incidents in the US in 1974, 63 were directed against utilities. Furthermore, the recent trial of a young man for damaging a meterological tower used in a western Massachusetts reactor-siting study suggests that nuclear facilities may become a target not only of malicious saboteurs and terrorists but also of those nuclear opponents who believe that conscience compels them to practice civil disobedience. (The cited case was dismissed because the indictment was defectively drawn, so no verdict bearing on the defendent's arguments was obtained.)

85. Comptroller General of the US, B–164052, US General Accounting Office, 29 May 1968 (declassified Dec 1970) and 29 Jan 1971; Gillette, R, *Science 181*:728 (1973). Approximately 10 percent of the Hanford high-level waste tanks have leaked. The record in other countries is said to be better. Boring holes to trace the diffusion of leaked wastes underground unfortunately creates new channels for such diffusion, just as boring holes to test the geological suitability of a formation for waste storage tends to make it unsuitable.

86. Pittman, F K (director, Division of Waste Management and Transportation, USAEC), "Management of Commercial High-Level Radioactive Waste", summer course on Nuclear Fuel and Power Management, MIT, Cambridge, Massachusetts, 25 July 1972, p 17.

87. In a stable nuclear economy, inventories of principal fission products would asymptotically approach equilibrium values rather than steadily increasing, though this would not occur appreciably for very-long-lived fission or activation products. On the other hand, the toxicity of mixed actinides *increases* with their age by nearly an order of magnitude, owing to the shifts in composition as some isotopes decay into others. Such decay tends initially to increase the physical quantities of some lower transuranics such as [239]Pu. Blomeke *et al.* give useful calculations of the amount of each nuclide in various parts of several fuel cycles at various times: ORNL–TM–3965 (Feb 1974).

88. Isaacson, R E and Brownell, L E, "Ultimate Storage of Radioactive Wastes in Terrestrial Environments", at p 955 in OECD–NEA/IAEA, *Management of Radioactive Wastes from Fuel Reprocessing*, OECD 66 73 02 3 (Paris, 1973). Many papers in this volume provide insight into such practical problems as these: (1) solidification of liquid wastes generally requires high temperatures but must entrain volatile fission products; (2) if solidification is not prompt,

in-process liquid inventories are large enough to offset much of its advantage, but if solidification promptly follows reprocessing, heat and radiation loads are much higher; (3) solidification is generally incompatible with later partitioning of actinides (see note 89); (4) it is hard to predict the long term properties of solidified wastes of which a substantial mass fraction is changing into other elements with different chemistry; (5) there are numerous uncertainties of other kinds in the long term behaviour of solidified wastes.

89. Kubo, A S and Rose, D J, *Science 182*:1205 (1973).

90. Claiborne, H C, ORNL–TM–3964 (Dec 1972) discusses some of the difficult problems of separating and of fissioning or transmuting actinides. For example, Am and Cm are chemically almost identical to abundant fission product lanthanides of high cross–section, notably Eu and Sm. In general, "the optimum grouping of radioactive elements for waste management does not correspond with natural groupings based upon chemical behavior", and the required separations demand extremely close process control, generate large volumes of contaminated reagents, and are plagued by the formation of colloids and precipitates. Efficient actinide recycling, if feasible, would complicate the logistics of fuel cycles by greatly increasing the concentrations of energetic neutron emitters such as ^{244}Cm, ^{242}Cm, and (perhaps more avoidably) ^{252}Cf. (Such problems are discussed at pp 59–98 of USAEC CONF–700502 [May 1970].) As S Halaszovich *et al.* of Kernforschungsanlage Jülich GmbH point out (OECD–NEA/IAEA, *supra* note 88, p 723), "An absolute seclusion of the very long-lived alpha-emitters from the biosphere over periods of thousands or even millions of years cannot be guaranteed by any storage philosophy known today besides . . . launching into outer space. . . ." The incentives for partitioning and recycling actinides are therefore large; unfortunately, "[i]t is uncertain at this time whether economical processes for the partitioning of the wastes can be developed" (Perge, A F and Ramsey, R W Jnr [USAEC], *Ibid.*, p 290), and no such process will ever avoid small losses of 0.1 percent or 0.5 percent at each pass, yielding a total loss of 0.5 percent or 2.5 percent respectively. These are still very large amounts of substances that remain biologically active (and concentratable) for geological periods; their toxicity, if thus reduced by 206× or 42.5× (additional recycles do not help), remains formidable. These calculated reductions, too, are overoptimistic because they do not allow for a few percent of the actinides being lost at each pass by "leaks" in the form of fabrication plant losses and the like (estimated *e.g.* by Pigford, *infra*). Thus when WASH–1250 (July 1973) says at p 4–73 that "The 99.5 percent recoveries [of uranium and plutonium from spent fuel at the reprocessing plant] represent the practical limits of the processing methods currently in use" and that though special "process steps can be added to recover additional plutonium should this be deemed necessary", "the cost of these added steps would greatly exceed the fuel value of the recovered plutonium", the substantial loss—generally several percent—of actinides from portions of the fuel cycle *outside the reprocessing plant* is being wholly ignored. (See Pigford, T H, *Ann Rev Nucl Sci 24*:515 [1974].) With repeated recycling, these "leaks" from the recycling loop become dominant sources of residual hazard and substantially defeat the purpose of the recycling.

91. This might no longer be necessary if actinides were fissioned by neutrons from a fusion reactor or from a nonthermonuclear reactor where, for example, a ^{3}H beam impinges on a ^{2}H plasma (both methods whose development would create difficult new safeguards problems). The burnup physics of mixed actinides in such a flux will be complex, with some isotopes activating by neutron capture while others fission, and the practical details of recycling, burnup, and process residuals do not seem to have been assessed. Alternatively, actinides might be partitioned for extraterrestrial disposal on a trajectory that will not intersect the earth during the relevant period (a surprisingly hard task—OECD–NEA/IAEA, *supra* note 88, pp 413, 428; and NASA TM X–71557 [May 1974]). Such a scheme would require both dramatic economic improvements and the development of accident-proof encapsulation. Skeptics of the latter feature are bound to recall the SNAP series in which two out of three launches did not go as planned: on 21 Apr 1964, an aborted SNAP launch resulted in the vaporization of 17 kCi of ^{238}Pu in the upper atmosphere, almost trebling the global free inventory of this isotope (Hardy, E P *et al.*, *Nature* 241:444 [1973]). K Z Morgan has remarked that he was assured before the event that the probability of such a failure was less than 10^{-9}, but in the event it was 10^{-0}.

92. Committee on Geological Aspects of Radioactive Waste Disposal, Division of Earth Sciences, untitled report to USAEC Division of Reactor Development and Technology: National Academy of Sciences (Washington, DC, May 1966). This report notes that "... none of the major sites at which radioactive wastes are being stored or disposed of [in the USA—*i.e.*, the same sites still in use] is geologically suited for safe disposal of any manner of radioactive wastes other than very dilute, very low-level liquids." See also Gera, F and Jacobs, D G, ORNL–4762 (Feb 1972). The more obvious contingencies include glaciation, submersion, vulcanism, mountain building, and the sorts of processes that enrich barren rock into metallic ores. (Professor Sir Kingsley Dunham, director of the Institute of Geological Sciences in London and an authority on such enrichment processes, has stated that in his opinion no place on earth can be guaranteed not to undergo such changes within the periods of isolation required, and that terrestrial disposal is accordingly unacceptable.) In OECD–NEA/IAEA, *supra* note 88, at pp 1173–4, D W Clelland of British Nuclear Fuels Ltd states: "I would like to record, that there are many experts who have severe reservations about the safety of disposal operations. If disposal without retrieval is to be employed, extremely high standards of guarantees must be provided. Many feel that it will be extremely difficult, and some would go so far as to say that it is impossible, to obtain the guarantees which would be necessary to justify highly-active waste being allowed to pass beyond control. We should always provide a means of getting the waste back as a final safety measure, even in very long term geological systems." (See also his paper at pp 241–2.) At pp 878–80, *Ibid.*, G D DeBuchanane of the US Geological Survey lists (as potential "catastrophic events") "the seismic potential of the area, the surface ... and subsurface erosion and solution of an area, and the effect of extreme hydrologic events, such as floods or extended periods of high precipitation leading to changes in ground water regime. Any or all of these events could happen at any management facility within the period of time that the high-level waste would be toxic to

man[,] and the potential of such events to destroy or severely damage the safety of man-made or natural storage facilities should be considered.... Diastrophism, the process or processes by which the earth crust is deformed, has caused concern to many who are involved in the consideration of the long time management of high-level waste. In the geologic past all parts of the United States have undergone major changes one or more times in response to some form of diastrophic forces.... The fact that salt was deposited or evaporated from water some 60 million years ago and is still found today is indicative that it has not been exposed to circulating waters. Diastrophic forces in the next million or 60 million years could expose these deposits to circulating waters." At p 986, *Ibid.*, R E Isaacson of Atlantic Richfield Hanford Co (the USAEC site contractor) is more specific about that site: "Evidence indicates that flood basalts recurred at 500,000 to 2,000,000-year intervals. The youngest basalt is about 8,000,000 years old.... There is evidence ... of the region being swept by catastrophic floods on several occasions due to the sudden release of large impoundments of glacial melt waters. Geologic evidence indicates that the Hanford plant site has been submerged by such floods at least four times in the past 40,000 years (approximately). The last such flood occurred about 14 to 16,000 years ago." The high-level waste inventory at Hanford amounts to about 1/4 million m^3 and is presumably in the GCi range.

93. Schneider, K J and Platt, A M, eds, *Advanced Waste Management Studies, High-Level Radioactive Waste Disposal Alternatives*, BNWL–1900 (4 vols), USAEC, May 1974; summarized in WASH–1297, USAEC, May 1974. USAEC policy of 1974 is summarized in WASH–1539 (DRAFT), Sept 1974, rejected by USEPA as "inadequate" and withdrawn by ERDA on 9 Apr 1975 (*Wkly Energy Rpt 3*, 15, 14 [14 Apr 1975]). *Not Man Apart 5*, 10, 9 (mid–May 1975), FOE Inc (*supra* note 3), reports that the Retrievable Surface Storage Facility proposal has apparently been abandoned and that high-level waste is to be stored in salt beds without an intervening period of mausoleum storage as proposed by WASH–1539 (DRAFT). Salt beds in New Mexico are being explored. Some lay views of options and problems can be gathered from *Business Wk*, p 70, 3 Mar 1975, and *Newswk*, p 56, 18 Nov 1974.

94. USAEC *News Releases 5*, 38, 1 (18 Sept 1974). The proposal is limited to transuranic concentrations > 10 nCi/g—a figure whose odd history is given in Appendix B of WASH–1539 (DRAFT), Sept 1974. Data in "Waste Management Practices in Western Europe" (OECD–ENEA, Paris, 1972) suggest that the current UK limit for soil burial at Drigg, near Windscale, is ∿120 nCi/g. Low-level alpha waste is bulky and chemically diverse, but in aggregate contains substantial amounts of actinides which could be leached or blown away, digested by microorganisms, or otherwise released, and then reconcentrated. According to Pigford, T H, "Radioactivity in Plutonium, Americium and Curium in Nuclear Fuel" (Dept of Nucl Eng, Univ of Calif at Berkeley) (a June 1974 paper for The Energy Policy Project), the Pu content of the low-level wastes from reprocessing, conversion, and fabrication can exceed the Pu content of the high-level wastes. "Permanent isolation ... is as important for these low-level wastes as it is for the high-level reprocessing wastes." The same is true in the UK: *Nucl Eng Intl 19*:975 (1974). Soil sorption and environmental pathways of actinides,

especially those other than Pu, are highly variable, strongly dependent on chemical circumstance, and poorly understood (Price, K R, BNWL–B–148 (Dec 1971), pp 18–29; UCRL–50564 Rev 1 (1972); Dunster, H J, personal communication, 23 Apr 1975); indeed, "Whether a long-term continuing increase in transuranic element availability might result from reactions with soil organic matter or from microbial transformations is not known" (WASH–1535, Dec 1974, at pp II.G–26–7). And since "it is not intended that low level wastes would ever be transmuted" (*Ibid.* at p V.22–7)—if indeed this could be done without producing large amounts of new activation products—perpetual terrestrial storage seems to be logically required.

95. Bair, W J and Thompson, R C, *Science 183*:715 (1974).

96. Tamplin, A R and Cochran, T B, "Radiation Standards for Hot Particles", NRDC (*supra* note 73), 14 Feb 1974; Long, A B, *Nucl News 14*, 6, 69 (1971).

97. Geesaman, D P, UCRL–50387 and Addendum, Lawrence Livermore Laboratory, 1968.

98. Pu toxicity is formidable even if the hot particle hypothesis is wholly rejected: animal experiments whose clinical response was saturated even at the lowest Pu doses suggest (see note 95) that the 10^7 kg of Pu to be generated in the next few decades would correspond to about 3×10^{15} lung cancer doses, and show that lung cancer is induced within ten years in dogs whose terminal lung burden of Pu aerosols is about three times the presently allowed human maximum. The essence of the geometric argument put forward by Tamplin and Cochran, Long, and Geesaman is that a single $^{239}PuO_2$ particle one μm in diameter (0.28 pCi) irradiates not the entire 1–kg lung as present standards assume, but only tens of μg of it—thus giving a local tissue dose not of 0.3 mrem/yr but of about 4–11 krem/yr. That seems to be generally agreed. The carcinogenetic potential of such a dose, which is the point at issue, is plausible but not directly proven: Lovins and Patterson, note 99 *infra*. (Any particle bearing at least 0.07 pCi of long-lived alpha activity would be capable of providing a one krem/yr local tissue dose in a half-inflated lung, and would thus qualify as a "hot particle" under the Feb 1974 Tamplin–Cochran definition, later redefined in the 24 Feb 1975 Supplemental Submission to USEPA; such a particle could be *e.g.* $^{239}PuO_2$ 0.6μm in diameter or $^{238}PuO_2$ 0.09 μm in diameter. The hypothesis says nothing about risk from smaller particles.) For fundamental statistical reasons, lung burdens below $\sim$1 nCi—perhaps corresponding to tens of burdens certain to induce cancer if the hot particle hypothesis is correct—are undetectable *in vivo*. The present maximum permissible lung burden, 16 nCi, is just within the range of convenient detection; far more stringent standards would be unenforceable. Likewise, maximum permissible concentrations of particulate actinides in air are already extremely difficult to monitor (Long, *supra* note 96), and it would be impossible to demonstrate compliance with far stricter standards.

99. On 10 Oct 1974 the USAEC published WASH–1320 (an expansion of the Jan 1974 Healy report LA–5482–PR), a rejoinder to Tamplin and Cochran which W J Bair *et al.* had prepared without consulting them or (apparently) noting their comments on Healy's findings. Tamplin and Cochran, who found WASH–1320 unconvincing and largely irrelevant, responded in Nov 1974 with a

cogent 48 page memorandum available from NRDC (see note 73). They seem to show that all the evidence cited in WASH–1320 is either irrelevant to or consistent with the hot particle hypothesis. In the author's opinion, the same is true of the evidence cited by the UK National Radiological Protection Board (NRPB–R29, Sept 1974) and by the UK Medical Research Council ("The Toxicity of Plutonium", HMSO, London, 1975). The controversy will doubtless persist, as in *New Scient 66*:497, 501 (29 May 1975) and in J W Gofman's 14 May 1975 dosimetric report CNR 1975–1 (Committee for Nuclear Responsibility, P O Box 2329, Dublin, California 94566), and is reviewed by Lovins, A B and Patterson, W C, *Nature 254*:278 (1975). Meanwhile, on quite unrelated grounds, the MRC (*op. cit.*) have suggested that whole body Pu standards be made more restrictive by a factor of perhaps five, and K Z Morgan, by a factor of about 400 (EPA Public Hearings on Plutonium and the Transuranium Elements, 10 Dec 1974), and new animal experiments in related areas are continuing (Little, J B *et al.*, *Science 188*:737 [16 May 1975]) to test E A Martell's hypothesis about smoking: see *e.g. Nature 249*:215 (1974), *250*:158 (1974), *Am Scient* (forthcoming, July 1975), and Martell's 10 Jan 1975 evidence to the USEPA Denver hearings on Pu standards (available from Martell at National Center for Atmospheric Research, Box 3000, Boulder, Colorado 80303).

100. Rose, D J, *Science 184*:351 (1974).

101. Willrich, M and Taylor, T B, *Nuclear Theft: Risks and Safeguards*, Ballinger, for the Energy Policy Project (Cambridge, Massachusetts, 1974); Willrich, M, *Bull Atom Scient 31*, 5, 12 (1975). Confirming Taylor's statements about ease of design, a television program by John Angier ("The Plutonium Connection", *Nova*, WGBH–TV, Boston, 9 March 1975) discusses and evaluates a crude bomb design computed by a commissioned chemistry undergraduate in five weeks, working alone and entirely from the open literature, and assuming reactor grade plutonium. A considerably simpler design could have been achieved (see note 109). (This one has led to a congressional bill, HR 4994 / S1197, to ban plutonium recycle for three years, though the bill may now be superfluous (see note 120).)

102. Gillette, R, *Science 185*:1027 (1974), *185*:1140 (1974); Cochran, T B and Speth, J G, "NRDC Comments on WASH–1237", NRDC, *supra* note 73), 30 Oct 1974, especially pp 10–17; Cochran, T B, *Bull Atom Scient 31*, 4, 2 (1975); Tucker, A, *The Guardian* (London), 13 Jan 1975.

103. Shapley, D, *Science 174*:569 (1971); *cf. 178*:208, 351 (1972). There appears to have been little sustained histological or epidemiological study in appropriate depth to seek possible effects of Pu release in the Rocky Flats or Denver area. Even the measured magnitudes of release are disputed: Poet, S G and Martell, E A, *Health Phys 23*:537 (1972), *26*:120 (1974). In Subcommittee *Hearings on the Supplemental Appropriations Bill, 1971*, Committee on Appropriations, US House of Representatives, 1 Oct 1970, General Giller (then director, Division of Military Applications, USAEC) testified that the Rocky Flats fire was "a near catastrophe" and that "hundreds of square miles" could have been contaminated if the fire had burned through the roof. "If the fire had been a little bigger, it is questionable whether it could have been contained."

104. Inspection of published cross–sections and neutron yields at the appropri-

ate energies suggests that fast critical assemblies can be made from reasonable quantities of certain isotopes which are not "fissile" (*sc.* by *slow* neutrons), and some of which are not now safeguarded. This study accordingly refers to "strategic materials" rather than to "fissile material" or to "special nuclear material" as defined by regulation. Moreover, officially defined "significant quantities" of strategic materials appear to assume an unwarranted degree of crudity of design, as critical mass is proportional to the inverse *square* of density, and published equations of state suggest that rather large Hugoniot compressions are not too difficult to achieve. J S Foster Jnr (*Encyc Americana 20*:521 [1970]) mentions compressions "to several times normal density" by using Chapman–Jouguet pressures of at least 0.7 Mbar; the open literature on C–J pressures obtainable with various high explosive configurations, on hypervelocity metallic equations of state, and on methods of avoiding instabilities during implosion is extensive and explicit.

105. Theft might become unnecessary if there were continued rapid progress in laser enrichment (Gillette, R, *Science 183*:1172 [1974]; Metz, W D, *Science 185*:602 [1974]; Sullivan, W, *N Y Times*, 24 Apr 1975). One hopes that the materials problems of this method turn out to be very awkward: otherwise, a generation hence, an exceptionally ingenious schoolboy will probably be able to enrich significant amounts of uranium in the cellar. In this event it would be necessary to treat even uranium ore as a strategic material subject to Baruch-style controls.

106. McPhee, J, *The Curve of Binding Energy*, Farrar, Straus, & Giroux (New York, 1974); originally a "Profile" in *The New Yorker*, 3, 10 and 17 Dec 1973. See also Burnham, D, *N Y Times*, p 26, 29 Dec 1974, in which it is stated that "there already were two known instances where Government employees were discovered to have smuggled out of guarded facilities enough special nuclear materials to fashion a nuclear weapon." A carefully worded denial appears in USAEC Press Release U–3, 2 Jan 1975. A well-documented 1970 case of nuclear blackmail by a 14 year old schoolboy without any strategic material is described by Lapp, R, *N Y Times Magazine*, 4 Feb 1973; and by Ingram, T H, *Washington Monthly*, p 20, Dec 1972.

107. Rosenbaum, D M *et al.*, "A Special Safeguards Study", internal Task Force Report to the director of licensing, USAEC, 1974; reprinted in 120 *Congr Rec* S6621–30 (30 Apr 1974).

108. Geesaman, D P, "Plutonium Diversion", presented to the Energy Panel on Radiological Issues Related to Nuclear Power Plants, Science and Technology Council, California State Assembly, 15 June 1972. Much of this compilation consists of remarks by prominent members of the Institute of Nuclear Materials Management (Tenth Annual Meeting, Apr 1969, *q.v. Stockholm Conference Eco 2*, 11, 4 [8 Sept 1972]: FOE Inc, *supra* note 3; and *Environment 14*, 8, 14 [1972]; Eleventh Annual Meeting, May 1970; INMM Report "Nuclear Materials Safeguards in Transportation", 15 May 1970). See also Shapley, D, *Science 172*:143 (1971); WASH–1147 (USAEC, 1969); *Nucl News*, p 16, Dec 1969, p 36, July 1970, and pp 112–3, June 1974; USNRC Regulatory Guide 5.31, Rev 1 (Apr 1975).

109. Mentioned (see note 106), but fortunately not yet described, in the

literature is a design approach (based on oxide powder) of such simplicity that reduction to and fabrication of fissionable metal are eliminated.

110. Hall, D B, "The Adaptability of Fissile Materials to Nuclear Explosives", Oct 1971 MS (out of print); slightly revised version reprinted at p 275 in Leachman, R B and Althoff, P, eds, *Preventing Nuclear Theft: Guidelines for Industry and Government*, Praeger (New York, 1972).

111. Mark, J C, "Nuclear Weapons Technology", in Feld, B T *et al.*, eds, *Impact of New Technologies on the Arms Race*, MIT Press (Cambridge, Massachusetts, 1971).

112. Jauho, P and Virtamo, J, "The Effect of Peaceful Use of Atomic Energy upon Nuclear Proliferation", Helsinki Arms Control Seminar, Finnish Academy of Arts and Letters, June 1973.

113. Comptroller General of the US, B–164105, US General Accounting Office, 7 Nov 1973 and 12 Apr 1974; Gillette, R, *Science 182*:1112 (1973); *Nature 246*:241 (1973).

114. In many countries, amateur weapons fabrication is officially considered not to be credible. This is apparently because the government experts responsible for these matters are so impressed by the difficulty of designing compact, lightweight, efficient, and reproducible weapons that they cannot readily conceive of the potential effectiveness of far simpler design philosophies, particularly those in which generous margins are substituted for elaborate calculations.

115. Thus the Rosenbaum Report (see note 107) states: "Just the normal errors of transposed figures and misread instruments are a continuing problem, and the confusion which can be introduced by a person skilled in the analytical arts and the physics and chemistry of a process is frightening. The standard samples to labs can be altered to force a bias on the whole process. Interfering materials can be added to samples and process lines. Instruments can be made to give erroneous results. The very complexity of the process invites tampering of a kind which defies detection." This concern is not academic: an analytic laboratory used by the Japanese nuclear industry to monitor effluents has recently been shut down by the government for falsifying and fabricating test results (*Nucl Eng Intl 19*, 214, 123 [Mar 1974]). Even without tampering, the inherent imprecision of assays has already produced a cumulative US total of strategic "material unaccounted for" that is measured in tons (see note 106).

116. Kriegsman (*infra* note 121) states that "serious consideration is being given to the concept of co-location of various nuclear operations—fuel reprocessing, fabrication, and storage—in nuclear centers. *** While from the safeguards standpoint, such co-location seems to offer many advantages over the relatively disparate system now operating, we must give closer attention to whether a centralization of various nuclear facilities may be disruptive environmentally and unfeasible economically. And, of course, public acceptance is another important consideration. The entire concept is still under review. *** For the foreseeable future, . . . we plan to continue to keep careful watch on the transportation of nuclear materials." Careful watch, and vault storage, did not prevent the theft of an England-to-Canada gold shipment (*The Times* [London], p 1, 22 Feb 1975) nor innumerable similar thefts of valuable materials in transit. Moreover, co-location exposes all the facilities to common hazards, would change the basic struc-

ture of many utility industries, and is inconsistent with their well-advanced plans for dispersed siting.

117. On 24 Nov 1973, *The Times* (London) and the *Washington Post* both reported that according to the leading Egyptian commentator M H Heykal, Egypt had tried to develop, and Libya to purchase, nuclear weapons. (Heykal's memoirs—*The Road to Ramadan* [Collins, London, 1975]—recount the details.) Libya seems to continue to entertain nuclear ambitions (AP, 13 Jan 1975). Of course, governmental diversion of civilian nuclear materials under the control of nonnuclear states presents problems (see note 101) somewhat different from those of external theft by or on behalf of governments, groups, or individuals, but the prognosis is essentially the same in both cases. See SIPRI, *Nuclear Proliferation Problems* (Stockholm, 1974); Feld, B T, *Bull Atom Scient 31*, 5, 5 (1975); Halstead, T A, *Ibid.*, p 8; *Nucleon Wk 16*, 18, 8 (1 May 1975). In a speech reported in *The Times* (London), 17 Jan 1975, Dr Ikle, director of the US Arms Control and Disarmament Agency, estimates that in 20 years "the fissionable material in foreign transit each year will be enough to make some 20,000 bombs." The spread of strategic materials may take strange forms, as when one of many (see note 108) misrouted shipments of strategic material, in this case travelling across a California city, ended in Tiajuana, Mexico (the AEC report was entitled "Inadvertent Export of Special Nuclear Material"). It has been claimed, and officially denied, that one US commercial airliner hijacked to Cuba contained a strategic shipment; new regulations banning such shipments came into effect about a month later.

118. USAEC Commissioner Larson, addressing the Tenth Meeting of the Institute of Nuclear Materials Management (*supra* note 108), remarked: "Once special nuclear material is successfully stolen in small and possibly economically acceptable quantities, a supply-stimulated market for such illicit materials is bound to develop. And such a market can surely be expected to grow once a source of supply has been identified. As the market grows, the number and size of thefts can be expected to grow with it, and I fear such growth would be extremely rapid once it begins."

119. A strong case can be made that despite the limited effect of IAEA safeguards, export of US reactors and licencing of US reactor technology abroad should be suspended until all nations involved have ratified the Non-Proliferation Treaty. (Likewise abroad: British plutonium exports to non-NPT-ratifiers in direct breach of the NPT, of which Britain is a Depositary State, have aroused much concern; see Wright, P, *The Times* (London), 10 Feb 1975.) The US Nuclear Regulatory Commission, to the dismay of the EEC (*Wkly Energy Rpt 3*, 15, 1 [14 Apr 1975]), has suspended action on all 82 pending import-export permit applications (Burnham, D, *Intl Her Trib* [Paris and London], p 3, 28 Mar 1975) but is free to approve them later, perhaps under different regulations (*Wkly Energy Rpt 3*, 16, 3 [21 Apr 1975]; *cf. Ibid. 3*, 18, 3–4 [5 May 1975]). Indeed, concern ought not to be limited to nations directly involved in such transactions, since nations as well as individuals or groups might become economic speculators: e.g., some nations now possessing strategic materials and knowledge of how to use them may have very strong incentives to sell such assets to nations now wholly outside the active nuclear community. See Steven-

son, A E III, *Foreign Affairs*, Oct 1974 (inserted in the *Congressional Record* by fellow Senator Muskie on 9 Oct 1974 at S18583–6). With a widely shared inconsistency, in his speech S–21–74 of 18 Dec 1974, USAEC Commissioner (now USNRC Chairman) Anders expresses considerable faith in international cooperation on safeguards, but simultaneously argues that unilateral US restriction of nuclear exports is pointless because "[s]ix other countries offer reactors for sale abroad, thus effectively undercutting our ability to demand a particular moral tone from the world in these matters." (*Cf.* Gillette, R, *Science 188*:911 (1975); Binder, D, *Intl Her Trib* (Paris/London), p 3, 27 June 1975.) Nuclear exports may also be involuntary: according to *The Times* (London), p 8, 2 May 1974, a smuggling ring has apparently been supplying uranium "metal" from the Jaduguda mine and mill in Bihar, India to Chinese or Pakistani agents in Nepal. The article concludes, "Five people, including two workers at the plant, were arrested . . . and 3.75 kilograms of highly finished uranium powder was recovered from one of them." A further report (*Ibid.*, 8 Oct 1974) states that the uranium concentrate stolen amounted to about $2.5 million worth—*i.e.*, perhaps some hundreds of tons, though later private reports indicate this is a gross exaggeration.

120. Mondale, Senator W F and Hart, Senator P A, letter to chairman, USAEC, 26 Sept 1974 (available from NRDC, *supra* note 73). On 8 May 1975, the Nuclear Regulatory Commission proposed to prohibit commercial Pu recycle for the time being, to issue a revised draft of WASH–1327 (the environmental impact statement on Pu recycle) in 1976 after the current safeguards review, and to reconsider Pu recycle in about 1978: Gillette, R, *Science 188*:818 (23 May 1975), *Wkly Energy Rpt 3*, 19, 13 (12 May 1975). As shown by M Resnikoff's "Is Reprocessing Cost-Justified?" (*Environment*, forthcoming, Aug 1975), and recently confirmed by industry studies, reprocessing of LWR fuel has become uneconomic anyhow, so it is not clear why there should be much incentive for Pu recycle. (See *e.g.* Wolfe, B and Lambert, R, "The Back-End of the Fuel Cycle," AIF Fuel Cycle Conference, 20 Mar 1975, and ERDA–33 (14 May 1975).)

121. Despite persuasive evidence to the contrary [101, 106–8, 113], USAEC Commissioner W E Kriegsman, in remarks before the American Society for Industrial Security on 18 Sept 1974 (AEC *News Releases 5*, 39, 3 [25 Sept 1974]), stated: ". . . I want to emphasize that while our safeguards systems cannot *absolutely eliminate* the risk, we are absolutely certain that we have minimized the risk to an acceptable level." Presumably the risk of the diversion scenarios considered feasible under the new Nov 1973 AEC regulations (WASH–1535 [Dec 1974] at p VI.37–8) is considered "acceptable". The nuclear industry has vigorously opposed as unnecessary and crippling many recently proposed improvements in US safeguards, though these fall far short of critics' recommendations (see notes 101 and 107): see *e.g. Nucl Ind*, pp 45–7, Feb 1973, and *Nucl News*, pp 48–52 and 97–8, Apr 1975.

122. Alfvén, H, *Bull Atom Scient 30*, 1, 4 (1974).

123. US National Academy of Engineering, "US Energy Prospects: An Engineering Viewpoint", NAE (Washington, DC, 1974). See also the National Research Council report of 12 Feb 1975.

124. MIT Energy Laboratory (Policy Study Group), *Techn Rev 76*, 6, 22 (1974).

125. Jacobs, S L, *Wall St J*, p 26, 19 July 1974. Similar constraints apply to many other centralized, large scale, high technology devices for energy conversion: *cf.* the recent suspension (*N Y Times*, p 1, 5 Oct 1974) of plans for oil shale development. But the special problems of electrical utilities have hit reactor ordering especially hard: nearly a third of US reactors announced, ordered, or being built had been deferred by 19 Sept 1974 (Muntzing, L M, Speech S–15–74, AEC *News Releases 5*, 39, 5 [25 Sept 1974]), and roughly half by Dec 1974. In Jan 1975, faced with 12 cancellations and at least 100 deferrals, President Ford proposed a 36 percent subsidy (by tax credit) for nuclear or coal-fired investment by utilities.

126. Parkes, C, *Wkly Energy Rpt 2*, 42, 10 (21 Oct 1974); Henry, C, *Le Monde*, 28 May 1975, and reply by Boiteux, M, *ibid.*, 11 June 1975; *Economist 253*, 6852, 74 (1974), and *The Times* (London), p 15, 31 Dec 1974 report large cuts in the French PWR program. A recent appeal by over 2000 French scientists (*Le Monde*, 10 Feb 1975, and *The Times* [London], 11 Feb 1975) suggests concern on other than economic grounds.

127. Price, J H, "Dynamic Energy Analysis and Nuclear Power", Friends of the Earth Ltd for Earth Resources Research Ltd (9 Poland St, London W1V 3DG, England), 18 Dec 1974, revised Mar 1975 and May 1975 and included in this volume. As with Chapman's article (note 134 *infra*), some readers have voiced methodological criticisms based on misunderstandings, and Price deals with these in an Epilogue appearing in this volume. No methodological errors have been found in the paper. Indeed, the Epilogue cites Westinghouse and Électricité de France computations giving even less favourable results. The Epilogue also surveys other new data.

128. Chapman, P F and Mortimer, N D, "Energy Inputs and Outputs for Nuclear Power Stations", ERG 005, Sept 1974, revised Dec 1974: Energy Research Group, The Open University (Milton Keynes, Bucks., England). This is an interim report presenting preliminary and incomplete results based on approximate data; a more definitive report is due in about a year.

129. With many colleagues, the author is engaged in efforts to develop generally agreeable conventions for energy analysis, under the auspices of the International Federation of Institutes for Advanced Study (Nobel House, Box 5344, S–102 46 Stockholm). A preliminary report (by M Slesser) of the August 1974 IFIAS Workshop at Guldsmedshyttan was drafted in Oct 1974 and published by IFIAS in early 1975. It will be further revised in a June 1975 Workshop. Other useful surveys are: Chapman, P F, *Energy Policy 2*, 2, 91 (1974); Chapman, P F *et al.*, *Ibid. 2*, 3, 231 (1974); and forthcoming articles *Ibid.*

130. Lem, P N; Odum, H T; and Bolch, W E, "Some Considerations that Affect the Net Yield from Nuclear Power", paper presented to 19th Annual Meeting, Health Physics Society, Houston, Texas, 7–11 July 1974; available from authors at Energy Center, 309 Weil Hall, University of Florida, Gainesville, Florida 32611.

131. Some authors seem to interpret the USAEC fuel cycle analysis (WASH–1237 and WASH–1248, which show that direct process inputs of energy to the

fuel cycle of LWRs amount to approximately 4–5 percent of the lifetime reactor output) as proof that the energy output-to-input ratio of such a reactor is about 20–25. This class of energy inputs, however, is only one of many significant terms in the total energy budget (see note 132). (Incidentally, the 4–5 percent figure is probably too low: Creagan, R J, "Net Output of Energy from Nuclear Sources", Westinghouse Power Systems Planning, Pittsburgh, Oct 1974, gives about 7 percent.)

132. Many colleagues have urged the author to publish an estimate of the sort he has given for heuristic value in seminars. He does so here—as Chapman and Mortimer have done (supra note 128)—with the greatest reluctance, as the available data are so extremely rough as to show only the need for far better data, and if published to reduce confusion arising from garbled word-of-mouth accounts, may be misinterpreted as authoritative. The following numbers, then, are purely illustrative back-of-the-envelope estimates, and must not be construed as correct, careful, complete, uniquely justified, nor even a statement of the author's technical opinion. From 100 percent of the lifetime gross electrical output of a US LWR, one may subtract the following inputs and losses, in any order, to arrive at net electrical energy available to consumers: 10 percent distribution losses, 6 percent on-site power (pumps, controls, etc), 8 percent to operate dry cooling towers, 7 percent enrichment and other fuel cycle process inputs (see note 131), leaving 69 percent. The energy input to build the reactor and its associated transmission facilities may be very crudely estimated thus: 10^9 W installed capacity $\times$ 1 \$/W capital cost $\times$ 6 $\times$ 10^8 J/\$ (typical of the energy content shown by US and UK Census of Production regressions for heavy engineering investment, and equivalent to spending a tenth of one's money on energy in the form of, say, products refined from \$8/bbl crude oil) = 6 $\times$ 10^{17} J = 10 percent of 25 yr lifetime output at 75 percent load factor (or 40 year output at 47 percent). Subtracting this 10 percent leaves 59 percent. From this must be further subtracted direct and indirect energy requirement for building transmission and capital support facilities, incremental energy requirement for administrative (and, under some conventions [see note 130] which the author thinks inappropriate, land use) overheads, energy requirement for R&D (amortized over all the reactors built with the technology before it becomes obsolete), and energy requirement for future services (see note 133). The result of this further subtraction is relatively small and very uncertain, and would not be much different for fast reactors than for LWRs. Obviously all these numbers, especially the larger terms, are probably wrong, perhaps by substantial factors, but their magnitudes nonetheless suggest a legitimate problem—perhaps even in the static case, but certainly in the dynamic case (see note 127), where net energy yields of a program are extremely sensitive to the net energy yields of the constituent reactors.

133. The possibility that single reactors may have zero or negative yields of net energy in the long run may sound bizarre but cannot yet be ruled out: the main uncertainty is future energy requirements for waste management and safeguards. These requirements may be small each year, but may be cumulatively significant if incurred for 10^6–10^8 yr, as Chapman and Mortimer (supra note 128) illustrate: "Now if a power station produces 1000 MW for 25 years

but leaves waste materials which require a power input for maintenance of 100 kW for 250,000 years then the net energy output will be zero. A power input of 100 kW is equivalent to an annual consumption of 90 tons of steel or 25 tons of rolled stainless steel." The author has calculated (see note 127) from Chapman's kWh/kg data (obtained by regressions through the UK Census of Production and to be published in 1975 as ERG 006) and from data in WASH–1539 (DRAFT) that the power requirement for storing by proposed surface storage methods the high-level waste produced by 10,000 reactor-years' operation is about 3–9 MW(t). Since 10,000 reactor-years' operation produces about 5–6 million MW-yr of electricity, it follows that this gross output (allowing for no other inputs, and for a zero discount rate of energy rather than the slightly negative one that the Second Law of Thermodynamics requires) would be consumed by the construction and maintenance of successive 100 yr surface storage facilities for a period of 10^6 yr, and would be consumed 100 times over if the isolation period required were 10^8 yr (see note 88). Of course, less energy-intensive methods of disposal may be devised, but in the absence of credible technologies already demonstrated and ready for assessment, one may perhaps be forgiven for assuming that proposed methods of storage might have to be used permanently in lieu of disposal. (Indeed, it is this very possibility that has led the USEPA to reject WASH–1539 (DRAFT) as "inadequate".)

134. Chapman, P F, *New Scient 64*:866 (1974). For comment, see *Ibid.*, *65*:51,:66,:97,:160,:230 (1975).

135. The Energy Policy Project of the Ford Foundation, *A Time To Choose: America's Energy Future*, Ballinger (Cambridge, Massachusetts, 1974); and numerous supporting documents: EPP, 1755 Massachusetts Avenue NW, Washington, DC 20036. *Cf.* Chapman, P F, *Fuels Paradise: Three Energy Scenarios for Britain*, Penguin, 1975.

136. Some social critics believe that equity is likely to suffer, not benefit, from further growth in energy conversion in rich countries: *cf.* WASH–1535 (Dec 1974) at p V.19–13.

137. The author believes this is even correct for Japan, as noted in his address ("Energy Strategies and Nuclear Power: An International Perspective") to the Centre Party / School for Adult Education Symposium on Energy, Development, and Future, Stockholm, 25–6 Nov 1974.

138. An elementary form of decentralization is the use of smaller units of generating capacity: thorough study of diseconomies of scale might suggest such action, and has indeed done so in a new Federal Energy Administration review: *Wkly Energy Rpt 3*, 10, 10 (10 Mar 1975). Analyses of the consequences of accidents in large reactors, too, seldom consider the social impact of an "economic calamity" (see note 100), as expressed not only through partial or total loss of a large investment, but also through loss of a large block of generating capacity, with concomitant grid instabilities and supply shortages. Accidents or strikes, too, have the gravest effects in highly centralized systems whose energy output is in a form that cannot be readily stored in large quantities—a fact that some militant electrical trades unionists in the UK already appreciate. One reportedly stated: "The miners brought the country to its knees in eight weeks; we can do it in eight minutes."

139. US Environmental Protection Agency, "Environmental Statement Comments: LMFBR Program", Apr 1974; see Gillette, R, *Science 184*:877 (1974). See also the Apr 1975 USEPA comments on the "Proposed Final Draft" of WASH–1535, urging a delay in the LMFBR program, and the May 1975 LMFBR hearings by the Joint Economic Committee, US Congress.

140. Bupp, I C and Derian, J–C, *Techn Rev 76*, 8, 26 (1974).

141. Holdren, J P, "Uranium Availability and the Breeder Decision", EQL Memorandum 8, Environmental Quality Laboratory, CalTech (Pasadena), 1974. Three further references on this subject are cited in *Nucleon Wk*, pp 6–7, 24 Oct 1974. See particularly Electric Power Research Institute EPRI SR–5 (Nov 1974) and National Petroleum Council, "US Energy Outlook—Nuclear Energy Availability" (1972).

142. Hammond, A L, *Science 185*:768 (1974).

143. Several analysts have also suggested that large LMFBRs cannot be made sufficiently reliable (or safe or economic) in commercial service, especially given the degree of technological sophistication of most utilities: *e.g.* Carpenter, E W *et al.*, "Sodium-cooled fast reactors: an electricity utility's perspective", *Proc Intl Conf Fast React Power Stations*, British Nuclear Energy Society (London), 14 Mar 1974, p 631 (reported in *The Times* [London], 15 Mar 1974).

144. *Wkly Energy Rpt 3*, 10, 1–10 (10 Mar 1975). The staff of The Energy Policy Project have recommended (*supra* note 135) "that the present open-ended government funding commitment [see note 145] to the LMFBR demonstration plant be terminated immediately. In addition, an independent assessment of the state of reactor technology and its associated health, safety, and environmental problems should be undertaken by the National Academy of Sciences on an urgent basis. . . ." A wide-ranging study by the US General Accounting Office is due to report in Spring 1975.

145. Lovins, A B at pp 120–30 in "Hearings on the LMFBR Demonstration Plant", Joint Committee on Atomic Energy, US Congress, 8 Sept 1972; excerpted *Bull Atom Scient 29*, 3, 29 (1973); full text in *Stockholm Conference Eco 2*, 11, 2 (8 Sept 1972), FOE Inc, *supra* note 3.

146. Ebbin, S and Kasper, R, *Citizen Groups and the Nuclear Power Controversy*, MIT Press (Cambridge, Massachusetts, 1974). According to NRC News Release 75–80 (8 Apr 1975), the NRC has retained consultants to explore possible financial aid to intervenors; but other sources of inequity would remain. Perhaps reflecting the limited range of substantive issues that intervenors can now cause to be explored in depth—and hence intervenors' limited impact on licencing decisions—the speech of L M Muntzing (Director of Regulation, USAEC) to the 13th USAEC Air Cleaning Conference (San Francisco, 14 Aug 1974) concluded that "[b]y and large . . . intervenors have become a positive force in the regulatory process and we hope to obtain increasing benefit from their constructive contributions. *** Opponents of nuclear power, by and large, deserve credit for their ever more constructive contributions to regulatory processes and to public discussion of the issues." (Speech S–13–74, AEC *News Releases 5*, 34, 5, 21 Aug 1974.) Legal flanking attacks continue, however; in a particularly interesting case now pending before the US Court of Appeals in Washington DC (Citizens for Safe Power, Inc. v. USAEC, No. 74–1186), the

parties have stipulated that operation of the Maine Yankee reactor will present residual risk to the public even though it will be in full compliance with the AEC's regulations, and the petitioners accordingly seek to make the AEC (now the NRC) develop a record explicitly setting out the size and nature of the risk in order to support findings (required by law) that licencing the facility will not endanger, or be inimical to, the health and safety of the public. (Heretofore the AEC has treated these findings as mere surplusage and has only made findings of compliance with its regulations.)

147. Lilienthal, D E, "Whatever Happened to the Peaceful Atom?" Lecture III, Stafford Little Lectures 1963, Princeton University, 19 Feb 1963.

148. Green, H P, *71 Mich L Rev* 479 (1973); *cf.* the discussion in *Nucleon Wk*, 28 Nov 1974, of the 1974 veto of the renewal of the Price-Anderson Act limiting liability for US nuclear accidents. Current political efforts in several places— *e.g.* by the "People for Proof" referendum effort in California—seek to restore unlimited liability for nuclear accidents and to place upon nuclear operators the burden of substantive public proof that the risk is as small as they claim. The logic is broadly that which the UK Select Committee on Science and Technology found persuasive in ¶19 of their 1974 report (*supra* note 41): "In view of the conflict of opinion on the safety of LWRs, it is, in our opinion, for the proponents of light water technology to prove its safety beyond all reasonable doubt, rather than for their opponents to prove the contrary." Such logic may be expected to be more widely applied as controversy persists. See also Green, H P, remarks to the Conference on Growth and Technology, *supra* note 3.

149. Roddis, L H, remarks to Atomic Industrial Forum (International Conference, Washington, DC, Nov 1972), reported by Bird, D, *N Y Times*, 19 Nov 1972; also Bird, D, *Ibid.*, 3 Feb 1974, and Burnham, D, *Ibid.*, 9 Mar 1975.

150. USAEC, WASH–1139 (74), Feb 1974, at p 23.

151. "Data for Decisions: Operating Units Status Report" (Director of Regulation, USAEC): monthly series, *e.g.* 22 Nov 1974. The distribution list of 500 is all internal (including 40 to the Office of Information Services) save 130 to industry, 100 to utilities, 16 to federal agencies, one to the Public Document Room, and 50 to "other". There is no general public distribution, though it may begin soon. The data are oddly calculated (see note 171) and apparently not always reliable: Comey, D D, *Not Man Apart*, 5, 18, 12 (mid–Apr 1975), FOE Inc, *supra* note 3.

152. Comey, D D, *Bull Atom Scient 30*, 9, 23 (1974); *31*, 2, 40 (1975); and *Not Man Apart 5*, 18, 12 (mid–Apr 1975), FOE Inc, *supra* note 3 (see also May corrigendum); more recently, Commonwealth Edison have reportedly admitted that their nuclear electricity is indeed 27 percent more costly to produce than is their coal-fired electricity, as Comey concludes in his BPI memo 750308–A (8 Mar 1975). Similarly, the president of the Japan Atomic Industrial Forum reportedly agreed in Jan 1975 that the Japanese nuclear program, with a 1974 average capacity factor of 37.2 percent, is uneconomic (*Not Man Apart 5*, 10, 9 [mid–May 1975], FOE Inc, *supra* note 3). As noted in note 44, Comey is preparing for publication some of his extensive analyses of malfunctions. These support his hypothesis that the infirmities of LWRs tend to proceed promptly from the pediatric to the geriatric.

153. As reactors age, their structure activates and deposits of radioactive "crud" accumulate, making repair very awkward. In May 1970, for example, a cooling pipe in the Indian Point 1 reactor needed repair. In a fossil-fuelled power station, a similar repair would have taken 25 men two weeks, but at Indian Point, because of the radiation hazard, it required the use (for a few minutes each) of 700 men over a 7 month period (*supra* note 149). In slightly different circumstances, there would not have been enough qualified welders in the country to do the job: Comey (*supra* note 152, mid–Apr 1975) reports that a 1973 repair at Indian Point required "a large portion of the Atlantic coast" to be "scoured" for 2000 welders, who took six months to do a repair that would normally take "slightly over a week". Comey cites a further incident in which 350 men were required for repairs at the Dresden station.

154. Bupp, I C *et al.*, "Trends in Light Water Reactor Capital Costs in the United States: Causes and Consequences", Center for Policy Alternatives CPA 74–8, MIT, 18 Dec 1974: *Techn Rev*, 77, 2, 15 (1975). If realistic values of capital cost, capacity factor, lead time, and capital carrying charges are considered *together*, US nuclear electricity is probably more expensive than coal-fired electricity: Investor Responsibility Research Center, "The Nuclear Power Alternative", Special Report 1975–A, IRRC (Suite 866, 1522 K St NW, Washington, DC 20005), Jan 1975; *Wall St J*, 13 Feb 1975; *Nucleon Wk*, 20 Feb 1975; Harding, J, *Not Man Apart 5*, 6, 10 (mid–Mar 1975), FOE Inc, *supra* note 3 (see also May corrigendum). Based on capital-cost estimates that may prove too low, a recent financial meeting concluded that the world nuclear industry would need $1–1.5 million million by 1990 (*Nucleon Wk 16*, 17, 6 [24 Apr 1975]). Even the R&D investments may be too big for most countries: Garner, M, *Electr Rev*, p 390, 28 May/4 Apr 1975.

155. Ackerman, A J, *Trans IEEE (Aerosp Electr Syst) AES–8*, 5, 576 (1972).

156. As James Madison remarked (*supra* note 135) in 1822, "Knowledge will forever govern ignorance. And a people who mean to be their own governors must arm themselves with the power knowledge gives. A popular government, without popular information or the means of acquiring it, is but the prologue to a farce or tragedy." *Cf.* Muntzing, L M, "Good Government", speech S–20–74 to Atomic Industrial Forum Workshop on Reactor Licensing and Safety (San Diego, 12 Dec 1974) and "To Protect the Public Interest: The Regulator's Quest", speech S–1–75 to Butcher & Singer–S M Stoller Corp's 4th Annual Nuclear Energy Conference (NY, 15 Jan 1975). Information is particularly restricted in countries, like France and the UK, where official secrecy rather than freedom of information is the general legal principle, but even the opposite principles of US law are not always enough, as Ford, D F and Kendall, H W point out in *Environment* (July 1975).

157. Gillette, R, *Science 177*:771,:867,:970,:1080 (1972); Burnham, D, *N Y Times*, p 1, 10 Nov 1974.

158. Even today, there may be relevance in Weinberg's remark (*Bull Atom Scient 22*, 8, 299 [1956]): "There is an understandable drive on the part of men of good will to build up the positive aspects of nuclear energy simply because the negative aspects are so distressing. *** There are very compelling personal reasons why atomic scientists sound optimistic when writing about their impact

on world affairs. Each of us must justify to himself his preoccupation with instruments of nuclear destruction (and even we reactor people are only slightly less beset with such guilt than are our weaponeering colleagues)."

159. The supporting econometric study described in Appendix F to the EPP Final Report (*supra* note 135) is summarized by Shepard, S B, *Bus Wk*, pp 69–70, 1 June 1974.

160. Sjoerdsma, A C and Over, J A, eds, *Energy Conservation: Ways and Means*, publication 19, 12 June 1974, Stichting Toekomstbeeld der Techniek (Prinsessegracht 23, The Hague); see also citations in reference 3 and in Schipper, L, "Energy Conservation: Its Nature, Hidden Benefits and Hidden Barriers," UCID 3725 ERG 2 (Room 112, Bldg T–5, University of California, Berkeley, CA 94720), 1975.

161. *Dagens Nyheter* reported on 13 July 1974 that a poll conducted in Jan 1974 by the Swedish power industry showed that 57 percent of the sample thought nuclear power should be abandoned and that more than 80 percent thought they did not need more energy. A further poll reported on 23 Jan 1975 showed opposition to nuclear power running two to one. Such results suggest eventual political action perhaps beyond the extensive cuts already announced in the Swedish energy and nuclear projections. Accordingly, the Danish Ministry of Trade and Industry's report on energy policy (*Danmarks Energiforsyning*, Apr 1974) treats on an equal footing alternative projections with and without nuclear power. A Nov 1974 Gallup poll in Norway showed 76 percent against and 17 percent for local siting of an imaginary nuclear power station, and on 13–14 May 1975 the Norwegian Parliament rejected by 136–4 a proposal to begin construction licencing for a commercial nuclear station. Sentiment appears to be similar in many parts of the Netherlands, France, and Japan (*Far Eastern Econ Rev*, p 33, 11 Apr 1975).

162. On Christmas Day 1974, a hijacker was overpowered after threatening to crash a Boeing 747 jet into the centre of Rome. More such incidents can be expected. In Jan 1972, Gofman remarked (*supra* note 81): "If, two years ago, one had been asked about the likelihood that three huge airliners would be successfully hijacked to the Middle East *within one week* by terrorists, I am sure the probability estimate would have been vanishingly small. Until it happened."

163. O'Toole, T, *Wash Post*, p A3, 28 July 1974 reports the Nike–Hercules incident. See also Schneider, B, *Bull Atom Scient 31*, 5, 24 (1975) at p 27. (At p 28, Schneider cites 11 major US accidents with nuclear weapons.) Emphasizing that military bases outside the US are also not immune from crime, *The Times* (London) reported on p 1, 16 July 1974 that "More than a dozen Admiralty civilian employees were being questioned . . . in connection with a theft of metal and ship fittings valued at more than £10,000 from Rosyth dockyard. Some of the metal was stolen from inside the dockyard's top security nuclear submarine dock where the Polaris submarine Revenge is being refitted and refuelled. . . . [A]n officer said . . . : 'several tons of metal and fittings are involved. Several people have been charged with offences. None of the fittings stolen from inside the nuclear dock was of a classified nature.' " Contrary to this report, a Commons written answer on 19 July 1974 (*Hansard* 276–7) said "There is no evidence as yet that any of the metal was removed from the nuclear refitting area."

Nuclear submarine fuel is highly enriched uranium, the simplest material for weapons fabrication (see note 101).

164. Other analysts have suggested various alternatives to a moratorium—*e.g.* limits on siting or size or power density, derating of reactors already operating or being built, interim bans on certain types of reactors, rate-of-change limits on some technical parameters, government ownership and operation of nuclear facilities, etc. Such measures would have complex costs and benefits that have been little studied. It is not the purpose of this paper, however, to propose or assess any specific policy recommendations, but merely to stimulate an informed discussion which must precede any decision for or against fission, and which in most countries has barely begun (but see Gillette, R, *Science 187*:1058 [1975]).

165. The US nuclear industry now considers a moratorium credible (*Nucleon Wk 16*, 3, 1 [16 Jan 1975]). Interestingly, the EPP staff state explicitly (*supra* note 135) that they do not recommend a nuclear moratorium in the USA at this time, though they present ample grounds for doing so. This is perhaps because the US nuclear expansion already in hand exceeds that required for any scenario that includes significant conservation efforts—which EPP does strongly recommend—so that the wisdom of any expansion not already committed can be examined at some leisure. In WASH–1535 (Dec 1974) the AEC pointedly ignore this conclusion, and assume that US electricity demand will increase $\sim 15\times$ —or a "conservative" minimum of half that much—by 2020: an heroic assumption apparently requiring drastic price cuts (*op. cit.* at p V–19.4, and Chapman, D *et al.*, *Science 178*:703 [1972]).

166. Kneese (*supra* note 16) points out that if alternatives to fission fail, "we would still have fission at hand as a developed technological standby, and the ethical validity of using it would then perhaps appear in quite a different light." Meanwhile, the comments of some fission advocates on their critics' proposals might be applied to their own ideas. Thus Weinberg points out ("Long-Range Approaches for Resolving the Energy Crisis", ASME Symposium: The Energy Crisis, Long Term Solutions, NY, 29 Nov 1972, revised 14 Dec 1972) that "we find, among the community of long-range solution enthusiasts, a sort of messianic attachment to various ways of providing infinite, cheap, clean, safe energy. The messiahs may be right; but it would be a catastrophic error if we were to allow our overall energy policy to be based on the influence of such advocates." Yet later in the same speech Weinberg argues that "it would be imprudent to base energy policy on the availability of any ["soft"] . . . options at some definite time. This leaves us, really, with only two firm alternatives—clean energy from coal and nuclear energy. I have little doubt that, with enough effort, we shall get clean energy from coal. . . . In the very long term, however, our fossil fuels will have run out and, if one discounts all the other technologies, we shall be left with the breeder. . . . Nuclear breeders very probably will be the long-term energy source, and man, if he is to survive in anything like his present numbers, will have to adjust his social institutions to the requirements imposed by this technology." Likewise, G N Walton and M L Brown were presumably not thinking of their own nuclear advocacy when they wrote (*The Guardian* [London], p 10, 13 Jan 1975): "We have a duty not only to distant generations but

also to the next two or three to ensure that they do not suffer from change accelerated by unthinking idealism."

167. Kendall, H W and Moglewer, S, for the Joint Review Committee, Sierra Club / Union of Concerned Scientists, "Preliminary Review of the AEC Reactor Safety Study", UCS, *supra* note 35, 24 Nov 1974.

168. Health physics errors by RSS are dealt with more fully in comments prepared by T B Cochran and submitted to the AEC (less the citations, which Dr Cochran at NRDC can supply in case of difficulty) by Resources for the Future Inc. The comments on WASH–1400 (DRAFT) by the US Environmental Protection Agency (27 Nov 1974) generally support and amplify the RFF and UCS/SC conclusions about health physics, and raise many other points omitted by both: Gillette's partial summary appears in *Science 186*:1008 (1974). The APS review (*supra* note 43) concludes that the RSS estimate of latent cancers in the "reference" LOCA "PWR–2" (said by RSS to have a probability of $5 \times 10^{-6 \pm 1}$/reactor-yr) are $\sim 50 \times$ too low, though RSS staff apparently disagree (*Wkly Energy Rpt 3*, 18, 6 [5 May 1975] and *3*, 19, 8 [12 May 1975]): WASH–1400 (DRAFT) may be substantially revised, and indeed has already been revised owing to programming errors (*supra* note 43). It is not clear whether RSS can adhere to its intention (*Nucleon Wk 16*, 18, 5 [1 May 1975]) of confining changes to about a factor of three.

169. The high pressure coolant injection systems (HPCS) designed to deal with small pipe breaks are calculated by RSS to fail 7.8 times per 1000 demands. In 47 tests at four reactors near Chicago, the observed HPCS failure rate was 2.1 per 10 demands. Moreover, HPCS called upon four times (at three working reactors) proved to be inoperable twice, and HPCS called upon during accidents at two other working reactors proved to be unavailable both times. (*Supra* note 167 at pp 86–8.) According to Comey (personal communication, 16 May 1975), HPCS failures are occurring at a rate of perhaps one per week. In a recent HPCS failure (Zion 2, 23 Oct 1974), one valve failed because a four foot section of half inch pipe was stuck inside it, another froze shut (its design is being reviewed), and a third failed because of a blown diode: a check revealed that owing to the fail-safe design of protective circuitry, tests of diodes gave positive results while simultaneously destroying the diodes. The piece of pipe is only one of many foreign objects found in reactors: on 8 May 1972, for example, Commonwealth Edison reported to the AEC (docket 50265–71) that they had retrieved an entire heliarc welding rig, complete with 7½-m cables and hose, from inside a malfunctioning jet pump. In another instructive incident, the logic circuits controlling the safety injection system at Zion 1 and 2 (and similarly at a third reactor) were recently found to be wired in reverse so that the system could never work: the blueprints had been changed to conform to the incorrect wiring (USAEC, Office of Operations Evaluation, "Operating Experience: Wiring Error in Safety Injection Logic System", 1974).

170. Lovins, A B, letter to Mr. Saul Levine (RSS, USAEC), 25 Oct 1974.

171. Capacity factor is how much electricity a power station sends out in a given period, expressed as a percentage of the amount it would have sent out if it had operated for the whole period at its full rated design power. Definitions

vary: calculated capacity factor can be increased by making an allowance for de-ratings from full design power, or for maintenance and off-load refuelling time. In reference 151, calculated cumulative average capacity factors are increased by an average of two percentage points (maximum 7.7) by using not the design power rating, but the "maximum dependable capacity" (based on the least favourable temperature of condenser cooling water) (Comey, D D, *Bull Atom Scient 31*, 5, 3 (1975)). Capacity factor is not the same as availability, an even harder-to-define measure of what fraction of the time a power station (or a part of it, such as the steam supply system or the turbogenerators) is available for use if desired, either at full power or at any power level. Costly "baseload" plant is generally operated whenever it is available, but not always, owing to insufficient demand, strikes, etc. Persons anxious to prove a point about capacity factor or availability are free to choose the mix of definitions and comparisons they find most congenial; many do just that.

172. Brennan, D G, *Arms Control & Disarmament 1*:59 (Pergamon Press, 1968).

173. A 7¼ hour cable tray fire under the control room of the Browns Ferry reactors on 22 Mar 1975, caused by a candle being used to check airflow, shut down Unit 2 and disabled five supposedly redundant ECCS elements of Unit 1: the high and low pressure coolant injection systems, core spray, core isolation cooling system, and residual heat removal system. (Comey has calculated from RSS methods and data (*supra* note 30) a probability of about 10^{-13} for such a common mode failure.) Much instrumentation and other equipment was also disabled. Meltdown was prevented by manual control of pumps and valves not intended for safety functions. See *e.g. Wkly Energy Rpt 3*, 13, 1 (31 Mar 1975): "One Candlepower Knocks Out 2200 Megawatts"; NRC News Release 75-79 (3 Apr 1975). A small fire, caused in the same way, had been extinguished 38 hours earlier: *The Tennessean* (Nashville), 9 Apr 1975.

Part Two

Dynamic Energy Analysis and Nuclear Power

John H Price

An initial inquiry (intended for the persevering layman) into how the net energy balance of exponential programs of energy conversion facilities varies in time; what are the energy inputs and outputs of commercial nuclear reactors, both singly and in such programs; what are the possible errors and omissions in this analysis; and what are the policy and research implications of the results.

This edition is virtually identical to the preliminary edition of 18 December 1974 save in the following respects: (1) the discussion inserted into the preliminary edition as a mimeographed sheet has been incorporated as a Preface; (2) for ease of reading, Section 3 has been replaced by a short summary (Chapter Eleven) and its original text relegated to Appendix II–2; (3) data on the projected growth rates of some national nuclear programs have been brought up to date and treated more fully in Appendix II–3; (4) an Epilogue summarizing and responding to methodological criticisms of the preliminary edition has been added. (It would have been possible to revise the text so as to eliminate the sources of misunderstanding that gave rise to the criticisms, but it was thought that treating all the criticisms explicitly in a separate section would do more to help readers to understand the issues.)

Nuclear power generation must take over a large part of the increase in energy demand by 1980.

—The Institute of Fuel

"There's no use trying", she said, "one can't believe impossible things."

"I daresay you haven't had much practice", said the Queen. "When I was your age, I always did it for half-an-hour a day. Why, sometimes I've believed as many as six impossible things before breakfast."

—Lewis Carroll

Decrease does not under all circumstances mean something bad. Increase and decrease come in their own time. What matters here is to understand the time and not to try to cover up poverty with empty pretense. If a time of scanty resources brings out an inner truth, one must not feel ashamed of simplicity. For simplicity is then the very thing needed to provide inner strength for further undertakings. Indeed, there need be no concern if the outward beauty of the civilization . . . should have to suffer because of simplicity. One must draw on the strength of the inner attitude to compensate for what is lacking in externals; then the power of the content makes up for the simplicity of form. . . . Even with slender means, the sentiment of the heart can be expressed.

—I Ching

Acknowledgements

Dr Peter Chapman and his colleague Nigel Mortimer provided the stimulus for this research with their often-cited paper ERG 005, brought it up to date with valuable new data, and generously provided essential help, advice, and encouragement throughout. Dr Chapman also wrote the original draft of Chapter Thirteen. Amory Lovins edited the text, drafted Chapters Twelve and Fourteen and the Preface and Epilogue, and gave indispensable technical advice and moral support. The many contributions of these three virtual co-authors are acknowledged with gratitude.

Gerald Leach, another leading practitioner of energy analysis, suggested useful amendments to the draft Epilogue, and raised some important theoretical questions which he and others will (the author hopes) pursue in detail as part of the next phase of research into dynamic energy analysis. Walter C Patterson also kindly offered technical comments and other help on the manuscript, and, with Colin Blythe, Richard Sandbrook, and Graham Searle, commented usefully on matters of style.

Thanks are also due to various persons within the nuclear community for their cooperation in locating obscure data; to Paula Quirk for her patient hospitality during production; and to Jane Price, Richard Sandbrook, Amory Lovins, and the FOE Ltd office staff for their hard work on production and distribution.

All facts and opinions stated in this study remain the sole responsibility of the author, who would be glad to receive any comments that might help to improve it.

Preface

Many influential energy policymakers continue to believe that energy growth is essential for social welfare, that increasing energy use is a strategic social goal, that energy demand must and will continue to grow more or less exponentially (i.e., by a fixed percentage each year) even though the rate of growth may somewhat decline, and that very rapid growth in nuclear power is essential for the next few decades if we are to develop a substitute for oil before it runs out. The number of nuclear power stations is officially projected, over the next two to five decades, to double every two and one-half to three and one-half years in Japan, four to five in the USA, three to four in the EEC, and four and one-third in the UK. Such rapid growth is caused by trying to keep up with assumed rapid growth in demand for energy (especially in the form of electricity) while *simultaneously* trying to substitute quickly for oil and gas and *simultaneously* taking aggressive measures to keep energy prices from rising.

This study analyzes in detail the net energy output of nuclear programs *during periods of sustained rapid growth*. In general, most or all of the output of these programs is not available to society as useful energy because a very large amount of energy needed to build and fuel new power stations must be offset against it. This energy consumption by nuclear programs can even exceed their output, sometimes by a substantial factor. The study also considers, though more briefly, the formidable practical problems of slowing growth after it has been rapid for a significant period.

Men of good will (and limited vision) continue to promote a crash program of nuclear construction even though they know it is difficult. They are probably not so aware that reactors can only *stretch* fossil fuel resources, not wholly *substitute* for them; nor that reactors can be a more resource-efficient way of *using fossil fuels to generate electricity* without also being necessarily an efficient *source of energy*. But the argument for mounting crash programs of nuclear construction is that the resource-stretching benefits of nuclear power may be obtained soonest if many reactors are built as quickly as possible.

Thus the policy which probably yields most net energy most quickly in the long run is the most painfully energy-consumptive in the short run, when energy supplies are already limited. Short and medium term energy goals conflict, and it is not clear from a purely energy-analytic point of view when and how rapid nuclear growth should abate—though it is clear that political and economic forces favour both continuation of growth and stimulation of demand to meet available supplies.

But these considerations turn only on net energy, not on the more important social, political, and ethical reasons not to commit oneself to a large (or any) nuclear program—e.g., catastrophic accidents or sabotage, proliferation of nuclear weapons (both military and civilian), risks in long term waste management, large capital requirements, social vulnerability and fragility, and erosion of traditional freedoms as societies try by sophisticated police action to reduce some of these risks.

These points aside, building enough nuclear capacity to provide a substantial fraction of a nation's total energy is extremely slow and costly—so much so that the purely logistical problems seem all but insuperable. It appears that no country can sustain a nuclear doubling time of three or four years for long enough to provide the major alternative energy source desired before the oil runs out. But it also appears that at rates and costs comparable to those of nuclear power, other options, more useful and attractive in the long run, may be available with even less technical uncertainty.

Thus two very different policy paths now present themselves for choice and are rapidly diverging. The first, a business-as-usual policy, leads via extrapolation and self-fulfilling prophecy to a very energy-intensive society; to a massive and irreversible commitment to nuclear power; to a highly centralized, highly bureaucratized, high technology society very vulnerable to both internal and external disruption; and to profound and unwelcome changes in our political and social structures. Many thoughtful analysts see this type of future more and more as a social trap fraught with dangers and tyrannies rather than as a utopia of liberty and wealth.

Another type of policy path leads to a lower energy society that is less centralized, relies mainly on renewable energy sources, is relatively resistant to disruption from within or without, and could offer greater personal freedom and social diversity. Achieving such a pluralistic low energy society would be difficult, but probably not nearly so difficult or coercive as achieving an unstable high energy society—and far more lasting. Though no future avoids all problems, some kinds of problems are preferable to others. Analogously, withdrawal from heroin addiction is unpleasant (far more so than withdrawal from energy addiction need be) but is preferable to the costly alternative of increasing the dose.

Many observers of industrial societies today are suggesting that traditional notions of endless growth in material consumption are no longer viable and are bound to lead to even greater crises of social equity, food supply, urban stability, and the like. So too with energy growth: but the fundamental choice of policy path must be taken very soon, before commitments of scarce resources and time to nuclear power have destroyed in practice our present opportunity to choose other options.

—JHP

London
18 December 1974

Chapter Nine

Introduction: Why Energy Analysis Matters

Since 1971, the staff of Friends of the Earth Ltd have been studying problems of energy policy. A team of experts, "Energy 2000+", was assembled in late 1973 to examine the strategic options available to the UK. One member of the team, Dr Peter Chapman of the Open University's Energy Research Group, has for several years been working with colleagues to determine how much energy is needed to produce various goods and services, especially energy itself: mining raw materials, putting up buildings, and preparing fuel all consume energy which must in some way be offset as a debit against the output energy of the plant in calculating its net output of useful work for society. Of course, these energy inputs can be, and often are, supplied by some energy source other than the one being analyzed; but they still come out of society's total energy budget and must be debited somewhere, for in effect, the new energy source is supplying less energy to society than it was supposed to do. We must therefore find out how much energy our energy technologies consume at what times; we can then calculate the energy versions of a cash-flow account and of a profit-and-loss account.

This study outlines the methods used to perform this energy analysis (Chapter Ten), then analyzes [1] six types of nuclear reactor systems both as individual power stations (Chapter Eleven) and in programs (Chapter Twelve). The word "program" denotes a sequence of reactors built according to some pattern, and dynamic energy analysis is concerned with the profitability (in terms of energy) of the entire program as a function of time.

Originally it was intended that the findings of this analysis should appear in a forthcoming paper on the viability of the nuclear energy option for the UK. That paper will complement a recent assessment [2] of certain nuclear policy issues (accidents, sabotage, waste management, security of strategic materials, etc) by considering economies and diseconomies of scale, social and economic implications of centralization, and other broad problems. However, energy policy decisions are now being made in which the *energy* profitability of nuclear power systems and programs has apparently not been considered at all. The implications of Dr Chapman's work are so important for these current decisions that it would be irresponsible not to make them known now. The author, Dr Chapman, Mr Amory Lovins, and several colleagues also hope to prepare a technical version of this study (more complete and rigorous than this version for the layman) for publication in a scientific journal. Meanwhile, corrections of some errors in the initial report [1] by Chapman and Mortimer have been incorporated into a second edition [1] and into this study, which also extends the theoretical treatment of programs designed to satisfy exponentially increasing energy demand.

Let us begin with some comments on the nature of the problem facing energy supply utilities.

The energy and money needed to obtain utilities' raw materials (crude oil, coal, uranium, etc) are tending to increase as the higher grade, more easily won reserves are depleted. For example, the capital and operating costs of extracting a barrel of oil from the North Sea are about ten times those for extraction from the Middle Eastern fields [3].

At the same time, the demand for energy, especially in the form of electricity, is officially predicted to increase rapidly, and the energy supply utilities claim to have to try to meet this projected demand. Figure 9-1 shows the demand for electricity in England and Wales until the year 2000 as projected in 1973 by the Central Electricity Generating Board. Figure 9-1 also shows how the CEGB plan to meet this demand: they expect nuclear power to take over the main burden of electricity supply as fossil fuels become less readily available. The combination of assumed rapid growth in demand together with declining availability of fossil fuels implies exceptionally rapid sustained growth (Figure 9-2) for nuclear power; and it is the burden of this paper that such conditions raise important and novel problems which dynamic energy analysis is well suited to address. Unfortunately, the data available for such analysis are sometimes of dubious quality or have to be estimated indirectly from financial data. The author nonetheless believes that dynamic energy analysis lends much confidence to the conclusion that traditional views of nuclear power as an abundant source of energy in the future are a myth.

Figure 9–1. CEGB Projection of UK Electricity Supply to 2000

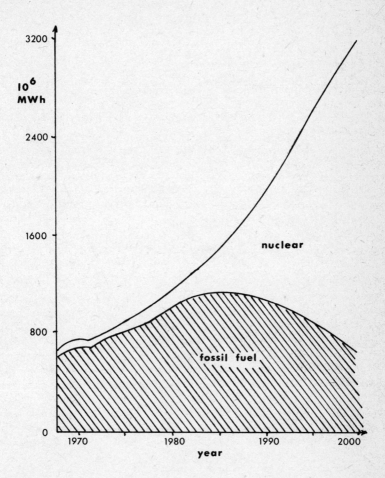

A CEGB estimate [4] of electricity demand until the year 2000—and how they expect to meet it. The energy units have been altered.

Figure 9–2.   CEGB Projection of UK Nuclear Output to 2000

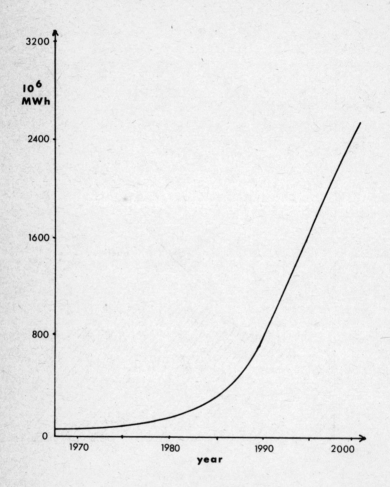

A CEGB estimate [4] of electricity demand from nuclear power stations until the year 2000 (derived from Figure 9–1).

This myth finds implicit expression in a statement by Professor D C Leslie [4], who, after acknowledging that it is impossible to quantify the risks or consequences of accidents, remarks: "If you are hearing this statement for the first time, your reaction may be that this state of affairs is quite unacceptable. If so . . . weigh this against the risks implied by a decision not to have nuclear power; these latter include cold, starvation and social chaos." Comments like this tend to portray nuclear systems as the magical source of virtually infinite energy, or at least as an incredible untapped source that we cannot afford not to exploit. This report examines such assumptions and finds them unproven and probably untrue. Before Britain or any other country embarks on expensive nuclear construction programs, it must be clearly demonstrated that these programs are part of the solution rather than part of the problem.

(Throughout most of this report, power—in the physicist's sense—is referred to as energy/year. The author realizes that he could use the ambiguous word "power", but feels that his meaning is clearer if he does not.)

Chapter Ten

Energy Evaluations of Energy Conversion Processes

Energy conversion processes change a natural energy flow (such as sunlight) or the energy locked in a raw material (such as coal) into a form that can be conveniently used by a consumer. These processes require plants to be built, fuel prepared, and output energy distributed to the users. Each of these operations requires inputs of energy. The present analysis is concerned with three questions:

1. How much time does it take before one energy conversion plant has produced more cumulative energy than it has consumed?
2. How much time does it take before a *program* of several such plants has produced more cumulative energy than it has consumed?
3. What fraction of the energy output of such a program must be offset against energy needed for continual investment in that program?

The analysis can be used for any conversion process. In Chapter Eleven and Chapter Twelve of this report the analysis will be performed for nuclear power stations; but it can be readily applied to other systems such as those that convert North Sea oil in situ, or solar or wind energy, to various kinds of useful energy.

ENERGY PROFITABILITY OF A SINGLE ENERGY CONVERSION PLANT

Energy inputs to a plant come in two main categories: investment inputs and process inputs. (A few examples of energy inputs to nuclear power that do not, strictly speaking, fit into either category are noted in the second part of Chapter Twelve.) The concepts of *investment* and *running costs* are familiar ones in economics. Any business requires an investment of capital before it can begin operation, and it also requires expenditure on raw materials or stock throughout its period of operation. *Energy investment* and *process inputs* are exactly analogous to these economic costs. The energy investment includes all energy expenditures, for example, to build energy conversion plants before they can start to operate. The process energy inputs are required for the plant to continue in operation, and must be supplied during the period of operation. More specifically:

1. *Investment*: Before the plant can give any energy output, the site must be prepared, buildings constructed, machinery made, and the initial fuel charge (where applicable) made and supplied. Each of these operations consumes energy. Accordingly, during the construction period the plant is a consumer of energy rather than a supplier.

2. *Process inputs*: After the plant has begun production, it still needs energy inputs for maintenance and for preparing further fuel. These inputs are considered as deductions from the output of the plant.

Such a plant is profitable in energy terms when its cumulative output of energy (gross output less process inputs) exceeds its total energy investment. A typical plant may take, say, five years to construct, we shall assume that the investment is (5 years $\times$ P_i) units of energy/year), P_i being the average energy consumed per year during the construction period. After construction, a delay of one year is assumed for checking, adjustment, etc before the plant is turned on. During its operating lifetime (typically 25 years) the plant will produce an average output of energy at a rate P_o/year. Input and output are illustrated in Figure 10-1 for the construction, delay, and

Figure 10-1. Net Output Energy of a Single Energy Conversion Plant

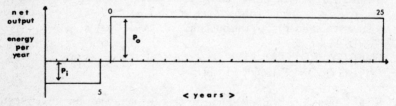

A simple illustration of output energy/year during construction and operation of a single energy conversion plant.

operating periods: we assume for convenience that P_i and P_o are uniformly distributed over the construction period and the lifetime respectively.

Though the output energy/year is positive as soon as the plant is operating (after six years), the energy debt incurred in its construction will not be offset until after it has been operating for some time. The energy debt incurred is $5 \times P_i$, and after t years of operation the cumulative output of energy from the plant will be $P_o \times t$. Clearly the time at which the plant becomes a net producer of energy is $t = 5P_i/P_o$. If, for example, the output energy/year of the plant, P_o, is twice the energy investment/year, P_i, then $P_o/P_i = 2$ and $t = 2.5$ years: that is, if the plant produces energy twice as fast during operation as it consumes energy during construction, then the energy investment will be paid back twice as quickly as it was paid out, or in half the time (five years) during which it was paid out. Completing our example, since the period of operation required for the plant to recover the energy invested in it is 2.5 years, the plant will begin making an *energy profit* 8.5 years after the start of its construction.

Clearly the time that elapses before an energy conversion plant shows an energy profit depends strongly on its ratio P_o/P_i. In Chapter Eleven, and in more detail in Appendix II-2, this ratio is estimated for six types of nuclear power stations.

ENERGY PROFITABILITY OF A PROGRAM OF PLANTS: A SIMPLE EXAMPLE

Often more than one plant is required to satisfy the projected demand for energy in the form that the plant is to produce. Normally the energy supplier plans a building program with anticipated demand in mind. (He may later have to stimulate enough demand to use the output of his program—a problem ignored in this paper.) In this and the following section we shall explore, for such programs, the time taken to achieve energy profitability.

By way of illustration, consider a program of plants each requiring (as in the preceding section) energy investment/year P_i for five years, then neither requiring nor producing energy for a year, and then producing an output/year P_o (from which process inputs have been subtracted). Let us also assume that the construction of one plant is begun each year. Thus

in year 1 the number of plants under construction is 1
in year 2 the number of plants under construction is 2
in year 3 the number of plants under construction is 3

Table 10-1.   Energy Investment, Output, etc for a Program in which Construction of One Conversion Plant is Begun Each Year.

(1) Year	(2) Energy invested in this year (in units of P_i)	(3) Output energy in this year (in units of P_O)	(4) Total energy invested up to and in this year (in units of P_i)	(5) Total energy output up to and in this year (in units of P_O)	(6) Ratio P_O/P_i required if instantaneous input is to equal instantaneous output in this year	(7) Ratio P_O/P_i required if cumulative energy output is to exceed cumulative energy input after this year
1	1	0	1	0	—	—
2	2	0	3	0	—	—
3	3	0	6	0	—	—
4	4	0	10	0	—	—
5	5	0	15	0	—	—
6	5	0	20	0	—	—
7	5	1	25	1	5/1 = 5.00	25/1 = 25.00
8	5	2	30	3	5/2 = 2.50	30/3 = 10.00
9	5	3	35	6	5/3 = 1.67	35/6 = 5.83
10	5	4	40	10	5/4 = 1.25	40/10 = 4.00
11	5	5	45	15	5/5 = 1.00	45/15 = 3.00
12	5	6	50	21	5/6 = 0.83	50/21 = 2.38
13	5	7	55	28	5/7 = 0.71	55/28 = 1.97
14	5	8	60	36	5/8 = 0.62	60/36 = 1.67
15	5	9	65	45	5/9 = 0.56	65/45 = 1.44
...	...	...	...	...	...	...

(The entry in column 6 for a particular year is the ratio P_O/P_i required for the entry in column 3 to equal the entry in column 2. Similarly, the entry in column 7 is the ratio P_O/P_i required for the entry in column 5 to equal the entry in column 4.)

in year 4 the number of plants under construction is 4
in year 5 the number of plants under construction is 5
in year 6 the number of plants under construction is 5
in year 7 the number of plants under construction is 5

and so on. Note that after year five, as one plant is completed, another is begun, so that the number being built is constant and equals five. Hence after year five the annual energy input is $5 \times P_i$.

In year seven the first plant begins operation so that

in year 7 the number of plants operating is 1
in year 8 the number of plants operating is 2
in year 9 the number of plants operating is 3

and so on. Thus the energy output is $1 \times P_o$ in year seven, $2 \times P_o$ in year eight, and so on. (After plants reach the end of their lifetime—which could be, say, 25 years—one plant will be retired one year as a new one is commissioned, so that after year 32 the number of plants operating will be constant and equal 25.)

We can now build up a table of energy invested and produced per year as the program progresses (Table 10-1).

Figure 10-2 shows the variation in energy/year output from such

Figure 10-2. Net Energy Output of a Linear Program of Building Energy Conversion Plants

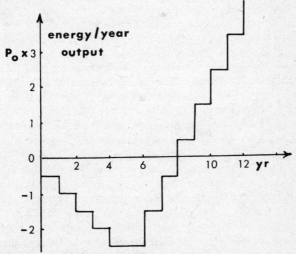

The variation in energy/year (in Table 10-1, column 3 minus column 2) resulting from a program in which one plant is built each year and $P_o = 2 \times P_i$.

a program during its early years, assuming $P_o/P_i = 2$. For a single plant, the energy/year output is positive as soon as the plant begins operation—i.e., at the beginning of the seventh year after its construction begins; but the effect of putting the plant into the program is to delay for a further year the achievement of positive annual energy output from the program. Table 10–1 shows that the cumulative energy profit is achieved after 13 years, compared to 8.5 for the single plant.

It is clear from Table 10–1, and shown further in Figure 10–3, that the ratio P_o/P_i is very important in determining the time that will elapse (1) before the program will produce more energy/year output than is required for investment (column 6) and (2) before the accumulated energy debt is repaid (column 7).

A constant rate of construction has been assumed so far in order to provide a simple illustration. Now to the real world!

Figure 10–3.   Instantaneous and Cumulative Energy Payback Time for a Linear Program

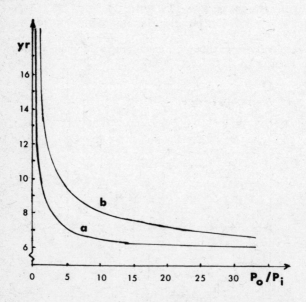

Plots of the dependence of the time that elapses before (a) the program produces more energy/year output than is required for investment and (b) the accumulated energy debt of the program is repaid, for various values of the ratio P_o/P_i, and assuming one plant is built each year.

ENERGY PROFITABILITY AND
EXPONENTIAL GROWTH

As a general rule, energy supply utilities aim to supply energy to match expected demand for their product. Often these estimates of future demand display a good approximation to exponential growth: the projected demand increases each year by a fixed percentage of the demand of the previous year, a process familiar to people who earn or pay compound interest on money. Another way to look at exponential growth in demand is to note that if the time taken for the demand to double is T_D, then in each subsequent interval T_D the demand will double again. In this discussion the rate of growth will be characterized by this doubling time T_D. A good rule of thumb is that T_D equals 69.315 divided by the annual rate of growth in percent.

Figure 10-4 compares the curve in Figure 9-2 (a CEGB estimate

Figure 10-4.   Exponential Fit to CEGB Projection of UK Nuclear Output

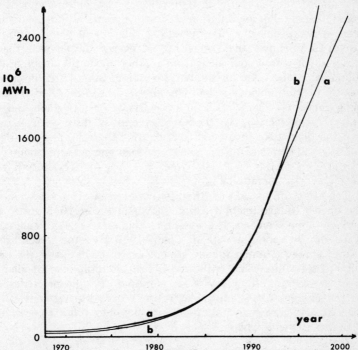

The curve (a) of Figure 9-2, compared to an exponential curve (b) with T_D = 4-1/3 years.

of English and Welsh demand for electricity from nuclear power stations) with an exponential curve that has T_D = 4-1/3 years; the two curves are nearly identical until about 1995. (Figure 10–4 is included only as an example at this stage. In this section we are considering the profitability of energy conversion plant and programs in general; we shall discuss nuclear power specifically in Chapters Eleven and Twelve.)

For the moment it is *assumed* that energy supply utilities treat the energy investment for their plant under construction as a demand on supply like any other, even though it is necessary for their own program to be carried out. In other words, the steel, concrete, coal, copper, and other inputs needed to establish a finished power station or other energy conversion facility will be treated as an ordinary part of final demand by society.

Appendix II–1 analyzes numerically a theoretical program of plant construction and operation intended to produce an exponentially increasing amount of energy output. The analysis shows that the fraction of annual energy output whose equivalent is required for investment in the construction of further plants is independent of time, if we assume that the operational lifetime of plant is infinite. Figure 10–5 shows the percentage of energy output/year that is required (or whose equivalent from another previously uncommitted source is required) for investment, for various values of P_o/P_i characteristic of the individual plant. The plot has been repeated for doubling times T_D = 2, 3, 4, 5, and 8 years. (For this graph and the others in this section, save the noted exceptions, it has been assumed that the plant takes five years to build, that there is a one year delay before it is commissioned, that its average energy investment/year during construction is P_i, and that its average energy output/year throughout its operational lifetime is P_o.)

The effect of considering the lifetime of each plant is to increase the output-to-investment fraction shown in Figure 10–5 during the period of replacement. The extent of this increase is calculated in Appendix II–1 and illustrated in Figure 10–6. Here the percentage of output energy required for investment is plotted against P_o/P_i, both with (dashed lines) and without (solid lines) retirement of plant at the end of its lifetime. For a given ratio P_o/P_i, the percentage of output energy that is equivalent to the required investment can be read from the graph for programs with doubling times T_D = 2, 3, 4, 5, 6, and 10 years, where

1. the lines marked (a) give the exact percentage for the operational lifetime until T = 25 years, which is assumed to be the life of

Figure 10–5. Investment Energy for Exponential Programs With Infinite Plant Lifetime

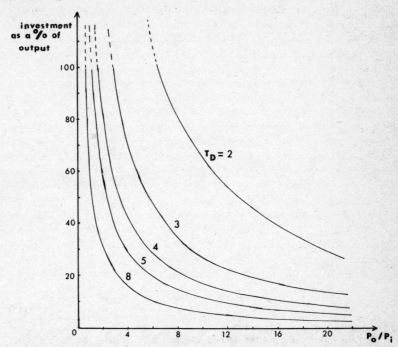

The percentage of energy output that would be required for investment, plotted against the ratio P_o/P_i for plant used in exponential programs with characteristic doubling times $T_D = 2, 3, 4, 5,$ and 8 years. (As will be shown later, it is difficult in practice to achieve P_o/P_i greater than about 2 or 3 with nuclear power stations.) Values greater than 100% on the vertical axis correspond to values of P_o/P_i and T_D for which deployment of plant requires a continuing external subsidy. The curves are all calculated from Equation AII–1.6 in Appendix II–1.

individual plant. The percentage is also approximately correct for $T > 25$ if $T_D = 2$ or 3.

2. the lines marked (b) give the exact percentage for the period from $T = 25$ to $T = 50$ years. The percentage is also approximately correct for $T > 50$ if $T_D = 4, 5,$ or 6.

3. the line marked (c) gives the exact percentage for the period from $T = 50$ to $T = 75$ years. The percentage is also approximately correct for $T > 75$ years.

These percentages are applicable during the period of operation of the program. However, before the program has produced any out-

Figure 10−6.   Investment Energy for Exponential Programs With Replacement

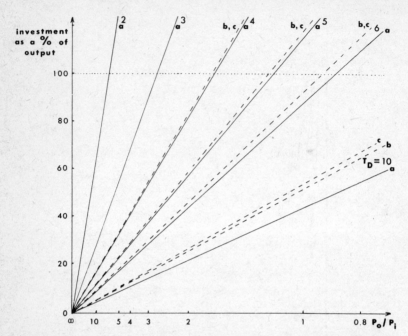

The percentage of energy output equivalent to the energy that would be required for investment, plotted against the ratio P_o/P_i (this time using a reciprocal scale) for plant used in exponential programs with characteristic doubling times T_D = 2, 3, 4, 5, 6, and 10 years. The dashed lines show how the percentage will change if the programs retain these rates of growth until the first (b) and second (c) replacements of obsolete plant occur (see text). The dashed lines are omitted in the cases T_D = 2, 3 because they would fall essentially on top of the solid lines, which show the effect of assuming infinite plant lifetime. All the dashed lines shown are valid for times outside of short periods when early transients in the program are "echoed" (Appendix II−1, Equation AII−1.6), but the correction in these periods would not greatly change the results shown.

puts, energy has been consumed to construct initial plant. One question of interest is how much time is taken before the program produces more cumulative energy than has been used in this initial construction period. Figure 10−7 plots against P_o/P_i the time required for various programs (with doubling times T_D = 2, 3, 4, 5, 6, and 10 years) to make an energy profit, assuming that plant life is infinite. (If plant life were assumed finite, the programs shown would gradually become less energy-profitable, in term of percentage of output to investment [Figure 10-6], as successive generations of

Figure 10–7.   Energy Payback Time for Exponential Programs With Infinite
Plant Lifetime

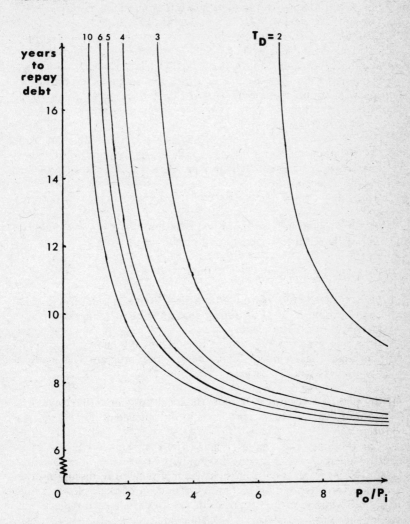

The time that elapses before the accumulated energy debt is repaid for plant
used in exponential programs with characteristic doubling times T_D = 2, 3, 4, 5,
6, and 10 years and with various P_o/P_i. (Calculated from Equation AII–1.10
in Appendix II–1.)

retired plant had to be replaced. The position would of course be more complex if new types of plant were brought into use so that P_o/P_i varied in time; the present analysis is merely illustrative and is not designed to deal with such complexities.)

Consider three examples. First, suppose that an energy supply utility has a conversion plant whose lifetime is 25 years and whose annual energy output-to-investment ratio P_o/P_i is three. If the utility is planning to use such a plant in a program designed to produce an output that doubles every five years ($T_D = 5$), Figures 10-5, 10-6, and 10-7 show that

1. from the time the first plant begins operating until 25 years from the beginning of its construction, the energy required for ongoing construction of plant will be equivalent to 38.5 percent of the program's output/year;
2. from then on the percentage will be approximately 40 percent; and
3. the time taken before the program has produced more cumulative energy than it has consumed will be about 8.5 years.

If the plant has a ratio $P_o/P_i = 2$, then

1. for the productive period of the first 25 years (i.e., $6 < T < 25$ years) the percentage of output that must be offset against investment will be 57.5 percent;
2. from then on the percentage will be 60 percent; and
3. the time that will be taken before the program has made a "profit" is about 13.5 years.

If the plant has a ratio $P_o/P_i = 1$, then the program will always consume more energy than it produces in output and will never make a profit.

For these three examples, Figure 10-8 shows the net and gross output energy/year from the beginning of construction of the first plant. Each graph shows, in slightly simplified form, discontinuities in output corresponding to (1) the operation of the first plant and (2) the beginning of construction of additional plant to replace that which becomes obsolete. The shaded area shows the energy/year required for construction of plant as a function of time, and the black area shows the energy/year required to replace obsolete plant.

If investment energy were mistakenly assumed to be negligible in these examples, then the energy/year made available to society by the program would be approximately that shown by the upper (gross

Figure 10–8. Illustrative Gross and Net Outputs from an Exponential Program (pp. 131–133)

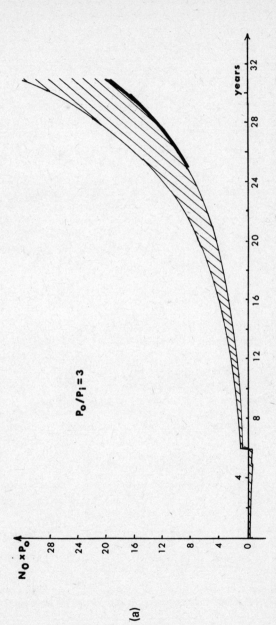

(a)

Net and gross energy/year output from a program designed to produce a gross output increasing exponentially with a doubling time $T_D = 5$ years. The construction time for each plant is assumed to be five years, and one further year's delay is assumed before commissioning. The shaded area represents the energy required for investment in construction of new plant, and the black area represents the energy required for further construction to replace obsolete plant after a lifetime of 25 years. N_o is the number of plants whose construction is undertaken in the first year; P_o is output/year from one plant. (As will be seen later, the five year doubling time assumed here is longer than that of virtually any current nuclear program.)

Figure 10—8 continued

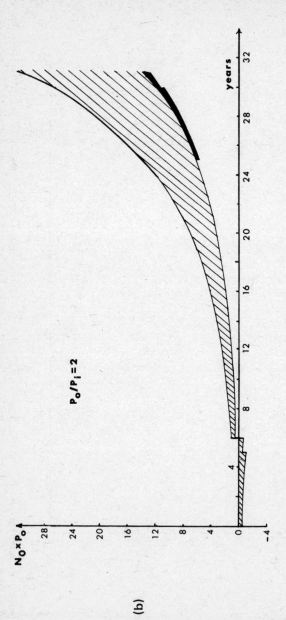

(b)

Figure 10–8 continued

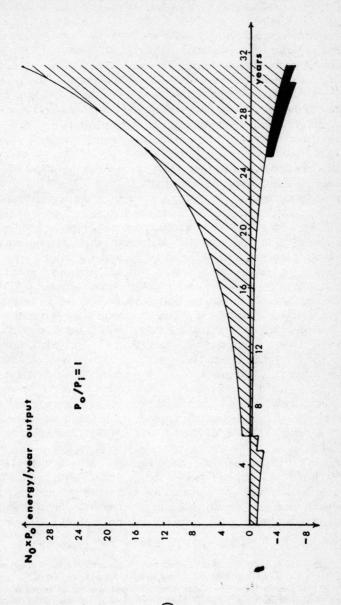

(c)

energy) curve. But the energy/year *actually* available for purposes other than building and fuelling new plant is shown by the curve forming the bottom edge of the shaded and black areas. (For exact values, use Equation AII–1.7 in Appendix II–1.)

For the case where the ratio $P_o/P_i = 1$, there is clearly no energy left—indeed, for the program to continue it must receive an ongoing energy subsidy from some other source. *Yet a single plant with this $P_o/P_i = 1$ is a perfectly profitable plant which produces in its operational lifetime five times[†] more energy than was required in its construction.* It is the speed and pattern of the program of construction and operation that can turn a respectable energy producer into just another consumer.

This discussion has assumed that, in devising programs of plant construction and operation, the supply utility has taken into account the energy demand of the program itself.[‡] (Essentially, in this treatment we have been concerned with the rate of increase of demand, not with its magnitude.) If the utility has *not* properly included this investment demand as part of total demand, then the program must of course be augmented accordingly by building the equivalent of more than one plant in place of each one that had been planned. This will increase the output of energy available for societal use, but will also increase the demand for energy to be invested in new plant. Moreover, there is no way in which a nonprofitable program can be made profitable: the best that can be achieved is not to start it at all.

These examples assume a program with a characteristic doubling time $T_D = 5$ years. Figure 10–9 plots the energy/year required for investment (as a percentage of annual output) against various doubling times for different values of the ratio P_o/P_i. For these plots plant lifetime has been assumed infinite, construction time five years.

Figure 10–10 plots the time elapsed before the cumulative energy debt is repaid for the same values of T_D and P_o/P_i used in Figure 10–9.

Figures 10-9 and 10-10 relate program profitability to T_D and P_o/P_i. For types of plant representative of the ratios P_o/P_i considered, the faster rates of growth shown are clearly unrealistic if intended to increase rapidly the supply of energy; for though each plant is individually energy-profitable, a program of such plant can

---

[†] Eight times more if the plant lifetime is not 25 years but 40 as is commonly assumed in the USA (and if the construction time remains five years).

[‡] I.e. it is assumed that the utility considers final demand by consumers other than the nuclear industry to be defined by the lower, not the upper, boundary of the shaded and black areas in Figure 10–8.

Figure 10–9. Investment Energy for Exponential Programs With Infinite Plant Lifetime

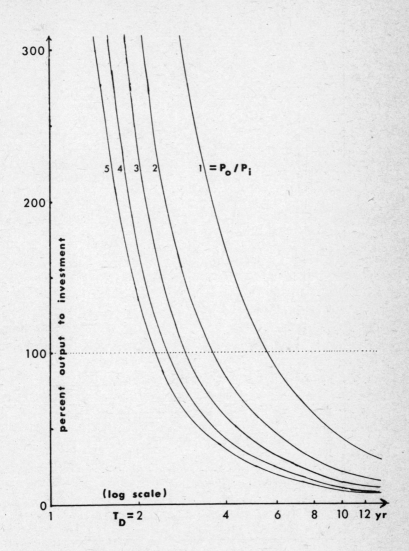

Energy/year required for investment (as a percentage of output/year) versus exponential doubling time T_D, for various values of P_o/P_i (and infinite plant lifetime). (Calculated from Equation AII–1.6 in Appendix II–1.)

Figure 10–10.   Energy Payback Time for Exponential Programs With Infinite Plant Lifetime

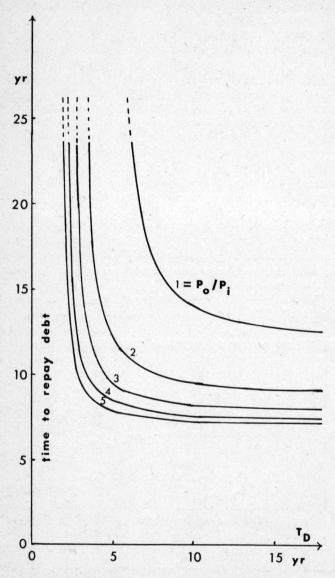

Time before cumulative energy debt is repaid, with assumptions as in Figure 10–9. (Calculated from Equation AII–1.10 in Appendix II–1.)

become a major net energy consumer if the rate of deployment exceeds certain limits which we shall now consider.

Figure 10-11 shows these limits in a way that energy policy-makers might find useful. For varying P_o/P_i, Figure 10-11 plots doubling times which would result in a given percentage of energy output being offset against investment energy in the program. For example: (1) the policymakers wish to build a program of plant whose P_o/P_i is two; (2) they are prepared to invest in the program up to the equivalent of 75 percent of its output energy.

Then from Figure 10-11 the fastest sustained exponential rate of

Figure 10-11. Energy Investment for Exponential Programs as a Function of Doubling Time and Power Ratio

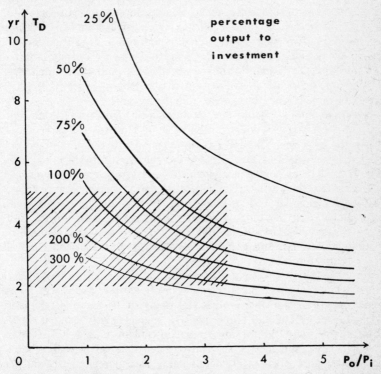

Exponential doubling times T_D which, for given values of P_o/P_i, will require that the indicated percentages of program output/year be offset against investment in the program. (E.g., the curve labelled "25 percent" would be appropriate if it were desired that 75 percent of the program output be available for purposes other than investment in new plant.) Plant lifetime is assumed to be infinite. The shaded area will be explained in Chapter Fourteen.

construction which would give this result is that with a doubling time T_D = 4.4 years.

If the percentage of output they were prepared to invest were only 25 percent, then the minimum sustained doubling time allowable would be 8.8 years.

This study assumes that individual plant takes five years to build and a further year to commission. Since P_i is defined as the average energy investment/year during the construction period, the ratio P_o/P_i is affected if the construction time changes. If the construction time has some value T_c other than five years, then the corresponding new value of P_o/P_i can be found by multiplying the P_o/P_i shown in the graphs by the quantity $5/T_c$.

For purposes of demonstrating the effect of a change in the assumed construction time, let us take as an example a program of plants which have a ratio P_o/P_i = 2, a construction time initially taken to be five years, and a characteristic doubling time T_D = 5 years. What, then, will be the percentage of energy output required for investment for plants under construction, and how much time will elapse before the accumulated energy debt is repaid, if the construction time is something other than five years?

This percentage (Figure 10–12) and time (Figure 10–13) are plotted against a range of construction periods. The effect of altering the delay time between the end of construction and the commissioning of individual plant is also shown, in each of the plots, by dashed curves for a delay time of two years (a) and zero years (b) along with the assumed delay time of one year (the solid curve). Figure 10–12 (but not Figure 10–13, for which the result would be far off scale) also shows how the plotted sensitivity increases steeply with doubling times T_D shorter than five years. (Note that the shorter the doubling time T_D, the greater the effect of delays in construction and commissioning.)

These graphs show that the shorter the construction period and time delay are, the more profitable in energy terms is the program and the shorter the time required to repay its energy debt. Thus if, with T_D = 5 years, the above analysis had correctly estimated the total energy required for investment in a plant as E_i (= 5 × P_i) but had wrongly assumed that the construction time is five years when it was really four, then investment energy as a percentage of output energy would be 53 percent instead of 57 percent. The change in the time that would elapse before the energy debt was repaid would be from 12.2 years (construction time five years) to 10.5 years (construction time four years). If, on the other hand, the construction time had been *under*estimated, the effect would be slightly larger in

Figure 10–12. Sensitivity of Energy Investment to Construction Time and Delay Time

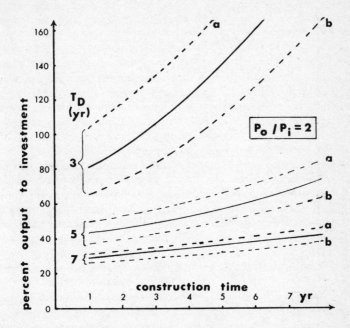

Percentage of output/year required for investment versus construction time, for delay time of one year ———, two years ————(a), and zero years ————(b). (Equation AII–1.6, Appendix II–1.)

the other direction. For $T_D < 5$ years, the sensitivity would be greater than just stated (Figure 10–12).

This section has discussed the implications of exponential growth programs on the basis of the analytical treatment presented in Appendix II–1. This in turn has assumed that the number of operating plants is given by a smooth exponential function. In fact, this condition can only be approximated in reality; but the author has checked the analytic approximation by unsmoothed simulation and has found it to be quite close, particularly after the first few years.

SUMMARY

For the two types of programs considered—linear and exponential—the above analysis shows that energy profitability depends strongly on the ratio P_o/P_i, where P_i is the average annual energy investment

Figure 10–13. Sensitivity of Energy Payback Time to Construction Time and Delay Time

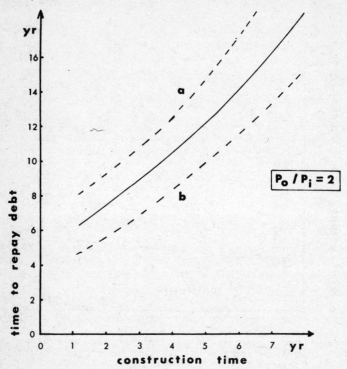

Time elapsed before the cumulative energy debt is repaid versus construction time, for delay time of one year ————, two years — — — (a), and zero years — — — — (b). (Equation AII–1.10, Appendix II–1.)

in the construction of a single plant and P_o is the average annual output of energy from that plant throughout its operational lifetime (less its process inputs).

Quite respectable types of plant which produce far more energy in their lifetime than is required in their construction can collectively become net energy consumers as part of a program. At a time when energy production is requiring increasing inputs of energy, care must be taken if programs are not to become significant consumers of the energy they produce, or even of further subsidies besides.

The next chapter will describe estimates of the ratio P_o/P_i for six types of nuclear reactor; Chapter Twelve will discuss the implications of using such reactors in the sorts of programs we have considered here.

Chapter Eleven

Static Energy Analysis
of Nuclear Reactors

The analysis described in Chapter Ten is rather simple; the difficulties begin as one tries to quantify the actual energy inputs and outputs for a singular and particular energy conversion system in isolation. This is called a *static* analysis to distinguish it from the *dynamic* analysis that considers inputs and outputs for a program as a function of time.

This chapter summarizes a static analysis performed by Chapman and Mortimer [1] for six types of nuclear power stations. (For convenience, each power station is considered to be designed to produce 1000 MW of electrical output, net of electricity consumed by pumps, controls, etc at the power station itself.) Details of the analysis are given in Appendix II–2, and only the broad outlines and results are shown here.

The energy requirement to provide a new nuclear power station ready to operate—that is, the "investment energy" required to build the station and to prepare its initial fuel charge—is not precisely known. In the absence of extremely detailed assessments of all the goods and services needed (both directly and indirectly) to build the station, the most reliable method available for estimating the construction energy is to use financial data. Costs for electrical equipment, for buildings and services, and for the nuclear steam supply system are multiplied by corresponding kWh/£ coefficients [8, 9] which represent the average total energy intensity (both direct and indirect) for appropriate sectors of the British economy in 1968, corrected for inflation to 1973. Formally, these coefficients are derived by regressions through the 1968 UK Census of Production, with due allowance for import/export and other transactions. Despite the obvious shortcomings of such a procedure, it is likely to be more reliable than crude application of average kWh/kg coefficients to the aggregate materials inputs to build a nuclear power station, largely because the actual kWh/kg values can vary enormously according to the composition, purity, physical form, and method of fabrication of materials. In general, the special requirements of nuclear technology demand materials with kWh/kg values considerably higher than those prevalent in other applications; and this increased energy intensity is more likely to be reflected in a kWh/£ assessment.

The energy investment required to prepare the initial fuel charge of a nuclear power station depends on the type of reactor (hence the amount and degree of enrichment of the fuel) and on the grade of uranium ore mined. Given these values, the energy invested can be calculated by a direct physical analysis of the main inputs of goods and services needed to prepare the fuel. The direct and indirect energy requirements to mine and mill uranium ore, extract U_3O_8, convert it to UF_6, enrich this in the rare isotope ^{235}U, reconvert it to UO_2, and fabricate this into fuel elements can be estimated with a fair degree of accuracy, and likewise for other nuclear fuel cycles which use different chemistry or do not require enrichment. Chapman and Mortimer [1] have performed such an analysis for six types of reactors, assuming two grades of uranium ore: 0.3 percent U_3O_8 (slightly richer than the present average for US mines) and 0.007 percent U_3O_8 (typical of Chattanooga Shale, a large very–low–grade resource which, though not necessarily typical of the future of uranium mining, has at least been the subject of some detailed mining-engineering assessments). Chapman and Mortimer [1] have also estimated the energy required to make the heavy water required by the SGHWR and CANDU designs.

So far we have considered only the energy investment required to provide a nuclear power station that is ready to operate. Once it is operating, it will not continuously produce electricity at its full design power (which we assume to be 1000 MW); sometimes it will not operate or will operate at a lower power level. We assume that the average capacity factor of the station over its lifetime is 62 percent [7]—that is, that over its lifetime the station sends out 62 percent as much electricity as it would if it operated continuously throughout its lifetime at its full design power level. A further deduction must be made for the total losses of electricity between the power station and the consumer; we take these losses to be 11.25 percent. These two corrections reduce the effective usable output of a 1000 MW power station to 550.25 MW. But one further deduction must still be made: the *process* energy inputs (see the last section of Appendix II–2) required to operate the nuclear fuel cycle after the *investment* energy inputs have established it. These process inputs—the energy needed to provide fresh "reload" fuel and to make good any operating losses of heavy water—are subtracted from the gross usable output of the reactor to yield its net output. Thus, to use a financial analogy, the process inputs are counted as a debit on current account.

The results of these calculations are summarized in Table 11–1 for six types of reactors and for two grades of ore. The table shows the average energy/yr P_i that must be invested in the reactor and its initial fuel charge during the five year construction period; the average energy/yr P_o of net output from the reactor during operation; and the "power ratio" P_o/P_i. (Note that the total energy investment in the reactor, E_i, is $5 \times P_i$, and that the total lifetime net output from the reactor, E_o, is $25 \times P_o$ for the 25 year lifetime generally assumed in the UK.) The table also shows the total lifetime "energy ratio" of output to input, E_o/E_i, which under these assumptions is simply $5 \times P_o/P_i$; this "energy ratio" is shown because Chapman and Mortimer give their results [1] in that form rather than in the form of the "power ratio" P_o/P_i used in this study.

For both investment and process inputs, some of the energy requirement is in the form of electricity, mainly for enriching uranium. Electricity itself has an energy requirement: in the UK today, for example, each unit of electricity requires an input of four units of primary energy. For *investment* inputs of electricity, this is taken into account by using a 4:1 conversion factor. For *process* inputs of electricity, however, including the electricity used to enrich reload fuel, a 1:1 conversion is used—that is, the electricity required is subtracted directly from the gross usable output of the nuclear power station.

Bearing in mind the possible errors but *not* the possible omissions of this analysis, we can draw the following conclusions:

1. For high grade ore (0.3 percent U_3O_8), it is impossible to distinguish significantly between the six types of reactors in terms of energy profitability.
2. The energy ratios of all the reactors are much reduced if their fuel has to be processed from very low grade sources such as Chattanooga Shale. In this case the energy requirements for mining and milling are very significant.

Using the power ratios determined in Appendix II–2 and summarized in this section, we can now examine the implications of incorporating the various types of reactors into the types of programs discussed in Chapter Ten.

Table 11–1. Average Energy Investment/Year P_i, Average Annual Energy Output (Less Distribution Losses and Process Inputs) P_o, Power Ratio P_o/P_i, and Energy Ratio E_o/E_i (Assuming Five Year Construction Time and 25 Year Lifetime), both for Fuel From 0.3 Percent Uranium Ore and for Fuel From 0.007 Percent Chattanooga Shale *(numbers in italics)*.

Reactor Type[a]	P_i (10^6 kWh/yr)	P_o (10^6 kWh/yr)	Power Ratio P_o/P_i and Error Estimate[b]	Energy Ratio E_o/E_i[b] and Error Estimate
Magnox	1566	4734	3.02 ± 0.6	15.1 ± 3
	3469	*3114*	*0.85 ± 0.04*	*4.27 ± 0.2*
SGHWR	2048	4603	2.25 ± 0.4	11.3 ± 2
	3483	*3448*	*0.99 ± 0.08*	*4.96 ± 0.4*
PWR	1394	4604	3.30 ± 0.6	16.5 ± 3
	2406	*3665*	*1.52 ± 0.16*	*7.62 ± 0.8*
AGR	2154	4541	2.11 ± 0.4	10.5 ± 2
	4193	*3212*	*0.77 ± 0.06*	*3.83 ± 0.3*
CANDU	2145	4750	2.21 ± 0.4	11.1 ± 2
	2669	*4167*	*1.56 ± 0.24*	*7.81 ± 1.2*
HTR	1397	4445	3.18 ± 0.6	15.8 ± 3
	2086	*3170*	*1.52 ± 0.12*	*7.60 ± 0.6*

Table 11-1. continued (Notes)

[a]Magnox = CO_2-cooled, graphite-moderated reactor fuelled by Magnox-clad natural uranium metal; SGHWR = steam-generating heavy water reactor cooled by light water; PWR = pressurized water reactor cooled and moderated by light water; AGR = advanced gas cooled reactor, CO_2-fuelled, graphite-moderated, fuelled with enriched UO_2; CANDU = Canadian deuterium uranium reactor, heavy-water-moderated, heavy-water-cooled, fuelled with natural uranium; HTR = high temperature reactor, graphite-moderated, helium-cooled, fuelled with ceramic particles.

[b]In making this analysis, assumptions have had to be made and conventions adopted (see Appendix II-2). Because precise energy requirement data are not now available, some estimates have had to be based on relatively aggregated financial data. Dr Chapman estimates the errors inherent in such methods to be ± 20 percent for energy requirements estimated from financial data, ± 10 percent for the analysis of energy requirements for uranium processing, and ± 5 percent for the net energy output estimation (before subtracting the process energy required to prepare replacement fuel charges). Owing to the varying importance of the different types of energy requirements for each system, these sources of error will not make the same relative contributions to total error. Dr Chapman's estimates of total error for the ratios P_o/P_i, and the corresponding ($5 \times$ larger) estimates of total error for the ratios E_o/E_i, are shown. For, say, the Magnox reactor using fuel prepared from 0.3 percent ore, the ratio P_o/P_i is calculated as being 3.02 with an error estimate of ± 0.6. This means that we can only confidently say (subject to the important caveat below) that the power ratio lies between 2.42 and 3.62. It is hoped that further analysis will narrow the error limits. Meanwhile, however, the results are not precise enough to permit *detailed* comparison of reactor types.

These error estimates assume that *all* significant energy requirements have been identified and considered, and that the data used are a fair representation of the types of reactors shown. The error estimates are also *not* intended to cover possible omissions from the analysis; these are discussed in the second section of Chapter Twelve and may significantly alter the energy and power ratios shown here. Accordingly, any reference to these ratios should take account of the numerous conservatisms discussed in Chapter Twelve.

Dynamic Energy Analysis of Nuclear Power Programs

ENERGY PROFITABILITY OF EXPONENTIAL NUCLEAR POWER PROGRAMS

Estimates of the ratio P_o/P_i for six types of reactors have been given in Chapter Eleven. This chapter will consider the implications of using such reactors in a program which aims to satisfy an exponentially increasing demand—a problem discussed in general terms in Chapter Ten. The following section will consider the conservatism of the P_o/P_i estimates.

If high grade ores are processed to fuel the reactors considered, the ratio P_o/P_i is found to range from 2.11 to 3.30. Table 12-1 shows, for these values, how much continuing energy investment is required by the program (expressed as a percentage of the program's output), and how much time elapses before the initial energy debt is repaid, for programs designed to achieve an exponential growth in gross energy supply with characteristic doubling times $T_D = 4$, 5, or 6 years. Such rates are chosen here because they seem representative of the thinking of the CEGB (see Figure 10-4), Sir John Hill [23] (chairman of the UK Atomic Energy Authority), and Bainbridge and Beveridge [24] of the UKAEA.

If low grade ores are processed, then each reactor considered in isolation will produce more energy in its 25 year lifetime than was required in its construction. Yet considered dynamically in the same exponential programs just described, the reactors will perform as in Table 12-2 which again shows the best and worst ratios P_o/P_i.

In Chapter Ten the energy profitability of programs was considered for energy conversion facilities in general. Figures 10-5 and 10-6 plotted investment as a percentage of output for varying P_o/P_i.

Table 12–1. Energy Investment in an Exponential Program as a Percentage of Energy Output from the Same Program, and Time Required Before the Program's Output has Repaid the Cumulative Investment Energy, for the Best (P_o/P_i = 3.30) and Worst (P_o/P_i = 2.11) Reactors Using Fuel Processed from High Grade Ore

P_o/P_i	$T_D = 4$ Years		$T_D = 5$ Years		$T_D = 6$ Years	
	Percent Output to Investment[a]	Years to Pay Debt	Percent Output to Investment[a]	Years to Pay Debt	Percent Output to Investment[a]	Years to Pay Debt
2.11[b]	78	14.7	54	11.7	42	10.7
3.30[b]	50	10.0	35	9.1	27	8.7

[a]These percentages apply from the start of operation until one must start to build new reactors to replace obsolete ones (after 25 years). The increase arising from such replacement is small (see Appendix II–1).
[b]These values may well be too high: see the second section of this chapter.

Table 12–2. Energy Investment in an Exponential Program as a Percentage of Energy Output from the Same Program, and Time Required Before the Program's Output has Repaid the Cumulative Investment Energy, for the Best (P_o/P_i = 1.56) and Worst (P_o/P_i = 0.77) Reactors Using Fuel Processed from Chattanooga Shale

P_o/P_i	$T_D = 4$ years		$T_D = 5$ years		$T_D = 6$ years	
	Percent Output to Investment[a]	Years to Pay Debt	Percent Output to Investment[a]	Years to Pay Debt	Percent Output to Investment[a]	Years to Pay Debt
0.77[b]	213	never	149	never	114	never
1.56[b]	105	never	74	~ 17	56	~ 14

[a]These percentages apply from the start of operation until one must start to build new reactors to replace obsolete ones (after 25 years). The increase arising from such replacement is small (see Appendix II–1).
[b]These values may well be too high: see the second section of this chapter.

The values of this ratio estimated for nuclear reactors in Chapter Eleven are such that marginal increases in P_i (or decreases in P_o) will significantly reduce the energy/year available for uses other than investment.

Increases in the actual value of P_i can occur because of declining ore grade, more stringent safety requirements [25], increased security measures, and the like. Decreases in the actual value of P_o can occur because of reduced station output rating (e.g., because of corrosion or revised safety analyses), reduced capacity factor (e.g., because of unexpected aging problems [26]), and the like. One or more of these factors could turn a profitable program into an energy consumer.

Of course, technological advance might lead to increased P_o/P_i, but the resulting improvement in program profitability would be much smaller than the loss due to an equivalent decrease, owing to the concavity of the curves shown in Figure 10–5. In dynamic energy analysis it is easier to go downhill quickly than uphill slowly.

The foregoing arguments suggest that the profitability of nuclear power programs in energy terms is far from established. Even for the best type of nuclear plant, the percentage of energy output required for investment is high—much higher than for equivalent nonnuclear power stations.

Dr Chapman has calculated that the ratio P_o/P_i for a modern coal-fired power station is about 8.0 compared to about 3.3 for the best nuclear power plant. In a program of coal-fired plant designed to achieve a doubling of output in $T_D = 5$ years, the percentage of output required for investment would be about 14 percent, compared with about 35 percent for the best nuclear plant in an equivalent program.

CRITIQUE OF METHODS AND DATA

In Chapter Eleven, and in the third section of Appendix II–2, error estimates were assigned to power and energy ratios, with the caveat that the error estimates take no account of possible omissions or methodological simplifications in the analysis; the discussion in the previous section of this chapter likewise assumed that the calculated ratios are correct. This section identifies and assesses these further sources of error which, if taken into account, may significantly change the results shown in Chapter Eleven and the preceding section.

The foregoing analysis has been deliberately biased in favour of high net energy yields from nuclear power programs: technical uncertainties have been rather consistently resolved in such a way as to give nuclear power the benefit of the doubt. Below are listed various technical and methodological changes which might be made in the course of a more detailed and sophisticated future analysis. (The categories shown are for convenience only and are not always exclusive.)

Investment Inputs

1. The present analysis has neglected the energy investment needed to build electrical transmission and distribution facilities, and to build any special equipment (e.g., hydroelectric pumped storage schemes) that might be needed to compensate for the effects of nuclear programs on the economics and security of the grid. The capital cost of transmission facilities is roughly comparable to that of an equivalent capacity of conventional generating plant, so the corresponding energy requirement is presumably large. Such an energy investment is of course also required for fossil-fuelled electrical networks, but not for decentralized energy systems (whether electrical or otherwise); and it is the comparison of large scale electrical generation with decentralized systems that is often of policy interest.

2. The present analysis has neglected the energy investment needed to build supporting facilities for the nuclear fuel cycle—enrichment plant, reprocessing plant, fuel conversion and fabrication plant, transport facilities, etc. In an expanding nuclear economy, substantial energy inputs are needed to build these components of the ancillary industry, often well in advance of obtaining the resulting electricity outputs. Moreover, some support facilities, though very costly in money and energy, have in the past operated at rather low capacity factors, thus making poor use of the energy invested in building them.

3. No allowance has been made here for recovering heavy water inventory, and perhaps components, at the end of reactor lifetime and reusing them in replacement plant. This is the only "unconservative" assumption the author has identified, and its effect (especially at small T_D) is very minor. Indeed, the effect of recovery and reuse can be seen by supposing that *all* the investment inputs of replacement reactors can be supplied by recovery from retired plant. The only effect of this assumption would be to delete the black areas in Figure 10–8. The percentages of output to investment and the payback times calculated earlier would be unaffected because they are already based on an assumption of infinite plant lifetime.

Process Inputs

4. Fuel cycle process inputs of electricity, for example for enrichment, have been assumed not to entail inefficient conversion of original fossil fuels to electricity, but have been subtracted directly from reactor output. In contrast, much of the present global enrichment capacity, including most of that in the UK and USA, is in fact fuelled by conventional fossil-fuelled power stations. The efficiency of producing electricity by such methods is about four times less than is assumed here.

5. Special process inputs to the fuel cycle have been neglected. They include production of hafnium-free zirconium, Magnox alloy, control rod materials, nuclear-grade graphite, etc; some significant special process inputs have probably not yet even been identified. In general, exotic materials may have disproportionately large energy requirements, whilst unusual components made of common materials (e.g., large steel pressure vessels) may have disproportionately low energy requirements. (In the UK economy, the energy requirement per £ value may vary more than 600-fold over the entire range of goods and services.) The fuel cycles treated here have been much simplified and it is likely that some significant energy inputs to them have been missed, particularly for Magnox and HTR systems.

6. Energy expended in safeguarding fissionable materials against theft or malicious release has been neglected in the present analysis, largely because the data are not available. For the same reason, maintenance energy has been neglected.

7. The grade of uranium ore assumed here (0.3 percent) is larger than the average grade of ore typically being mined today (about 0.2 percent); the assumed grade yields unrealistically low process and capital inputs for mining and milling. Process losses of materials throughout the nuclear fuel cycle have been neglected in computing both investment and process inputs of energy.

8. The enrichment energy per unit output assumed here is somewhat smaller than in most present gas diffusion technology, but probably larger than that which might be achieved by proposed gas centrifuge or laser enrichment technology. Process savings through the use of gas centrifuges would be partly offset by their increased investment inputs (perhaps further aggravated if the design lifetime proves overoptimistic), but the residual advantage might slightly reduce the energy requirements calculated here for enrichment.

9. Plutonium extracted in fuel reprocessing and recycled into new fuel for burner (nonbreeder) reactors has not been counted here as an energy credit against enrichment energy for the new fuel. Such a

credit, which would be partly offset by increased process and investment requirements for handling the more toxic plutonium fuel, would be appropriate if and when plutonium recycle was begun, and might decrease total fuel cycle process inputs by several percent if it became the nearly universal practice.

10. Process inputs have in general been calculated here on the basis of electricity sent out, not of gross electricity generated; hence process inputs needed to operate pumps, controls, active waste heat dissipating devices, etc at the power station could have been neglected here, resulting in significant underestimates of the required annual fuel inputs.

Other Inputs

11. The present analysis neglects all energy used in research and development, both past and ongoing. This energy, if it could be evaluated despite difficult boundary questions, ought probably to be counted mainly as an investment input, as most of it was supplied before much nuclear power was produced. Another method of treating this input might be as a process input amortized over the lifetimes of all reactors built using the technology before it becomes obsolete; but that method is not so relevant to the societal question of whether we should have been better off (in energy terms) not having a nuclear power program from the beginning.

12. Administrative overheads—design, safety analyses and precautions, other regulatory efforts, health physics monitoring, accountancy, etc—have been mainly neglected here, especially those arising not in the CEGB's offices but in central bodies such as the UKAEA, Nuclear Installations Inspectorate, Department of Energy, Treasury, etc.

13. The methodology used here does not consider land use as incurring an energy penalty. Some authors, such as Odum [27], would disagree, arguing that commitments of land for a purpose which excludes settlement or other uses displaces those uses onto other land—generally agricultural land—and thus increases the energy inputs needed to maintain the same level of productivity from the remaining pool of unaffected agricultural land. Odum would also argue [27] that net energy analyses should include contingent energy inputs arising from major accidents which contaminate large areas of farmland and thus entail large energy inputs to make up the lost biological productivity. The author of this study, lacking the data to calculate such a penalty, and uncertain whether such a penalty is appropriate, has omitted it.

14. Possible energy penalties resulting from accidents—e.g., energy

requirements for decontamination, evacuation, new construction, etc—have been neglected here: they might be considered an energy equivalent of insurance.

15. Energy inputs associated with decommissioning defunct reactors have been neglected.

16. Energy inputs associated with transport, treatment, storage, and disposal of low and medium level radioactive wastes (particularly noble gases and low-level alpha emitters such as cladding hulls) have been neglected.

17. All process and investment requirements for transporting, treating, storing, retrieving, safeguarding, and disposing of high-level wastes have likewise been neglected. The disposal technologies are still speculative, as is the appropriateness of the storage options proposed [2]. In the absence of credible disposal methods, one might calculate the energy which would be required for long term storage if it were to rely on the methods that are now proposed to be used for interim storage (for periods ranging from a few decades to a century): over the very long periods required, these energy inputs would be comparable to, or would exceed by as much as about an hundredfold, the lifetime gross output of the reactors served. The omission of all "future services" inputs from the present analysis may thus be significant even in the static case of one reactor in isolation.

Outputs

18. The present analysis has assumed that the lifetime average capacity factor of nuclear power stations is 62 percent—in effect, that the energy invested in them is used with 62 percent efficiency to produce useful outputs. However, the lifetime average capacity factor assumed for forecasting by the US Atomic Energy Commission [28] is 57.375 percent; and recent USAEC data suggest [26] that the actual value may be substantially lower, say about 50 percent, since aging problems (metal fatigue, corrosion, accumulation of dirt, etc) are more serious and are appearing earlier than expected. The present results are sensitive to the capacity factor assumed.

19. All nuclear power stations have been assumed to operate throughout their lifetimes at their full design power rating. In contrast, very many reactors in various countries have been derated owing to corrosion, new and less sanguine safety analyses, etc, and there is no guarantee that this will never happen again. Derating, like reduced capacity factor, has a direct effect on the energy ratio.

20. No account has been taken here of possible delays in construction and commissioning, nor of prolonged shutdowns not

considered in the average capacity factor (e.g., those due to strikes), nor of the possibility that all or part of the nuclear industry might be shut down in the event of a major accident or safeguards failure or of certain political developments at home or abroad.

21. The values assumed for construction time and delay time are substantially shorter than those actually experienced in most countries, and thus probably give rise to unrealistically favourable dynamic energy yields (see Figures 10–12 and 10–13 and accompanying text). Indeed, in many cases the construction and delay times are observed to be steadily increasing [25].

22. Advocates of nuclear power often postulate "learning curves" whereby increasing experience leads inevitably to improved reliability and quicker construction. Examples of such behaviour in other technologies can be found; but in the case of nuclear power, the "learning curve" hypothesis is inconsistent with much experience [25, 26] and must rest on causal relations that have not been proven. This is especially true since the doubling time of reactors is far shorter than the doubling time of the numbers and skills of the most competent and dedicated members of the nuclear community.

General Methodology

23. The present analysis does not give credit for large scale use of waste heat from nuclear power stations. Siting power stations near urban centers to facilitate district heating seems neither wise nor likely, and major uses for industrial process heat will probably be constrained by problems of reactor reliability (as failure of process heat can be very damaging to industrial equipment relying on it). If these difficulties can be overcome, the assumed energy outputs should of course be increased accordingly.

24. Contrary to experience, the present analysis has assumed that altered or additional supporting processes and facilities will not be required in future nuclear fuel cycles. The history of the nuclear industry shows that costly (in money and energy) new devices and processes are often required as more is learnt and as public controversy persists [25]. (It is also possible that future technical developments might decrease energy inputs to nuclear power, though it is not clear where, save in enrichment—*q.v.* ¶ ¶ 8, 9 above.)

25. The present analysis has assumed throughout that the energy required to produce a unit of each material (steel, copper, cement, etc) will remain constant in time. In practice, some energy requirements are likely to decrease through technical innovation whilst others increase through declining ore grade, geopolitical constraints, or the like.

26. Likewise, the energy requirements of producing energy inputs to the nuclear fuel cycle have been assumed to be constant. In view of present experience of increasingly marginal fossil fuel technologies, this assumption is probably overoptimistic even on a time scale of one to three decades; in the long run it is certainly too sanguine, owing to the requirements of the Second Law of Thermodynamics. More specifically, in the electricity-generating sector no allowance has been made for either existing fossil-fuelled plant or existing reactors being demoted in the merit order at any particular time (probably reducing both system efficiency and the capacity factor of older nuclear plant) as many new nuclear stations are commissioned.

27. The present assumption that reactor outputs are uniformly distributed over the lifetime and reactor inputs over the construction time may be unrealistic, though in which direction is unclear. It appears [26, 28] that outputs are likely to decrease during most of the reactor lifetime (after an initial increase during the first few years, owing to the resolution of "teething troubles") whilst process inputs gradually increase owing to increasing maintenance needs and to the increasing energy requirements per unit of energy and materials inputs.

28. The present study has presented analytic solutions rather than detailed (unsmoothed) simulations, and has not been able to deal with a mix of reactor types, such as possible mixes of burner and breeder reactors, or of different types or designs of burner reactors, or of reactors using thorium fuel cycles. Thus the analysis is indicative rather than definitive and is not a substitute for detailed simulation in any particular case.

Summary

A more detailed treatment of these matters, with the possible exception of ¶¶ 8, 9, 18, 22, 23, 24, 25, and 27, would probably lead to net energy calculations substantially less favourable than those presented in this chapter and Appendix II-2. The author believes that the energy ratios shown in Chapter Eleven are upper limits and are likely to be significantly reduced by further analysis, thus leading to even worse results than those given in the opening section of this chapter. As will be readily appreciated, however, it is probably not possible to quantify some of the important terms [2].

Chapter Thirteen

Some Questions and Answers

The initial report [1] by Chapman and Mortimer has elicited a wide range of reactions, among which are some recurring questions which seem worth answering here.

1. *If this analysis of nuclear power programs is correct in showing that they can be net consumers of energy, however can they appear economically attractive? Why does energy analysis give a different answer than economic analysis?*

This question, with variations, is the most common reaction to the analysis. Four points need to be made in reconciling the apparent conflict between energy and economic analyses.

a. The market only reflects people's perceptions. If people like those who need to ask the question do not perceive the dynamic net energy problems of nuclear programs, the market will not do so either.[†]

b. The economics of nuclear power are not as clearly favourable as some pundits would make out. Most economic analyses of nuclear power have been done in order to promote nuclear technology. This bias is reflected in omitting to take into account such items as the real capital costs of nuclear plant [25], the costs of future services (Chapter Twelve ¶ 17, and ¶ 10 below), the capital costs of support facilities, the increase in uranium costs owing to the increase in conventional fuel costs, and the capacity factors likely to be attained in practice [26]. It may be correct that when costed "properly" (but neglecting externalities), *single* nuclear power stations may be eco-

---

[†] As Chapman points out, it is no use assuming that prices can give information about the availability or viability of resources since the perfect market theory on which that assumption is based requires that the market already *have* this information in order to *determine* the prices.

nomically preferable to single fossil-fuelled power stations; nobody really knows. If the need to offset a substantial fraction of the output of a nuclear *program* against investment in it were treated as a cost overrun for the constituent power stations, they would probably look most unattractive.

c. The comparison made in economic analyses of nuclear power is between nuclear-generated *electricity* and electricity generated from fossil fuels. It is often said that if nuclear power were a net energy consumer, it could not compete with other sources of electricity. But look at those sources! Nobody would suggest building oil-fired power stations in order to relieve an oil shortage, for everyone knows that fossil-fuelled power stations are net consumers of energy, consuming between three and four kWh for every kWh of electricity sent out. So if a nuclear station consumed, say, two kWh of fossil fuel per kWh of electricity sent out, but if the energy content of the uranium also consumed were taken to be gratis, then it would appear, in energy terms, that nuclear fission is a preferable technology for generating electricity. Yet under these conditions neither fossil-fuelled stations *nor* nuclear stations would be considered a good method of increasing the world's fuel resources. (To show, by economics, that nuclear power is a net producer of energy would require a demonstration that the total cost per energy unit from a nuclear power station is less than the total cost per energy unit from a coal mine or oil well.) Let us compare two systems for generating electricity: one from fossil fuel alone, the other from uranium plus a fossil fuel subsidy. The latter system stretches the fossil fuel reserves and thus is a more resource-efficient way of using them to generate electricity; but that does not mean it is a good source of energy.

d. The final point concerns the objectives of energy analysis. It is not a system of allocating resources; it is not a replacement for economics. All that energy analysis can do is show the energy implications of policies. In contrast, economic analysis shows the financial implications of policies. These two approaches are not contradictory but complementary. The mistake implicit in the question is the assumption that a fuel industry which makes a fiscal profit must be a net producer of energy. The CEGB is a good example of why this assumption is wrong. Energy is just one of the resources that economics should consider, and can only be considered the most important one if the policy being analyzed demands that energy be so treated.

Thus, in summary, the answer to the question is that nuclear power can show a fossil fuel profit when compared to a fossil-fuelled industry which is a prolific net consumer of energy, but this does not imply that an expanding nuclear power program is a net producer of energy.

2. *It is not clear why this energy analysis is necessary, since if you are right, the price of uranium and of nuclear-generated electricity will rise, giving us due warning that we are heading for trouble.*

See answer (a) to question 1. Moreover, if you wait until the somewhat ponderous price mechanism has got round to reflecting the actual situation of net energy consumption—i.e., difficulties perceived as present or imminent—you are already so far into a net energy deficit that you are in real trouble. The market is notorious both for long perceptual delays and for vigorously signalling short term abundance of various resources when what matters for policy is the value corresponding to long term scarcity of the residual stocks.

3. *If your analysis is correct, what should be done?*

This analysis shows that the process of building large numbers of nuclear reactors does not increase energy supplies during the period intended; so do not build them.

To show that a policy is mistaken does not *oblige* the analyst to have an alternative policy. As it happens, however, the author and his colleagues do have ideas explored in past [2, 3] and forthcoming papers from Friends of the Earth, and hinted at in Chapter Fourteen of this study. According to these ideas, the human and fiscal resources now devoted to nuclear power can and should be redirected to other energy supply and conservation technologies with more favourable energetic and social characteristics.

4. *Your analysis has confused energy with welfare, and it is not obvious that this type of analysis is at all relevant to nuclear policy.*

This comment was not invented; it is an accurate summary of one received from the UK Department of Energy. The reply was that the report referred to [1] nowhere confused energy with welfare, and that the only justification for looking at the energy implications of nuclear power programs is that it is claimed (by their proponents) that they increase the supply of energy. If nuclear power stations are built for other reasons, then energy analysis may well be irrelevant to the formulation of nuclear policy.

5. *You have only demonstrated that nuclear systems are net consumers of energy under ridiculously high rates of growth. If you used a more sensible growth rate, your conclusions would be more favourable.*

Precisely. The UK nuclear growth rate assumed, however, is that officially projected by the CEGB, UKAEA, and similar authorities, all of whom are working hard to expand nuclear capacity with a doubling time of about 4.5 years for at least the next 20 years. This growth rate is *not* that projected by the same authorities for total energy demand; it arises because nuclear power is being put forward as a source able to take over the role of oil and other fossil fuels even as their availability may decrease. The results are indeed ridiculous, but are a straightforward extrapolation of historical trends [29] (see also Figures 9-1 and 9-2). It is noteworthy that the nuclear growth rate officially projected for the UK is among the lowest in the world: the approximate doubling times projected are about 3.5 years for the EEC, 4 for the USA, and perhaps 2.5-3.5 for France and Japan.

6. *Even if you have got the correct rate of growth, nobody is pretending that it will go on indefinitely, since breeder reactors will take over the growth within 15-20 years.*

This analysis does not pretend that growth in anything will continue indefinitely at the projected rate or at any other rate. This paper considers only a *transient* problem while the nuclear burner program is expanding rapidly, and shows only that burner reactors (relying on high grade uranium resources) are net consumers of energy during this period of rapid growth. Their future viability will depend on uranium ore grade, changes in nuclear technology, and other variables. (See also, however, the discussion in Chapter Fourteen on the recovery of cumulative energy debts after growth has moderated.)

If breeder reactors are to represent a large part of the new nuclear capacity installed, it will be necessary to continue to increase the number of burner reactors of the types considered in this paper. This is because a breeder reactor takes about 15-20 years in likely future practice (nearer 40 in present practice) to breed enough plutonium for the core of a second breeder reactor, and longer still (by 1.5-2.0X) to breed the "pipeline inventory" required for the fuel cycle of the second breeder. Breeder reactors by themselves are thus constrained to a doubling time of some decades. To build up a stock of breeders at a faster rate would require some source of plutonium other than breeders. The only other sources of plutonium are weapons stockpiles and the plutonium output of burner reactors. Fast growth in breeder reactors thus requires either the depletion of weapons stockpiles (which are too small to suffice for long) or earlier fast growth of burner reactors—coupled with concurrent operation of the breeder and burner programs for a very long time (typically about a century). The problem of plutonium stocks and flows in a breeder economy is closely analogous to the flows of energy in programs of nuclear power stations: just as the breeders, if built at an excessive rate, can no longer breed (collectively, not individually), so the nuclear stations, if built at an excessive rate, cannot provide their own energy investment.

Several more detailed comments and questions are also worth addressing here:

7. *Why is the initial fuel charge counted as an investment input?*

Because a nuclear power station cannot operate at all until the entire core has been assembled. This is a true investment: all the energy (and money) for the initial core must be paid out before any energy output can be obtained. The initial core actually represents about an eighth of all the fuel that the reactor requires over its 25 year lifetime. For a 1000 MW(e) coal-fired power station, this would be equivalent to a situation where of the order of 14 million metric tons of coal had to be mined and delivered before the station could be started up.

8. *Since the core is intact at the end of the reactor lifetime, it should be included as an energy credit in the total output of the reactor.*

If a reactor core is still intact when the reactor is decommissioned, then it could change the energy ratios for second generation reactors. It has absolutely no effect on the transient problem analyzed in the study: apart from anything else, it should be clear that in a growth period, the number of reactors being started up is always larger (and generally much larger) than the number being closed down (see also Chapter Twelve, ¶ 3).

It is also doubtful that anyone would continue to refuel a reactor with normal charges right up to the point of shutdown. It seems more likely that when a reactor is decommissioned, the recoverable fuel values from the core will be substantially lower than those from an equivalent amount of fuel during the normal operating lifetime.

9. *You have not given any credit for the plutonium produced.*

a. If you count the energy value of the plutonium as a credit, then to be consistent you should count the energy content of the uranium fuel as a debit, on the same principle used for fossil-fuelled stations. For both uranium and plutonium, the raw material is of no use to anyone until it has been converted into a useful form. This analysis is concerned with the energy profitability of energy *conversion* processes, not with the potential energy of the raw material.

In terms of real energy flow into an economy, the plutonium is irrelevant unless it is actually recycled (Chapter Twelve, ¶ 9). This study has shown that a rapidly growing population of burner reactors consumes more energy than it produces. It is not much use offering plutonium to people who want electricity. Thus plutonium is not relevant to the transient problem that concerns us here.

b. The plutonium is not normally considered a fuel for burner reactors (though it could be: see Chapter Twelve, ¶ 9). It also cannot be used in a large scale breeder program for a long time. If plutonium production were credited to burner reactors because it was actually being recycled and did actually save enrichment energy, or likewise for breeder reactors, the same plutonium could not be double-counted as a further credit in the systems thus served.

10. *You have not included any energy used in waste handling, storage, or disposal.*

This is because no realistic data on these operations are available. Any energy expenditure on these operations would only make the situation worse than portrayed here. In the long run, these energy inputs may be important, though they may have little immediate relevance to the transient problem analysed here.

The most abundant transuranic waste material is plutonium–239 with a half-life of 24,390 years. Although plutonium is recovered from spent fuel rods, 100 percent recovery is not economically or technically practicable (and is probably not energy-profitable either). Thus waste from spent rods contains some residual plutonium and must be stored at least, say, 240,000 years (ten half-lives)—probably a very conservative estimate [2]. Now if a power station produces 1000 MW for 25 years but leaves waste materials which require a power input for maintenance of 100 kW for 250,000 years, then the net energy output (neglecting all other inputs) will be zero. A power input of 100 kW is equivalent to an annual consumption of 90 metric tons of steel or 25 of rolled stainless steel. One hopes that designers of waste management schemes will be able to keep their average power consumption below 100 kW per reactor as well as develop an infallible system capable of surviving for geological periods [2].

It may be of interest that the waste storage methods now proposed in the USA (pending development of a viable method of permanent disposal) entail an average power consumption of about 12–35 kW. Specifically, if Chapman's data [8] for gross energy requirements of various materials are applied to the data in the USAEC's draft Environmental Statement on the proposed Retrievable Surface Storage Facility [30], then the continuous power input to build and operate such a facility (assuming the 100 year design life stated) is found by Lovins to be about 3–9 MW(t), depending on the design chosen. The facility will serve approximately 10^4 reactor years of PWR waste production, corresponding (at 1 GW(e)/reactor and 62 percent capacity factor) to a total lifetime output of the order of 6×10^6 MW(e) years. Thus the total energy inputs to a series of successive facilities of this type would be of the same order of magnitude as the total gross outputs of the reactors served if the required waste storage time were about 10^6 years (corresponding to the ^{239}Pu decay chain) and would be $\sim100\times$ larger than the total outputs if the storage time were about 10^8 years (corresponding to the ^{241}Am–^{237}Np decay chain [2]). Of course, less energy-intensive means of safe storage or disposal might be devised and demonstrated, but none appears to be available now for engineering assessment, and proposed methods for partitioning and recycling actinides may not be of much help [2]. Moreover, throughout this study it has been assumed that the energy requirement for supplying the energy inputs is constant in time; whereas the Second Law of Thermodynamics entails that a joule of free energy is easier to earn today than tomorrow (i.e., that energy has a small *negative* discount rate)—a conclusion fully borne out by recent experience with marginal energy technologies. This conservatism of the above calculation should become quite important over the very long periods relevant to waste management.

11. *You have counted electricity consumed in enriching initial fuel charges at the thermal rate based on conventional fossil-fuelled stations. However, as each 1000 MW(e) reactor is built, the average efficiency of generating electricity will steadily improve, thus making the energy requirements of reactors steadily decrease.*

While an excessively fast-growing nuclear power program is running at a net energy loss, the efficiency of generating electricity is actually declining. Thus by maintaining one efficiency throughout the growth period our calculation would be overgenerous. For nuclear programs operating always at a net energy profit, it would be correct to use a slowly improving efficiency of generating electricity, but the effect on the transient problem considered here would be quite small.

12. *You have only considered gas diffusion enrichment of uranium. If you had considered gas centrifuge enrichment, which requires a tenth of the power input, your conclusions would be changed.*

No reliable operating data seem to be available to confirm the estimated requirements of gas centrifuges. Even if the centrifuge has a tenth of the present operating power, its greater capital intensity may partly compensate (Chapter Twelve, ¶ 8). At the moment the enrichment process is the most energy-intensive step in uranium processing. The investment inputs to gas diffusion plant contribute about 10 percent to the total energy inputs to enrichment; the centrifuge process has been estimated to be more capital-intensive and to have some higher operating costs. Hence the energy requirement for centrifugation is likely to be substantially more than 10 percent of the energy requirement assumed here for gas diffusion. Moreover, though use of a gas centrifuge would increase the energy ratio for any *one* reactor, the shift of energy requirements from process inputs to investment inputs would make the *dynamic* problem worse. Thus, until better data are available, one cannot be sure whether or not the centrifuge process will improve the dynamic energy flows at all, let alone significantly.

13. *You have included uranium mining in your energy analysis, even though the UK does not mine any uranium. Surely this makes nuclear power very attractive as a net energy source for the UK.*

The energy requirements for mining uranium are an insignificant term (affecting the energy ratios by only about 0.2, well within the error estimates) if high grade ores are assumed. The important energy requirements—fuel enrichment and station construction—are supplied by the UK. In future, as the ore grade declines, the energy requirements for mining will increase until, at grades less than about 0.01 percent, they will dominate the analysis. Before this point one must ask whether it is reasonable to expect uranium exporters to subsidize one's own fuel production system. This is essentially a political question: energy analysis can only show the energetic implications. It is unpalatable to have to decide whether dependence on uranium exporters is preferable to dependence on OPEC.

Chapter Fourteen

Conclusions and Policy Implications

This study presents a conservative assessment of the net energy yields from various thermal reactors, neglecting a number of terms whose inclusion would be likely to make the results worse by a significant but presently (and to some extent perhaps perpetually) unknown amount. This optimistic assessment shows that reactors fuelled by uranium from high grade ores typically yield output energy about two or three times as quickly during their operating lifetime as they consume input energy during their construction. If the uranium is derived from low grade ores (in particular, Chattanooga Shale), this power ratio becomes about 0.8–1.6, and an isolated thermal reactor produces (in most cases) only a few times as much energy as is required to fuel it.

In the dynamic rather than the static case—that is, if reactors are considered not singly but as part of a multireactor nuclear power program whose *total* inputs and outputs at various times are of interest—the requirements on the output-to-input power ratio of the individual reactors are far more stringent. If the number of reactors increases too quickly, the energy/year that must be continuously invested in new construction is a large fraction of the program's output. For example, if a nuclear power program based on the most energy-profitable type of reactor studied (assuming high grade uranium ores) is to yield to society *half* of the energy/year that it was expected to yield (the other half being offset against investment in the program), then the doubling time of the number of reactors cannot be less than 4.0 years; the corresponding figure for the least energy-profitable reactor studied is 5.5 years. And if the doubling time of reactor population is less than 2.6 years for the most energy-profitable reactor, or 3.5 years for the least, then the nuclear power program will continuously consume more energy/year than it produces. For comparison, the doubling time widely proposed for the British nuclear program is about 4.3 years (Figure 10-4); for the EEC, about 3.5 years; for the USA, about 4 years; and for France and Japan, about 2.5-3.5 years. All these programs will therefore produce, as output to society, energy/year equivalent to about half or less of the demand they were intended to meet, and the output of at least the last two programs (the Japanese and French) will be negative.

The shaded area in Figure 10-11 shows the constraints imposed by nuclear doubling times that are short enough to achieve a significant measure of substitution for oil within several decades. The doubling times included in the shaded area—from two to five years—cover the range of historical and officially projected nuclear growth in nearly all countries. All these doubling times are short enough to ensure, with attainable power ratios ($\leq$ 3.3), that *no more than about two-thirds of the expected output is available to society for purposes other than investment in new nuclear plant, and that in most cases this available energy is far smaller or even negative (corresponding to continual subsidy from fossil fuels to nuclear power).*

In the British case, with reactor population proposed to double every 4.3 years or so, and assuming high grade uranium ores fuelling SGHWRs, only about a third of the energy which the program is supposed to produce would actually be left over for general use after reinvestment in the program. This can be interpreted as meaning that to meet a given final demand by society in general (excluding the nuclear industry), *about three times as much capacity must be built as was expected*; alternatively, that a unit of *net* output to society from the nuclear program *will cost about three times as much as had been claimed.* With uranium from low grade ores (Chattanooga Shale), it is likely that a sustained program of SGHWRs with a 4.3 year doubling time *would always be a net consumer of energy: the more reactors we built, the more energy we should lose* (see Figure 10-11).

Two types of policy conclusions flow from these considerations. The first is that doubling times of a few years (two to three and probably four) are certainly not sustainable with nuclear power if it is to produce net yields; indeed, this is probably true of all other major new energy technologies. Such rapid doubling times are the result of trying to meet assumed rapid growth in demand while *simultaneously* substituting rapidly for traditional sources (such as Middle Eastern oil). Major new energy technologies can, for a time, do *one or the other but not both*; or at least if they do both they cannot also produce net energy. This is a good argument (if one more were needed [3]) for stabilizing or reducing energy demand if one wishes to buy the time needed to substitute—a need many people had already perceived owing to the intractable rate-and-magnitude problems [3] of a purely logistical nature that impede very rapid proliferation of any complex technology.

This argument has special force in countries like Britain which are contemplating several kinds of substitution at once: North Sea oil for Middle Eastern oil, synthetic fuels for original coal, nuclear power for oil and coal, etc. These substitutions, too, have their net energy implications and rate constraints, entangled at the root with added demands for money, materials, technical skills, and other scarce resources.

Another set of policy conclusions is suggested by the question: When are more favourable cumulative net yields of net energy obtained if an exponential program, initially too rapid, is later moderated or terminated? No exponential process can continue forever; but what are the energetic consequences of reductions in growth rate? The answer depends in detail on the conditions assumed, but in general the time taken to recover cumulative energy deficits incurred by too rapid initial growth is long; it may exceed the lifetime of the energy facilities being built. Moreover, it appears to be true that at least in the early stages of a too rapid program that is incurring a deficit, it is less painful in the long run (and a more efficient use of national resources) to stop the program and promptly redirect its resources in a more rewarding direction than merely to slow the program in the hope of recouping losses incurred so far. (This conclusion is tentative: much more work is needed in this area.)

An analogy from economics may be helpful here. If an industrial economy with a fixed rate of capital formation grows exponentially at an excessive rate, its rate of internal capital formation will be too slow to support investment, so an exponentially increasing external subsidy (bearing a fixed proportion to output) must be obtained. If growth rates are later reduced, or if the profit margin available to repay the external debt is increased (an analogue of improving the power ratio of energy conversion facilities), then one may be able to obtain enough surplus money to pay back the debt over some period. But if the surplus income disposable in this way is not very large, the time required to repay the external debt may be very large; and if it exceeds the lifetime of the plants being built with the borrowed capital, there is a sense in which it would have been better not to build them: they contribute to a later profit, but are not themselves profitable during their lifetimes and do little to make one richer. The capital sunk in them can sink out of sight. (As noted in Chapter Thirteen, ¶ 6, there is also a material-flow analogy with plutonium in a breeder reactor economy: consider the case where the time required to repay the plutonium debt exceeds the reactor lifetime.)

Persons familiar with cash-flows and with profit-and-loss accounts will readily appreciate that accumulating a large external debt in the way just described is not sound management and should at least be confined to as short a period and as small a sum as possible. (Life is harder in the financial world, where one must pay interest at a high rate; but as pointed out in Chapter Thirteen, ¶ 10, there is a sort of interest rate on energy borrowings too, since one is borrowing high grade energy of low energy cost—e.g., Middle Eastern oil—but will repay the debt with lower grade energy of higher energy cost—e.g., North Sea oil or an even more marginal source. If one waits too long to repay the energy debt, the interest payable on it may be truly exorbitant and exceed the principal sum—e.g., the grade of uranium ore available may be very low, reducing P_o/P_i—so that the belated energy yields may no longer suffice to repay the debt.)

Unfortunately, managers who choose to retard or terminate excessively rapid exponential growth in, say, nuclear power may create serious new problems in their effort to solve present ones. For example, whatever rapid construction rate is chosen now must be essentially duplicated with an "echoing" increment of new capacity about 25 years later (or whatever the reactor lifetime may be), since reactors built within a short period will all have to be retired, and presumably replaced, within a similarly short period. If the final T_D was ten years, half the operating capacity will have to be replaced within a span of about ten years. If growth has been slow after the initial crash program, that "slump", too, will be "echoed" 25 years later. The result will be a violent oscillation of construction rate, not conducive to the smooth functioning of the national fiscal or industrial machinery. The oscillation can be gradually damped over several generations of reactors by retiring some before and others after their nominal lifetimes have expired (thus decreasing the energy ratio of the former and perhaps increasing that of the latter), but meanwhile the oscillation will be very disruptive to the nuclear industry and to economic functions related to it. Moreover, each "echo" of the initial rapid construction program will occur at a time when the fossil fuel subsidies used in the initial program are no longer readily available and when the investment energy must therefore be supplied from current nuclear output. Each "echoing" tranche of construction will entail a temporary but large decrease in the net energy available from the nuclear program for purposes other than maintaining the program itself, and this will entail a deep periodic "notch" in general demand. Conversely, at the end of the initial construction program and thereafter each time the stock of operating plant has just been replenished by a construction program, the sudden reduction in investment in new plant will effectively create a large transient increase in net energy output available from the program: reduced demand for energy input to the steel, concrete, and other industries that make and fuel nuclear power stations will result in a temporary surplus of generating capacity. Demand will drop at the moment of maximum output.

Clearly the best way to minimize these sorts of transient problems is to abandon crash programs as quickly as possible: the longer one waits, the worse the transients will be and the graver their social and economic implications[†]. Once a country is committed to nuclear growth that is rapid enough to run at an energy deficit, either the growth must continue (thus further enlarging the energy deficit) or the growth must slow down (thus producing embarrassing transients for some decades thereafter). One obvious way to avoid both problems is not to undertake the growth; urgently needed further research may reveal other and more complex strategies.

It has been noted above that reduced construction produces over-capacity by reducing energy demand. But this can be turned to advantage. It can be argued that as soon as investment in new plant is reduced or stopped, a tranche of new supply of energy (and money, materials, skills, etc) becomes immediately available for use in other energy supply or conservation efforts, or for other social purposes. It is often said that energy supply from, for example, North Sea oil and nuclear power should grow very quickly now so as to create capital for investment in other sources of supply, such as direct and indirect solar. Yet the sudden release of resources (previously committed to nuclear power) when rapid investment in nuclear plant abates, though it demands careful planning to minimize disruption, may be a readier and, in the long run, a less disruptive source of the energy and other resources needed to realize the long term goal of harnessing energy income (i.e., renewable and inexhaustible energy sources).

If nuclear power were a "soft" technology of smaller scale and smaller energy inputs, it would be less painful to reduce rapidly our investment in it, and we should have more room for mistakes, more leeway for exploration. But there is a connection between this explo-

---

[†] Implicit in this discussion is that short and medium term energy stringency means that whatever one's strategic goals, large amounts of immediate investment energy are simply not available.

ration and our nuclear policy: the British institution best suited to apply its undoubted talents to "unconventional" energy options [3] and to energy conservation [3] is probably the nuclear research and development establishment. This impressive technical resource could be usefully redirected to less centralized technologies with more favourable energy dynamics.

Traditionally it has been supposed that our energy problems can be solved only by substitution of fuels: wood, coal, oil, gas, uranium,—plutonium? But viewed from the broader perspective of modern strategic thinking about energy, this seems a rather shortsighted view that has arisen only recently through a series of historical accidents. Sophisticated societies in many parts of the world have worked for a very long time without large injections of fossil or fissile fuels, whose widespread use has lasted only a few centuries and whose massive use has been a very short term phenomenon of the past few decades. Today's energy problems arise not from shortages of energy but from shortages of our specifically habitual drugs of addiction—and from shortages of vision. Later papers in the current Friends of the Earth series on energy policy will explore in detail the problems and prospects of various sources of energy capital and energy income, and of their utility in achieving particular social goals.

The many causes [2] for anxiety about the proposed rapid expansion of nuclear power have often been brushed aside with the contention that whatever its failings, nuclear power is at least an abundant long term source of energy with which to cure our social ills. If, as the analysis in this paper suggests, nuclear power is not "an all but infinite source of relatively cheap and clean energy"[31], and under certain circumstances (e.g., deployment fast enough to seem a useful substitute for oil) is in fact an energy sink, then these familiar arguments for nuclear power must be reexamined.

The pioneering analysis [1] by Chapman and Mortimer has, like all first explorations of a new field, raised more questions than it has answered; so too has this study, which the author hopes has gone further to clarify basic principles of dynamic energy analysis. (Still further clarification at a greater level of complexity will be provided in a forthcoming joint technical paper.) Where this study has modified the data or approach of Chapman and Mortimer [1], it is not to denigrate their work, but to refine and enlarge it in the way that they themselves would wish and (in many cases) have directly suggested. Further refinement of methodologies and data is clearly needed for this study as much as for theirs: and if this study does nothing else, it should demonstrate the existence of legitimate and important net energy questions whose prompt and precise resolution is important to policy decisions now being taken throughout the world. It is long past time to resolve the ambiguity latent in the Institute of Fuel's recent conclusion [32] that "[n]uclear power generation must take over a large part of the increase in energy demand by 1980."

Appendices—Part Two

Exponential Growth: An Analytic Treatment of Energy Conversion Programs Designed to Satisfy Exponential Demand

If P_o is the annual output of energy (net of process inputs) from an energy conversion plant and $n_f(T)$ is the number of such plants operating at time T, then the energy output/year at time T is $E_o(t) = P_o n_f(T)$. Consider the case where the number of operating plants is given by

$$n_f(T) = N_O e^{a(T - T_c - T_p)} \qquad \text{(AII–1.1)}$$

where N_O = the number of plants operating at time $T = T_c + T_p$

   T_c = the time taken to construct a single plant

   T_p = the time pause or delay between the end of
            construction and the start of operation

   a   = $(\ln 2)/T_D$

where T_D is the exponential doubling time of the program. For the moment we assume that the operational lifetime of the plants T_ℓ is infinite. If $n_f(T)$ plants are operating at time T, then the number under construction then is

$$n_c(T) = N_O e^{aT} \qquad\qquad \text{for } T < T_c \qquad \text{(AII–1.2)}$$

$$n_c(T) = N_O e^{aT}(1 - e^{-aT_c}) \qquad \text{for } T \geq T_c$$

The annual energy investment in construction of plants at time T is then

$$X_i(T) = P_i n_c(T)$$

$$= P_i N_O e^{aT} \qquad \text{for } T < T_c \qquad \text{(AII–1.3)}$$

$$P_i N_O e^{aT} (1 - e^{-aT_c}) \quad \text{for } T \geq T_c$$

where P_i is the average annual energy investment per plant during the construction period. The energy output from operating plants at time T is

$$X_o(T) = P_o N_O e^{-a(T_c + T_p)} e^{aT} \qquad \text{for } T > (T_c + T_p) \qquad \text{(AII–1.4)}$$

If the operative lifetime of the plants is T_ℓ, then after T_ℓ years the building program must begin again to ensure that decommissioned plant is replaced. After each subsequent T_ℓ years, replacement must again be taken into account. The expression for $X_i(T)$ (Equation AII–1.3) is based on the assumption that the operational lifetime of the plants is infinite. For finite T_ℓ it becomes

$$\text{(AII–1.5)}$$

$$X_i(T) = P_i N_O e^{aT} \qquad \qquad\qquad \text{for } 0 < T \leq T_c \quad \left.\vphantom{\begin{array}{c}a\\a\end{array}}\right\}$$

$$P_i N_O (1 - e^{-aT_c}) e^{aT} \qquad\qquad \text{for } T_c < T \leq T_\ell \quad \left.\vphantom{\begin{array}{c}a\\a\end{array}}\right\} \text{first generation}$$

$$P_i N_O \left\{(1 - e^{-aT_c}) + e^{-aT_\ell}\right\} e^{aT} \quad \text{for } T_\ell < T \leq (T_\ell + T_c) \left.\vphantom{\begin{array}{c}a\\a\\a\end{array}}\right\} \begin{array}{l}\text{first and}\\\text{second}\\\text{generation}\end{array}$$

$$P_i N_O (1 - e^{-aT_c})(1 + e^{-aT_\ell}) e^{aT} \quad \text{for } (T_\ell + T_c) < T \leq 2T_\ell$$

$$P_i N_O \left\{(1 - e^{-aT_c})(1 + e^{-aT_\ell}) + e^{-2aT_\ell}\right\} e^{aT}$$

$$\text{for } 2T_\ell < T \leq (2T_\ell + T_c) \quad \left.\vphantom{\begin{array}{c}a\\a\\a\\a\\a\\a\end{array}}\right\} \begin{array}{l}\text{first, second,}\\\text{and third}\\\text{generations}\end{array}$$

$$P_i N_O (1 - e^{-aT_c})(1 + e^{-aT_\ell} + e^{-2aT_\ell}) e^{aT}$$

$$\text{for } (2T_\ell + T_c) < T \leq 3T_\ell$$

and so on. From Equations AII–1.4 and AII–1.5 the investment energy/year as a fraction of output energy/year is

$$\frac{X_i(T)}{X_o(T)} = \frac{M}{R} \qquad \text{(AII–1.6)}$$

$$\text{for } (T_c + T_p) < T \leq T_\ell$$

$$(1/R)\,(M + e^{-a(T_\ell - T_c - T_p)}) \qquad \text{for } T_\ell < T \leq (T_\ell + T_c)$$

$$(M/R)\,(1 + e^{-aT_\ell}) \qquad \text{for } (T_\ell + T_c) < T \leq 2T_\ell$$

$$(1/R)\left\{M(1 + e^{-aT_\ell}) + e^{-a(2T_\ell - T_c - T_p)}\right\} \qquad \text{for } 2T_\ell < T \leq (2T_\ell + T_c)$$

$$(M/R)\,(1 + e^{-aT_\ell} + e^{-2aT_\ell}) \qquad \text{for } (2T_\ell + T_c) < T \leq 3T_\ell$$

where $M = e^{aT_p}(e^{aT_c} - 1)$ and $R = P_o/P_i$. (Note that M is independent of time.) So that within each time period the fraction of the energy output/year that is required for construction of new plant is also independent of time. This fraction increases with the replacement of plant. In Table AII–1.1 the values of e^{-aT_ℓ}, e^{-2aT_ℓ}, etc are listed for a selection of exponential doubling times T_D and for both $T_\ell = 25$ and $T_\ell = 50$ years.

Analogous values are obtained for higher generations. (The table shows values less than 0.0001 as zeroes.) Clearly from Table AII–1.1 the effect of replacing obsolete plant is most important for programs with a long T_D. Consider a program with $T_D = 5$ years. If the plant lifetime is 25 years, then the fraction of annual energy output required for investment is

$$M/R \qquad \text{for } (T_c + T_p) < T \leq T_\ell$$

$$(1/R)\,(M + 0.133e^{a(T_c + T_p)}) \qquad \text{for } T_\ell < T \leq (T_\ell + T_c)$$

$$1.0133M/R \qquad \text{for } (T_\ell + T_c) < T \leq 2T_\ell$$

$$(1/R)\,(1.0133M + 0.0002e^{a(T_c + T_p)}) \qquad \text{for } 2T_\ell < T \leq (2T_\ell + T_c)$$

$$1.0135M/R \qquad \text{for } (2T_\ell + T_c) < T$$

But for $T_D = 20$ and $T_\ell = 25$ the equivalent fractions are

$$M/R \qquad \text{for } (T_c + T_p) < T \leq T_\ell$$

$$(1/R)\,(M + 0.4200e^{a(T_c + T_p)}) \qquad \text{for } T_\ell < T \leq (T_\ell + T_c)$$

$$1.4200M/R \qquad \text{for } (T_\ell + T_c) < T \leq 2T_\ell$$

$$(1/R)\,(1.4200M + 0.1764e^{a(T_c + T_p)}) \qquad \text{for } 2T_\ell < T \leq (2T_\ell + T_c)$$

$$1.5964M/R \qquad \text{for } (2T_\ell + T_c) < T$$

Table AII–1.1   Values of e^{-aT_Q}, e^{-2aT_Q}, e^{-3aT_Q} for Different Doubling Times and for T_Q = 25, 50 years

T_D (Years)	2		4		5		10		20	
T_Q (Years)	25	50	25	50	25	50	25	50	25	50
e^{-aT_Q}	0	0	0.0133	0.0002	0.0313	0.0010	0.1770	0.0314	0.4200	0.1764
e^{-2aT_Q}	0	0	0.0002	0.	0.0010	0.	0.0314	0.0010	0.1764	0.0311
e^{-3aT_Q}	0	0	0.	0.	0.	0.	0.0055	0.0002	0.0740	0.0055

and so on. If we now define $P(T)$ as the annual energy output at time T after subtracting that needed for investment, then

$$(AII-1.7)$$

$$P(T) = - (P_oN_O/R)e^{aT} \qquad \text{for } 0 < T \le T_c$$

$$- (P_oN_O/R)(1 - e^{-aT_c})e^{aT} \qquad \text{for } T_c < T \le (T_c + T_p)$$

$$(1 - (M/R))P_oN_Oe^{-a(T_c + T_p)}e^{aT} \qquad \text{for } (T_c + T_p) < T \le T_\ell$$

$$\left\{ (1 - (M/R))e^{-a(T_c + T_p)} - (1/R)e^{-aT_\ell} \right\} P_oN_Oe^{aT}$$
$$\text{for } T_\ell < T \le (T_\ell + T_c)$$

$$(1 - (M/R)(1 + e^{-aT_\ell}))e^{-a(T_c + T_p)} P_oN_O\, e^{aT}$$
$$\text{for } (T_\ell + T_c) < T \le 2T_\ell$$

$$\left\{ (1 - (M/R)(1 + e^{-aT_\ell})e^{-a(T_c + T_p)} - (1/R)(e^{-2aT_\ell}) \right\} P_oN_Oe^{aT}$$
$$\text{for } 2T_\ell < T \le (2T_\ell + T_c)$$

$$(1 - (M/R)(1 + e^{-aT_\ell} + e^{-2aT_\ell}))P_oN_Oe^{-a(T_c + T_p)}e^{aT}$$
$$\text{for } (2T_\ell + T_c) < T \le 3T_\ell$$

and so on. Figure 10–8 is plots of $X_o(T)$ and $P(T)$ for particular values of the parameters, and shows

1. the effects of changes in $R = P_o/P_i$;
2. the discontinuous nature of $P(T)$;
3. the effects of replacing obsolete plant on the energy/year available after investment.

The parameter values used are $T_c = 5$, $T_p = 1$, $T = 25$, $T_D = 5$ for each plot, with $P_o/P_i = 3$ (Figure 10–8(a)), $P_o/P_i = 2$ (Figure 10–8(b)), and $P_o/P_i = 1$ (Figure 10–8(c)).

Now if one wishes to calculate the total energy output, $W(T)$, up to a time T, one must integrate Equation AII–1.7, taking note of its discontinuities (which can be excluded as sets of measure zero). For simplicity let $(T_c + T_p) < T < T_\ell$:

(AII–1.8)

$$W(T) = -(P_oN_O/R) \int_O^{T_c} e^{at}\,dt - (P_oN_O/R)(1 - e^{-aT_c}) \int_{T_c}^{T_c+T_p} e^{at}\,dt +$$

$$(1 - \frac{M}{R})N_OP_o e^{-a(T_c+T_p)} \int_{T_c+T_p}^{T} e^{at}\,dt$$

$$= -(N_OP_oM/aR) + (1 - \frac{M}{R})(P_oN/a)(e^{a(T-T_c-T_p)} - 1)$$

If τ is the time that elapses before the accumulated investment energy is repaid, $W(\tau) = 0$, in which case AII–1.8 simplifies to

$$e^{a\tau} = e^{a(T_c+T_p)}R/(R-M) \qquad\qquad \text{(AII–1.9)}$$

(AII–1.10)

where
as before $M = e^{aT_p}(e^{aT_c} - 1)$ and $\tau = (1/a)\ln\left\{Re^{a(T_c+T_p)}/(R-M)\right\}$

For $M < R$ there is a solution to Equation AII–1.10, and if $M \geq 1$ the program will never repay the energy debt. That is, if the program is ever to repay the debt, P_o/P_i must exceed $e^{aT_p}(e^{aT_c} - 1)$.

It must be noted that this is not a sufficient condition because the replacement of obsolete plant must be taken into account. This requires integrating Equation AII–1.7 over more plant lifetimes. To some extent this is a purely academic question because for it to arise, the energy required for investment energy/year must exceed or equal the annual energy produced from the beginning of production.

Appendix II-2

**Static Energy Analysis
of Nuclear Reactors**

ENERGY INVESTMENT IN CAPITAL PLANT

The amount of energy required to build a nuclear power station is not now known precisely. Until detailed engineering analyses are available in a year or two, this energy investment must be estimated from aggregated financial data. To do this it is necessary to separate the capital costs of the power station into four parts:

1. *electrical machinery*, including the generator set, power transformers, control and switchgear, and distribution links to the grid;
2. *buildings and services*, including the site itself, office blocks, buildings to house equipment, cooling towers, service roads, and provision of an adequate water supply;
3. *the initial core assembly*, which is an initial supply of fuel amounting to about one-eighth[†] of the total fuel which the reactor will consume in its lifetime (for a nuclear power station, unlike a coal-fired power station, this initial fuel must be supplied *before* operation can begin, and is therefore an investment input rather than a running or process input); and
4. *the nuclear reactor and steam system*, including containment devices, safety and control systems, steam circuits, and heat exchangers.

Electrical machinery and the buildings and services are significant cost items for both conventional and nuclear power stations. The initial core assembly and the nuclear steam supply system (notably

---

[†] Assuming a 25 year lifetime; the $\sim 1/8$ would be $\sim 1/13$ if the lifetime were assumed to be 40 years according to US practice.

the reactor) are, however, special requirements of nuclear power systems, and reactors tend to cost more than equivalent fossil-fuelled boilers.

The CEGB have published [4] an approximate breakdown of capital costs for five types of nuclear power stations, showing separately the costs for total construction and for the nuclear steam system. By comparison with the known capital costs for electrical equipment [7] for coal-fired power stations, Dr Chapman has derived the division of the remaining costs of nuclear power stations into costs for electrical equipment and for buildings and services. The breakdown into the various categories is tabulated below for the five types of reactor described[†] by the CEGB [4] and for the HTR as described by TNPG.[†]

From statistical surveys of the total direct and indirect use of fuels, the average ratio of energy inputs/£ value for all UK industries has been computed [8, 9] for 1968. The energy consumed in the preparation of the initial fuel charge (see the following section) and of refuelling loads (see the third section of this appendix) varies considerably with the ore grade assumed, and also depends on whether the reactor uses enriched or natural uranium, so it must be considered separately, as must the energy requirement for heavy water (also discussed in the next section). For the other categories,

Table AII–2.1. Capital Costs (£/kW Installed Electrical Output Capacity; 1973 Price Levels)

Reactor Type	Electrical Equipment	Buildings and Services	Nuclear Steam System	Initial Fuel	Total
Magnox	52 ± 10	73 ± 5	116 ± 2	15 ± 2	256 ± 2
SGHWR	52 ± 10	31 ± 5	67 ± 2	18 ± 2	168 ± 2
PWR	52 ± 10	30 ± 5	50 ± 2	14 ± 2	146 ± 2
AGR	52 ± 10	30 ± 5	89 ± 2	19 ± 2	190 ± 2
CANDU	52 ± 10	31 ± 5	67 ± 2	12 ± 2	162 ± 2
HTR	52 ± 10	30 ± 5	60 ± 2	18 ± 2	160 ± 2

(Magnox = CO_2-cooled, graphite-moderated reactor fuelled by Magnox-clad natural uranium metal; SGHWR = steam-generating heavy-water-moderated reactor; PWR = pressurized-water-cooled-and-moderated reactor; AGR = advanced gas-cooled reactor, CO_2-cooled, graphite-moderated, UO_2-fuelled; CANDU = Canadian deuterium-uranium reactor, heavy-water-moderated, heavy-water-cooled, natural-uranium-fuelled; HTR = high temperature reactor, graphite-moderated, helium-cooled, ceramic-particle-fuelled)

[†] These data were slightly modified after communication with The Nuclear Power Group (TNPG), who also supplied the HTR data shown. Many US sources would give considerably higher estimates of capital costs.

the average UK ratios are used; corrected to 1973 £, these are: (1) for electrical equipment, 33 kWh(t)/£; (2) for buildings and services, 28 kWh(t)/£; and (3) for the nuclear steam system, 30 kWh(t)/£. The significance of errors associated with the use of these national industrial averages will be discussed later.

SPECIAL INVESTMENT INPUTS AND SOME CORRESPONDING PROCESS INPUTS

Uranium Fuel

The initial charge of uranium fuel represents a major energy investment in the construction of a nuclear reactor. The energy needed to prepare reactor fuel depends on the grade of ore mined and on whether the reactor uses enriched or natural uranium. For this reason two limiting grades of uranium ore have been considered here. The high grade ore (0.3 percent U_3O_8 by weight) is the average grade of ore being currently mined in some US mines. The second ore considered is Chattanooga Shale with an average grade of 0.007 percent U_3O_8 by weight: this source is chosen not because it will necessarily be typical of future low grade uranium sources, but because it is the low grade source for which the most detailed mining-engineering assessments are available.

For each of these grades of ore, the energy needed to process the ore for use in the reactor has been calculated by considering separately the following processes: (1) mining and milling to extract U_3O_8; (2) converting the U_3O_8 to UF_6; (3) enriching the uranium in the UF_6; and (4) converting the UF_6 to the solid fuel material and fabricating it into fuel elements. The detailed calculations are not included in this report, but a version sufficiently detailed for most purposes is available [1] and is based on published data [10–13].

The energy needed to extract a metric ton of uranium in a useful chemical form from uranium ore is shown in Table AII–2.2.

Table AII–2.2. Energy Required[1] to Extract Uranium From Ore in Place and Convert it to UF$_6$ *(in 10^6 kWh/metric ton U)*

Process Description	*Ore From Conventional Sources (0.3wt% U_3O_8)*	*Ore From Chattanooga Shale (0.007wt% U_3O_8)*
Mining and milling	0.265(t)	0.74 (e) + 8.22 (t)
Conversion to UF_6	0.016(e) + 0.054(t)	0.016(e) + 0.054(t)
Totals	0.016(e) + 0.319(t)	0.76 (e) + 8.27 (t)

Enrichment. The SGHWR, PWR, AGR, and HTR systems use enriched fuel. Uranium naturally occurs as a mixture of two main isotopes, ^{238}U (99.29 percent) and ^{235}U (0.71 percent). The enrichment process partially separates these isotopes so as to raise the proportion of ^{235}U in the enriched uranium produced for use in fuel. The amount of "separative work" required for this separation depends on the degree of enrichment (i.e., the percentage of ^{235}U required in the fuel). The separated ^{238}U (the "tails"), though partially depleted in ^{235}U, unavoidably contains some small residual percentage of ^{235}U (the "tails assay"), typically 0.25 percent [1, 14]. This paper will assume the 0.25 percent value throughout.

Table AII–2.3 shows the enrichment energy required per metric ton of enriched uranium in fuel and the natural uranium input to enrichment required per metric ton of enriched uranium in fuel for the SGHWR, PWR, AGR, and HTR.

Fabrication. Once the UF_6 has been enriched (as and if required) it must be converted to UO_2 or the like and then fabricated into fuel elements. The energy required (in units of 10^6 kWh/metric ton enriched uranium) for these processes is [1] 0.048(e) + 0.032(t): energy required in the form of electricity (e) has been left separate from other energy inputs which can be converted to thermal equivalents to give the (t) or kWh(t) total. The electricity required to process the uranium needed for *refuelling* can be directly subtracted from the reactor output: in this case kWh(t) and kWh(e) are assumed equivalent. For the *initial* fuel charge, however, the electricity itself has an energy requirement arising from the present efficiency of conversion of primary energy (mainly from oil or coal) to electricity. For the *initial* fuel charge only, this efficiency is taken into account by using a 25 percent conversion factor, so that one kWh(e) becomes four kWh(t). This value is derived from current UK statistics for the fuel industries, and includes both direct and indirect inputs of primary fuel for electricity generation.

Using this conversion factor and the energy requirements noted above, the energy needed to provide the initial fuel charge for a 1000 MW(e) reactor is shown in Table AII–2.4.

Heavy Water
The Heavy Water Division of Atomic Energy of Canada Ltd has estimated [20] that the energy required to make a metric ton of heavy water is 0.65×10^6 kWh(e) + 6×10^6 kWh(t). The CANDU reactor uses heavy water as a moderator (0.3 metric ton/MW(e)) and as a coolant (0.4 metric ton/MW(e)) [20]; the SGHWR reactor uses

Table AII–2.3.   Enrichment Data[a]

Fuel for	Enrichment (percent)	Metric Tons Natural Uranium Input Per Metric Ton Enriched Uranium Output[1]	Energy Required (10^6 kWh) Per Metric Ton Enriched Uranium Output[1, 13, 17, 18]
AGR initial core	2.45	4.78	6.53(e) + 0.259(t)
AGR refuelling	2.60	5.11	7.26(e) + 0.288(t)
SGHWR (both)	2.10	4.24	4.96(e) + 0.197(t)
PWR initial core	2.70	5.33	7.74(e) + 0.307(t)
PWR refuelling	3.11	6.22	9.78(e) + 0.388(t)
HTR initial core	6.50	13.59	27.30(e) + 1.083(t)
HTR refuelling	10.00	21.20	46.17(e) + 1.832(t)

[a]Energy inputs for different reactors depend on the net energy output, initial fuel charge, levels of enrichment, etc. No two authorities agree on *typical* values for these parameters for any given type of reactor. This analysis has used those data from the Directory of Power Reactors [15] which are most nearly consistent with those in the Nuclear Power Index [16]. Both sources give details of *actual* reactors which may not be fully characteristic. Wherever possible, model reactors for this analysis resemble those given by OECD [14] or by UKAEA and TNPG in private communications to Dr Chapman. The reactors chosen are Oldbury A (Magnox), Hunterston B (AGR), and Pickering (CANDU). SGHWR design characteristics are as published by Moore et al [19], and HTR characteristics are from TNPG (private communication to Dr Chapman). The data for the PWR vary greatly for different reactors, and Chapman [1] cites four examples; the data used here are for the most energy-profitable of these (Shearon Harris). Different choices of data are justifiable but lead to substantially identical conclusions.

Table AII–2.4.   Energy and Feedstock Requirements for Initial Core

Reactor Type	Fuel in Core (metric tons U)	Percent Enrichment	Requirement of Natural U (metric tons)[a]	Energy Requirement (10^6 kWh)					
				Mining, Milling, and Conversion		Enrichment	Fabrication	Total	
				0.3% Ore	0.007% Ore			0.3% Ore	0.007% Ore
Magnox	973.	natural	973	373	11005	0	218	591	11223
SGHWR	160.	2.1	657	252	7430	3206	36	3494	10673
PWR	87.	3.2	463	177	5240	2719	19	2915	7975
AGR	195.	1.9	932	357	10540	5154	44	5555	15739
CANDU	182.	natural	182	70	2060	0	41	111	2099
HTR	22.7	6.5	315	120	3565	2504	5	2629	6072

[a]The requirement of natural uranium is the amount that must be mined, milled, etc to be processed into the required amount of fuel; e.g. 657 metric tons of natural uranium are needed to produce 160 metric tons of uranium enriched to 2.1 percent with 0.25 percent tails assay.

N.B.: see the note to Table AII–2.3 regarding data.

heavy water as a moderator only (0.25 metric ton/MW(e)) [22]. The energy requirements for the heavy water inventories of reactors of 1000 MW(e) installed electrical output capacity are thus 6020×10^6 kWh(t) (CANDU) and 2150×10^6 kWh(t) (SGHWR). As noted in the next section, small process inputs of heavy water are also required to make up losses during operation.

Other Inputs

The other inputs are estimated using the capital-cost breakdown and kWh(t)/£ multipliers discussed earlier, and are incorporated into Table AII–2.6.

Because of the specialized nature of the technologies and the special materials used in building nuclear reactors, aggregated estimates of energy investment in reactors are liable to substantial error; but for the next year or two no better data will be available. Ideally the special investment inputs to nuclear reactors should be considered separately in full engineering detail. Dr. Chapman intends to do this for fuel cladding (e.g., hafnium-free zirconium), moderators and control rods, heavy water, pressure vessels, and perhaps other inputs (Chapter Twelve, ¶ 5).

OUTPUT OF ENERGY FROM A NUCLEAR POWER STATION

A nuclear power station designed to have 1000 MW installed electrical output capacity does not in fact supply 1000 MW-year of electricity per year to final consumers. The average energy/year supplied is much less and depends on the capacity factor, the distribution losses, and the use of electricity by the CEGB itself.

The working life of a power station is widely accepted in the UK as being 25 years, and the present analysis has assumed that

1. the average capacity factor of a nuclear power station over its lifetime is 62 percent [7], nearly the 64 percent assumed [4] by the CEGB (capacity factor is the amount of electricity sent out per year, expressed as a percentage of the amount which would be sent out per year if the station operated continuously at its full design rating); and

2. total losses of electricity between the power station and the consumer amount to 11.25 percent of the amount sent out. This is derived as follows. The distribution losses and use of electricity by the CEGB [21] account for 15 percent of all electricity generated. Of this 7.5 percent is classed as distribution losses. The

remaining 7.5 percent is used "by the CEGB and area boards in offices, showrooms, workshops etc". Half of this latter 7.5 percent will be assumed to be a loss incurred in activities that support electricity generation; the other half, used in CEGB offices, area board showrooms, etc, will be ignored here as an irrelevant overhead. Adding 7.5 percent distribution losses to 3.75 percent CEGB use yields a total loss of 11.25 percent.

Taking these assumptions into account reduces the effective usable power output of a 1000 MW(e) nuclear power station to 550.25 MW (= 550.25 × 10^3 kW). The annual energy output of such a plant is thus 4820 × 10^6 kWh. (Throughout this study it is assumed that a year contains 8760 hours, rather than the 8766 that would be needed to take account of the extra day in each leap year.)

To be offset against this annual energy output is the energy required[†] to process

1. the heavy water required to make good a loss of 0.7 percent/year for CANDU [20] and a loss of 0.5 percent/year for SGHWR [22]; the energy needed for this replacement is 42 × 10^6 kWh/year and 8 × 10^6 kWh/year respectively.
2. the uranium fuel required to refuel the reactor. The annual tonnage of fuel required and the energy needed to produce it are shown in Table AII–2.5 (see the note to Table II–2.3 regarding data.)

The total energy requirement/year of processing the replacement fuel has to be subtracted from the gross output of a nuclear power station to give its output energy/year, P_o. Table AII–2.6 shows this net output; the average energy investment/year throughout the construction period, P_i; and the resulting "power ratio", P_o/P_i. Table AII–2.6 also shows the "energy ratio", E_o/E_i, where E_o is the total lifetime output of each plant (net of process inputs) and E_i is the total energy investment in each plant. Clearly $E_o/E_i = (P_o/P_i) \times$ (plant lifetime/construction time); it is assumed here that the lifetime is 25 years and the construction time 5 years, leading to E_o/E_i equalling 5 × P_o/P_i.

[†]For each of these energy requirements, the energy needed per ton of product is as used in Table AII–2.2, but the electrical energy required is offset directly against the output of the power station without the use of any conversion factor.

Table AII-2.5. Energy and Feedstock Requirements for Reload Fuel

Reactor Type	Reload Fuel (metric tons U/year)	Percent Enrichment	Requirement of Natural U (metric tons/year)	Annual Energy Requirement (10^6 kWh/Year)					
				Mining, Milling, and Conversion		Enrichment	Fabrication	Total	
				0.3% Ore	0.007% Ore			0.3% Ore	0.007% Ore
Magnox	187.0	natural	187	62	1690	0	16.	78	1706
SGHWR	31.4	2.10	133	45	1200	162	2.	209	1364
PWR	17.4	3.11	108	36	975	178	2.	216	1155
AGR	30.0	2.60	153	51	1380	226	2.	279	1608
CANDU	67.0	natural	67	22	605	0	6.	28	611
HTR	6.8	10.00	147	49	1325	325	0.5	375	1650

Table AII–2.6[a]. Average Energy Investment/Year P_i, Average Annual Energy Output (Less Process Inputs) P_o, Power Ratio P_o/P_i, and Energy Ratio E_o/E_i, Both for Fuel From 0.3 Percent Uranium Ore and for Fuel from 0.007% Chattanooga Shale (numbers in italics)

Reactor Type	P_i[b] (10^6 kWh/yr)	P_o (10^6 kWh/yr)	Power Ratio P_o/P_i and Error Estimate[d]	Energy Ratio E_o/E_i[c] and Error Estimate[d]
Magnox	1566 / *3649*	4734 / *3114*	3.02 ± 0.6 / *0.85 ± 0.04*	15.1 ± 3 / *4.27 ± 0.2*
SGHWR	2048 / *3483*	4603 / *3448*	2.25 ± 0.4 / *0.99 ± 0.08*	11.3 ± 2 / *4.96 ± 0.4*
PWR	1394 / *2406*	4604 / *3665*	3.30 ± 0.6 / *1.52 ± 0.16*	16.5 ± 3 / *7.67 ± 0.8*
AGR	2154 / *4193*	4541 / *3212*	2.11 ± 0.4 / *0.77 ± 0.06*	10.5 ± 2 / *3.83 ± 0.3*
CANDU	2145 / *2669*	4750 / *4167*	2.21 ± 0.4 / *1.56 ± 0.24*	11.1 ± 2 / *7.81 ± 1.2*
HTR	1397 / *2086*	4445 / *3170*	3.18 ± 0.6 / *1.52 ± 0.12*	15.8 ± 3 / *7.60 ± 0.6*

[a]See the note to Table AII–2.3 regarding data.

[b]The average energy investment/year throughout the construction period, P_i, is calculated on the assumption that the construction period for each reactor is five years.

[c]Chapman and Mortimer [1] discussed their results in terms of this energy ratio, and assumed, as has this study, that the lifetime of each reactor is 25 years.

[d]In making this analysis, assumptions have had to be made and conventions adopted. Because precise energy requirement data are not now available, some estimates have had to be based on aggregated financial data. Dr Chapman estimates the errors inherent in such methods to be ±20 percent for energy requirements estimated from financial data, ±10 percent for the analysis of energy requirements of uranium processing, and ±5 percent for the net energy estimation (before subtracting the energy required to prepare replacement fuel charges). Owing to the varying importance of the different types of energy requirements for each system, these sources of error will not make the same relative contributions to total error. Dr Chapman's estimates of total error for the ratios P_o/P_i, and the corresponding ($5\times$ larger) estimates of total error for the ratios E_o/E_i, are shown. For example, for the Magnox reactor using fuel prepared from 0.3 percent ore, the ratio P_o/P_i is calculated as being 3.02 with an error estimate of ±0.6. This means that we can only confidently say (subject to the important caveat below) that the power ratio lies between 2.42 and 3.62. It is hoped that further analysis will narrow the error limits. Meanwhile, however, the results are not precise enough to permit *detailed* comparison of reactor types.

These error estimates assume that *all* significant energy requirements have been identified and considered, and that the data used are a fair representation of the types of reactors shown. The error estimates are also *not* intended to cover possible omissions from the analysis; these are discussed in the second section of Chapter Twelve and may significantly alter the energy and power ratios shown here. Accordingly, any reference to these ratios should take into account the numerous conservatisms discussed in the second section of Chapter Twelve.

Notes on Projected Growth in National Nuclear Programs

Dynamic net energy calculations for actual national nuclear programs are bound to be indicative, not precise, because both the power ratios and the doubling times are uncertain or disputed and because they may change over time. Indeed, it is precisely because growth projections keep changing that the analysis in Chapter Ten was presented in general terms, independent of any particular choice of data.

In an idealized case, the parameters—particularly power ratio and doubling time—would remain constant and one could plot a single point on, say, Figure 10-11 of this study as describing the behaviour of the system. But in practice the uncertainties and variations on both axes of Figure 10-11 are likely to blur this point into a region. The value of the graph is that it shows at least which region one is discussing, and whether the fraction of program output that must be offset against investment is negligible, significant, or larger than gross output. Such a conclusion, however imprecise, is far better than nothing, and helps one to decide how carefully the problem must be examined. Moreover, if low net energy yield is interpreted as a cost overrun for a program (Chapter Fourteen), the economic implications are generally large enough to make small marginal cost differences (the usual basis of economic comparisons) seem insignificant in comparison. Even if nuclear power ratios were, say, six, the effect of the initial nuclear fuel charge on power ratio would mean that the dynamic difference in net energy behaviour between nuclear and coal-fired power stations (whose P_o/P_i is in the neighbourhood of eight) would probably be of greater economic importance than the conventional economic differences between the same systems. (A similar argument could probably be made for capacity factors and engineering lifetimes, two other variables often treated superficially in economic comparisons of energy technologies.)

This appendix summarizes some recent data on the growth rates projected for selected national nuclear programs. These projections are in a state of flux because perceived economic and geopolitical incentives favouring nuclear power are said by some analysts to be rapidly increasing, while the practical constraints (mainly logistical, fiscal, and political) on rapid expansion are at the same time becoming more obvious. In general, current projections of future nuclear growth are considerably lower than those made two or three years ago. More revisions will doubtless occur. But the data shown in Table AII–3.1 at least give some idea of which region of Figure 10–11 (and similar graphs) is relevant in assessing present national plans.

In many national nuclear programs, growth is projected to slow down gradually; hence the current instantaneous doubling time is shorter than the average doubling time projected for some future period. For any particular time, however, the instantaneous doubling time can still be used to obtain from Figure 10–11 an instantaneous percentage-of-output-to-investment estimate (and likewise for other graphs). Analogously, using projected doubling times for future periods will yield representative values of percentage-of-output-to-investment over those periods. This "self-similarity", permitting use of the graphs in this study for instantaneous and period-average estimates interchangeably, is a general property of exponential growth.

Detailed dynamic energy analysis of systems whose growth rates are constantly changing, or whose growth does not approximate a linear or exponential curve, requires numerical calculations for which a computer simulation is convenient. Such simulations have been developed by *inter alios* Malcolm Slesser (*Nature 254*:170 [1975]) and George Merriam ("A Net Energy Study of Projections for American Nuclear Power", Dec 1974, revised Jan 1975: G R Merriam, LHRRB, Harvard University, 45 Shattuck St, Boston, Massachusetts 02115, USA). Such simulations, particularly if based on power ratios rather than on energy ratios, can accept arbitrary numerical descriptions of projected growth patterns and can be readily modified to take account of possible variation of power ratios over time, etc.

Simple manual calculations are often useful for exploring in an indicative way the likely magnitudes of net energy problems. Such a calculation by Lovins suggests that the US nuclear program sought by President Ford in early 1975—a good approximation to Case D of USAEC WASH–1139(74) (Table AII–3.1, note 3)—will require at least 50 percent of program output to be offset against investment. The corresponding figure for the British SGHWR program at a medium term doubling time of 4.3 years would be at least 65 percent. As a basis for international comparisons and for indicative estimates of the dynamic behaviour of some national programs, Table AII–3.1 presents some results of recent nuclear planning exercises, both national and international (the latter generally collated from data supplied by national authorities). Most other 1974 projections are broadly in agreement with those shown—which does not mean any of them is true, but only that they are a fair representation of official thinking in the main industrial countries.

Table AII-3.1.   Some Projections of the Future Growth of Nuclear Power

			Nuclear Installed Capacity GW(e)				Average Doubling Time yr	
			1975	1985	1990	2000	1975–85	1975–2000
OECD Europe	IAEA (1)	Early '73	26.5	184	373	1000	3.58	4.77
	OECD (2)	Basic	25.8	175	345		3.62	4.01†
		Accel.	25.8	227	480		3.19	3.56†
EEC	OECD (2)	Basic	20.6	129	264		3.78	4.08†
		Accel.	20.6	167	367		3.31	3.61†
Japan	IAEA (1)	Early '73	8.6	60	100	240	3.51	5.21
	OECD (2)	Basic	4.6	60	100		2.70	3.38†
		Accel.	4.6	67	138		2.59	3.06†
N America (USA and Canada)	OECD (2)	Basic	49.8	275	531		4.06	4.39†
		Accel.	49.8	358	743		3.51	3.85†
Canada	IAEA (1)	Early '73	2.5	15	31		3.87	4.13†
USA	IAEA (1)	Early '73	54.2	280	508		4.22	4.65†
	USAEC (3)	Case A	43.3	231	410	850	4.14	5.82
		Case B	47.3	260	500	1200	4.07	5.36
		Case C	52.0	275	575	1400	4.16	5.26
		Case D	47.3	250	475	1090	4.16	5.52
	USAEC (4)	"high"	56.9	332		1500	3.93	5.30
		"most likely"	54.2	280		1200	4.22	5.59
		"low"	52.1	256		825	4.35	6.27
	EPP (5)	"Historical Growth" High Import	29.0*	292		1172	3.60*	5.06*
		High Nuclear	29.0*	352		1465	3.33*	4.77*

Region	Source	Scenario						
	EPP (5)	"Technical Fix"						
		Environmental Protection	29.0*	146		88	5.15*	—
		Self-Sufficiency	29.0*	234		322	3.98*	7.77*
	EPP (5)	"Zero Energy Growth"	29.0*	146		88	5.15*	—
OECD	IAEA (1)	Early '73	92.0	542	1018	2550	3.91	5.22
		Accel.	92.0	705	1425	3820	3.40	4.65
USSR and E Europe	IAEA (1)	Early '73	9.5	104	246	670	2.90	4.07
		Accel.	9.5	117	290	930	2.75	3.78
World Except People's Republic of China	IAEA (1)	Early '73	104.0	693	1390	3580	3.65	4.90
		Accel.	104.0	888	1900	5330	3.23	4.40

*starting date 1975, not 1975
†ending date 1990, not 2000

1. Lane, J A et al., "The Role of Nuclear Power in the Future Energy Supply of the World", International Atomic Energy Agency (Vienna), 1 Oct 1974.

2. OECD, *Energy Prospects to 1985*, Organization for Economic Cooperation and Development (Paris), 1974.

3. US Atomic Energy Commission, "Nuclear Power Growth 1974–2000", WASH–1139(74), Office of Planning and Analysis, USAEC, Feb 1974. Case A assumes continued delays in construction, with two years for initial paperwork on each reactor, two years for construction permit approval, and six years for construction and startup. Case B assumes these times can be cut to 15 months, 15 months, and five and one-half years respectively. Case C assumes one year for the first step and six years for the next two (telescoped together). Case D combines the Case B assumptions with a modest reduction in the rate of growth of electricity demand.

4. US Atomic Energy Commission, "Nuclear Power 1973–2000", WASH–1139, Office of Planning and Analysis, USAEC, Dec 1972.

5. The Energy Policy Project of the Ford Foundation, *A Time To Choose: America's Energy Future*, Ballinger (Cambridge, Massachusetts, 1974).

N.B.: Growth rates in the early stages of national programs—*e.g.*, historical or even present instantaneous growth rates—may be considerably faster than those shown in the table.

Notes—Part Two

1. Chapman, P F and Mortimer, N, "Energy Inputs and Outputs for Nuclear Power Stations", ERG 005, Energy Research Group, Open University, Milton Keynes, Bucks., England, Sept 1974, revised Dec 1974. Dr Chapman's further revisions (June 1975) to the Chattanooga Shale values are reflected in the present text.

2. Lovins, A B, "Nuclear Power: Technical Bases for Ethical Concern", Friends of the Earth Ltd (9 Poland St, London W1V 3DG), 4 Dec 1974; 2nd ed., March 1975. Further revised and included in this volume.

3. Lovins, A B, *World Energy Strategies: Facts, Issues, and Options*, Ballinger (17 Dunster St, Cambridge, Massachusetts 02138) and Friends of the Earth International (529 Commercial St, San Francisco, California 94111), 1975; earlier edition in *Bull Atom Scient 30*, 5, 14–32 (May 1974) and *30*, 6, 38–50 (June 1974); earlier edition (now out of print) published by Earth Resources Research Ltd (9 Poland St, London W1V 3DG), Nov 1973.

4. CEGB evidence, p 44 in Select Committee on Science and Technology (House of Commons), "The Choice of a Reactor System", 73 i–vii, HMSO (London), Feb 1974.

5. Leslie, D C, p 78 in Inglish, K A D, ed, *Energy: From Surplus to Scarcity?*, Applied Science Publishers Ltd (Ripple Road, Barking, Essex) on behalf of the Institute of Petroleum, Great Britain, 1974.

6. CEGB, *supra* note 4, p 192.

7. Searby, P J, *Atom 178* (Aug 1971), p 185.

8. Chapman, P F and Mortimer, N, "Energy Analysis of the Census of Production 1968", ERG 006 (see note 1), in preparation, 1975.

9. Wright, D J, "Calculating Energy Requirements of Commodities from the Input/Output Tables", SARU, Department of the Environment (London SW 1).

10. Everett, F D, "Mining Practices at Four Uranium Mines", US Bureau of Mines IC–8151.

11. Bieniewski, C L *et al*, "Availability of Uranium at Various Prices from Resources in the US", US Bureau of Mines IC–8501 (1971).

12. Clegg, J W and Foley, D D, *Uranium Ore Processing*, Addison–Wesley, 1958.

13. "Fuel Cycles for Electrical Power Generation", Teknekron Inc (California), Jan 1973.

14. OECD, "Uranium: Resources, Production, and Demand", OECD (Paris), Aug 1973.

15. "Directory of Power Reactors", *Nucl Eng Intl* (April 1973).

16. "Index of Nuclear Reactors", *Nucl Eng Intl* (April 1972).

17. Barnaby, C F, *Science J* SA*(2)* (Aug 1969), p 54.

18. Roberts, J T, *Intl Atom Energ Bull 15*, 5, 14 (Oct 1973).

19. Moore, J; Bradly, N; and Rowlands, I T, *Atom 195* (Jan 1973), p 7.

20. Data supplied by letter to G Leach from manager, Heavy Water Plant Technology, Atomic Energy of Canada Ltd (see note 1).

21. Details in "Report on Census of Production 1968", vol 153 (Table 5); see also Chapman, P F in "Conservation of Materials", proceedings of conference, Harwell, 26–27 March 1974, p 125.

22. From estimates given to Chapman (see note 1) by TNPG and UKAEA.

23. Hill, Sir John, *Atom 180* (Oct 1971), p 231.

24. Bainbridge, G R and Beveridge, C, *Atom 155* (Sept 1969), p 248.

25. Bupp, I C *et al*, "Trends in Light Water Reactor Capital Costs in the United States: Causes and Consequences", CPA 74–8, Center for Policy Alternatives, MIT (Cambridge, Massachusetts, Nov 1974); summarized in *Techn Rev*, 77, 2, 15 (1975).

26. Comey, D D, *Bull Atom Scient 30*, 9, 23 (Nov 1974); *31*, 2, 40 (Feb 1975).

27. Lem, P N; Odum, H T; and Bolch, W E, "Some Considerations that Affect the Net Yield from Nuclear Power", paper presented to 19th Annual Meeting, Health Physics Society, Houston, Texas, 7–11 July 1974.

28. USAEC, "Nuclear Power Growth 1974–2000", WASH–1139(74), Feb 1974, at p 23.

29. Department of Trade and Industry/Government Statistical Service, "United Kingdom Energy Statistics 1973", HMSO (London), 1974.

30. USAEC, "Environmental Statement: Management of Commercial High Level and Transuranium-Contaminated Radioactive Waste", WASH–1539 (DRAFT), Sept 1974, pp 3.1–3, 3.1–10, 3.1–11.

31. Weinberg, A M, *Science 177*:27 (1972), p 34.

32. Fells, I *et al*, "Energy for the Future", The Institute of Fuel (London), 1973.

Epilogue: Some Criticisms and Responses

Various methodological criticisms of this study in its previous edition, of a contemporaneous article[a] by Chapman, and of the earlier paper[b] by Chapman and Mortimer have been made and are considered here. Each is quoted or paraphrased in italics, and its main source is cited if it has been published. Some repetition of points already stated in the text but ignored by critics is unfortunately unavoidable.

1. *Energy analysis is "just one of many tools that can be employed to prove whatever case you choose. . . . Clearly, the energy analysts disagree in their basic ground rules. . . . [The] practitioners have to agree on what they are talking about."*[c]

Energy analysts have devoted considerable thought to the ground rules of their new science. A special project of the International Federation of Institutes for Advanced Study (Nobel House, Sturegatan 14, S–102 46 Stockholm, Sweden) was initiated by Lovins in 1973 to devise generally acceptable conventions for energy analysis. An international workshop of experienced practitioners of energy analysis was held under IFIAS auspices in August 1974, and its report by Slesser[i] has been available since then from IFIAS, first in draft and then in a formal edition. A further IFIAS workshop in June 1975 is to refine and enlarge the substantial body of conventions already arrived at. This project has been given wide publicity in the field and is intended precisely to avoid the definitional confusion that has characterized many criticisms of energy analysis by persons unfamiliar with its concepts and terminology. The papers of Chapman, like this study, conform to the IFIAS conventions for enthalpic analysis of gross energy requirements exclusive of the potential energy of fissile materials. The criticisms made by Wright and Syrett[d] and by others of similar views[e, f] are based on misunderstandings of the purpose and methods of energy analysis, and use arguments inconsistent with the IFIAS conventions, presumably because the critics are not acquainted with them.

It is of course not a complete answer to methodological criticism to say that one's methodology conforms to the accepted conventions of the field. The IFIAS conventions have been used here not merely because they are authoritative and well thought out, but because they seem the appropriate conventions to use in asking the question asked here, namely, "How much external energy subsidy is required to produce a kWh of nuclear electricity?" and thus, "How much fossil fuel is required to produce a kWh of nuclear electricity?" (These are the basic questions in the static case; the questions in the dynamic case are strictly analogous.) Other questions could of course be asked for which a different choice of conventions might be appropriate; for example, "How does the social utility of a kWh of electricity compare with that of a kWh of coal combustion or of solar heat under stated conditions?" or, "What are the costs and benefits of nuclear versus fossil-fuelled electrical generation?" or, "What are the costs and benefits of electrical generation versus other forms of energy conversion and distribution?" The analysis presented here cannot answer, and is not intended to answer, such questions, and hence cannot tell the policymaker everything he needs to know; it only tells him the impact which rapid nuclear expansion will have on the supply of and demand for fossil fuels, and hence sheds some light on the feasible rates, independence, and economics of proposed nuclear expansion. The same methodology and the same conventions could also be used to compare the energy inputs and outputs of various nonfission energy conversion or conservation technologies, or could be extended to flows of resources other than energy.

2. *The inputs of thermal energy to build and fuel a nuclear power station should be compared not with its electrical output, but with its total thermal output; alternatively, a bonus (of approximately a factor of three) should be allowed for the electrical output to take account of the greater "value" or "efficiency" of electricity at the point of final use.*[d-f]

Chapman replies[g] that

... conventions have to be chosen to suit the purpose of the analysis. My purpose was to evaluate the amount of fossil fuel required to produce a kilowatt-hour of nuclear electricity, and my convention is consistent with this. I think my analysis could be improved, but not by adopting the absurd convention suggested by Wright and Syrett. Their convention, which counts the heat output instead of the electricity output, would make a conventional power station 100 percent efficient, and if applied rigorously to any closed system would simply confirm the law of conservation of energy. There are ways of allowing for the extra usefulness of electricity, but not by counting the waste heat as a useful output of a power station.

Chapman refers here to the difference between analysis of energy quantity alone and of energy quantity and quality—or, more precisely, enthalpy and free energy; this point is discussed at length below.

Wright and Syrett[d] first assume a threefold credit for nuclear output and then derive new values for the time required to pay back nuclear investment energy. These values are based on a misunderstanding of the purpose of the present analysis and are therefore of doubtful relevance. A mere bookkeeping exercise such as these values represent will not make a real nuclear program produce more useful energy nor consume less. Moreover, though Wright and Syrett consider a fictitious version of break even time, they nowhere consider a more important parameter—the percentage of the output of a nuclear program that must be devoted to investment in it—save obliquely in their final paragraph, where they admit that "much of the energy for nuclear construction and nuclear fuel production in the later years . . . would actually be obtained from nuclear energy." This would reduce the net output to society from the nuclear program during its growth phase, or would increase the effective cost of a unit of net nuclear output to consumers other than those engaged in the nuclear enterprise.

Finally, Wright and Syrett take for granted a certain incremental demand for electricity and go on to consider whether it should be produced by a nuclear or fossil-fuelled station. The present study and Chapman's analyses,[a, b] however, are more widely framed: they consider nuclear power as one of many sources of *energy*, not as one of two sources of *electricity*. Hence, they consider the behaviour of energy conversion technologies, not merely of different kinds of power stations, and they accept the possibility that projected demand is for performing an end use (not for performing it only with one form of energy) and may even be fictitious. Kenward,[c] like Wright and Syrett,[d] frames the question too narrowly: "There is no point in giving us coal or oil to run our light bulbs—we do not have the necessary equipment to turn them into clean light." Light bulbs require electricity; people merely require light, which can be obtained from light bulbs, oil lamps, coal gasification or organic conversion and mantle lanterns, windows, etc, each of which has various costs and benefits beyond the scope of this paper. (The "requirement" for light, too, is a social variable dependent on values and cultural patterns, not an inflexible absolute.) Indeed, Kenward's light bulb example is a pathological case, in that coal and oil can both be used directly—unlike uranium—to provide the great bulk of human energy needs (heat) without elaborate equipment. In the UK, and similarly in most industrial countries, probably more than half the energy at the point of final use is low temperature heat; perhaps about 15 percent is mechanical work; and all the rest is high temperature heat save about 5 percent. Only this 5 percent or so need be in a special form such as electricity—for operating aluminium smelters, light bulbs, electronic devices, etc—and even some of these uses (including light bulbs) are substitutable, with costs and benefits largely outside the scope of energy analysis. (The nonsubstitutable ones, too, seldom require large centralized power stations.)

An alternative form of the criticism stated above is that a factor of three bonus should be allowed for nuclear electricity *because each nuclear kWh(e) saves three kWh(t) of fossil fuel which would otherwise be burned in a power station*. In practice, however, the three kWh of costly fossil fuel would probably not be burned in a power station. Since, as stated above, about three-quarters of end use energy is in the form of heat and since fossil fuels can provide heat directly at high efficiency, it would be irrational to burn three kWh of fossil fuel to perform one kWh of end use unless the end use absolutely required it—which, as stated above, is rarely the case. In other words, the only reason to generate and use much more electricity is that nuclear power offers no other option; without nuclear power, pervasive electrification would not continue, partly because with scarcer fossil fuel supplies, the three to one conversion penalty would generally outweigh electricity's convenience.

3. *In the present study and in the Chapman analyses,[a,b] all the electrical inputs to the nuclear industry are multiplied by four to allow for the inefficiency of current fossil-fuelled power stations; but they should instead be charged at 1:1 conversion as a direct debit against nuclear output.[d]*

A 4:1 conversion penalty is assumed—explicitly for enrichment of the initial fuel charge and implicitly for the electrical component of reactor construction energy—only for these investment inputs, not for the considerably larger process inputs. The electricity needed to enrich reload fuel—about seven-eighths of the total lifetime enrichment demand of a reactor—is subtracted directly from nuclear output at 1:1 conversion, not multiplied by four as Wright and Syrett[d] imply. At present this is a fair, or if anything an overoptimistic, representation of how the system works. Of course any particular unit of electrical investment input to the nuclear industry can be considered to come from a nuclear source, but that is a mere bookkeeping exercise if (as is actually the case) the unit is very likely in fact to have come from a fossil-fuelled station, and nuclear output artificially assigned for this purpose would have to be replaced by fossil-fuelled output somewhere else in the grid.

As nuclear stations gradually replaced fossil-fuelled stations, the 4:1 conversion factor for investment inputs of electricity would gradually approach some approximation to 1:1, and a more sophisticated analysis could take this second-order correction into account. (It would have to include also an important third-order correction—the energy investment required to convert to electrical operation those energy-consuming devices, such as steel mills and cement works, that are now fuelled directly by fossil fuels.) But the term at issue here is minor for the next few decades—the period of this transient analysis—both because nuclear electricity is a relatively small component of national electricity supply and because over half of the energy needed for investment inputs is not electricity but directly burned fossil fuels, often in applications in which electricity could not readily substitute. Where substitution is possible, it could (but would not necessarily) be more efficient—another minor correction which would not significantly change the present results and which, as Slesser[h] points out, may not help:

If [the] . . . world were to be powered largely by nuclear reactors, then the basis of energy analysis would have changed. At the moment the convention in energy analysis is to take the prime unit of energy to be the amount of fossil fuel that must be withdrawn from the global stock in order to make the goods or service available to the consumer. In a nuclear predicated world, the prime unit will have changed. This will not necessarily make the sums more attractive. For example, a nuclear reactor is essentially a source of heat, and while most of [the available fraction of] this heat will be turned into electricity, some anyway must be turned into synthetic fuels like our present liquid and gaseous fossil fuels. Unless the current attempts at water splitting are made very efficient, such synthetic fuels will be relatively more costly in that future world than electricity is today in relation to oil energy.

Thus the cumulative inefficiencies in an all-nuclear economy can be large, owing to the need to use nuclear heat or electricity or both to generate synthetic fuels. In the "all-nuclear all-electric economy" the shift from 4:1 to $\gtrsim$ 1:1 conversion for electrical investment inputs does not mean that electricity has become four times as efficient as now, but only that the present forms of primary energy have disappeared.

4. *Many criticisms rest on a confusion of energy quantity with energy quality.*[†] Energy quantity is measured by "enthalpy" or heat content. But an amount of energy whose enthalpy is a kWh or a J or a BTU or a kg-cal can vary in quality: for example, a kWh of heat at a high temperature can do more and different things than a kWh of heat at a low temperature. (As an extreme example, there is probably more energy in the form of low temperature heat in the Atlantic Ocean than in the heat of combustion of the oil reserves of the Persian Gulf, but the quality or "grade" of the former energy is so low that it is not very useful.) Some critics have suggested that electricity is "higher grade" energy than fossil fuel energy and that a kWh(e) is therefore "worth more" than a kWh(t) of fossil fuel energy; or, in technical language, that a kWh(e) represents more "free energy" ("free" meaning not gratis, but available to do work) than a kWh(t) from fossil fuel. But the operational meaning of this concept depends entirely on the purpose to which the energy is put. If the end use of the energy is to be low temperature heat, as is very often the case, then the high quality of the energy is superfluous, and the use of a high grade energy source is thermodynamically wasteful. Determining the extra social value of high grade energy requires an exhaustive assessment of the extent to which that high grade is used to advantage, and hence requires a detailed knowledge of the patterns and thermodynamic nature of the energy uses in society. (It also requires value judgements of the relative social utility of those uses.) Undoubtedly such an analysis would be useful for some purposes, but it is far beyond the scope of this study and has little relevance to the question asked here, namely, *the practical impact of nuclear output and expansion on existing stocks of nonnuclear energy*.

Examples can of course be found where electricity is used to advantage and where its use results in greater efficiency. Conversely, using electricity for many important end uses (such as private trans-

---

[†]The author apologizes to thermodynamicists for an occasional lack of rigour in this section. Unfortunately, the only alternative would be a textbook incomprehensible to laymen.

port) requires extensive resource-consuming infrastructure and social change in order to match the end uses to the requirements imposed by the nature of the energy source. Perhaps three-quarters of our end uses of energy are in the form of heat, which electricity cannot supply much more efficiently than can fossil fuels directly. And some uses of electricity, e.g., in lighting, can be *less* energy-efficient than nonelectrical means of performing the same function. (They may be more convenient, but convenience is not measured by energy analysis.) Such is the inherent complexity of free energy analysis that simply weighting a unit of electricity—multiplying it by some assumed "efficiency factor"—is an unrealistic and technically invalid procedure. Moreover, many of the features of electrification that are extremely important for policy—convenience, centralization, vulnerability, capital intensity, etc—are no more reflected in free energy calculations than in enthalpy calculations.

It is also important to note that the fossil fuel energy being compared with electricity in the present study and in Chapman's studies[a, b] is itself of very high quality: it is coal, oil, and gas with high flame temperatures, not low temperature heat, and can perform many important functions directly at an efficiency not far below the maximum that is theoretically possible. From a technical point of view, the error introduced by equating the enthalpy of fossil fuel combustion (the amount of heat released) with the free energy of the fossil fuel (its ability to do work) is small—ordinarily less than 10 percent[i]—and the thermodynamic equivalence (in free energy terms) of a fossil fuel kWh(t) with a kWh(e) is surprisingly close in most cases. (Were electricity being compared instead with, say, geothermal heat or diffuse solar heat, this would not be the case.) The enthalpic equivalence is of course exact: one kWh(e) has precisely the same heat content as one kWh(t)—namely, 1 kWh = 3.6 MJ = 3413 BTU = 860 kg-cal.

In summary, therefore, while an analysis taking into account the quality of the energy produced by a nuclear power station, or by any other device, could in principle be done (but with great difficulty), such was not the intention of this study, and is *immaterial* to the questions addressed in this study. The practical output of a nuclear power station is electricity, whether we like it or not, and society's energy needs in a nuclear economy must therefore be met by electricity whether it is appropriate and efficiency-improving or not. This study merely explores the ways in which nuclear expansion will affect the actual depletion of other energy stocks, particularly fossil fuel resources. Claims that the electrical output of the nuclear power station is exceptionally useful in theory will not make it thermodynamically more efficient in practice, nor will it decrease the actual amount of energy stocks needed in practice to support the nuclear enterprise: *it is a bookkeeping exercise that does not affect the practical energy flows considered here.*

For similar reasons, comparing kWh(e) with kWh(t) is not dimensionally inconsistent as some critics suggest: both units have the dimensions of energy (or, more formally, both units as used here express an amount of enthalpy, or heat content, which has the dimensions of energy). It is no more incorrect in enthalpic terms to compare kWh(t) of input with kWh(e) of output than it is to compare kWh(e) at 220 volts with kWh(e) at 440 volts, or kWh(t) from coal in a grate with kWh(t) from gas in a kiln. The practical differences are neither large, nor independent of circumstances, nor relevant to comparisons of energy quantity (see any good text on thermodynamics).

It is interesting that these differences are not recognized in conventional projections of energy demand, where the units used are those of the heat content (enthalpy) of gross primary energy. Lamentably few if any projections even separate end use energy from total conversion losses; and no projections seem to say that since future energy supply will be increasingly in kWh(e) rather than kWh(t), and therefore presumably capable of doing more social work per kWh, fewer kWh will be needed. All conventional demand projections assume direct 1:1 substitution of kWh(e) for kWh(t) of direct fuel use; the projections do not assume that the greater free energy content (ability to do difficult kinds of work) of a kWh(e) should be reflected by crediting it with a greater social value than a kWh(t). Yet this is precisely the sort of exercise which some critics seek to perform. It involves broad and very complex problems of the social role of energy, both actual and hypothetical, and is outside the sphere of concern not only of this study but also of practically all energy planners. Their habit of correlating economic parameters with enthalpic requirements may not be ideally sophisticated, but it is a fact.

Analyses of energy quantity taking account of its quality are important and material for some purposes. Analyses of energy quantity exclusive of its quality are important and material for some other purposes. Neither energy quality nor energy quantity, nor both in combination, are the only things that the energy policymaker needs to take into account, but that does not diminish their relevance. That the present analysis considers the societal balance sheet of energy quantity without making allowances (which would generally be minor) for differences of energy quality does not make it invalid; that the present analysis does not consider nonenergetic features of energy technologies does not make it valueless. Its validity and value lie in its ability to provide fuller understanding of the energy dynamics of supplementing some energy conversion technologies with others. This scope is carefully defined in the study itself, and it is unfortunate that some readers have criticized the study for not doing what is explicitly states it is not intended to do.

A free energy analysis could be one of the many factors needed to help policymakers to decide whether a particular expenditure of fossil fuels for nuclear output and expansion is a good use of those fossil fuels. The present analysis does not go as far as that decision, but merely considers how large the expenditure of fuels would be.

5. Creagan[j] has not raised arguments of energy quality or free energy content. On the other hand, he claims that *"by any of Dr Price's criteria" the US nuclear power stations now operating have already paid off their energy investment* and *"the US nuclear program is a positive energy supplier"*.

The data that Creagan cites do not support this conclusion, though he uses them in various erroneous ways to try to show that they do. Firstly, he assumes that the doubling time now projected for future US reactor population, say four to five years (see Appendix II–3), has prevailed throughout the past program, whereas it has in fact been about two and one-half years or less until recently. (The first edition of this study cited such a figure as a future projection, but such projections are now out of date, and more recent figures are given and discussed in Appendix II–3.) Figure 10–11 and similar figures in this study can give correct results only if correctly applied (see Appendix II–3). Programs whose doubling time is changing require more elaborate calculations if the detailed energy dynamics are to be correctly computed.

Secondly, Creagan compares the energy investment in reactors now operating with their cumulative output to date; but he does not debit the energy investment in reactors now under construction. Thus he is doing not a dynamic analysis for a program, but a cumulative static energy balance for a large number of reactors at a single given time (now). Moreover, in this calculation he does not debit distribution losses and process inputs anywhere, but only investment inputs, and he counts electrical investment inputs at 1:1 conversion rather than 4:1. (In supporting calculations, too, he assumes an average capacity factor of 80 percent rather than the 62 percent assumed in this study or the 50–55 percent actually observed in the US program.) His calculations are based on these idiosyncratic choices of data and conventions.

Thirdly, Creagan tries to claim a positive energy balance because currently operational capacity exceeds the 23 GW[†] consumed by current construction; but that is an instantaneous power balance and has nothing to do with the cumulative energy balance he is computing. It is not even a correct power balance, because currently operational capacity is not a true measure of current output. The 37.25 GW(e) of US nuclear capacity which Creagan cites as operational on 1 Jan 1975 could yield an actual output (net of distribution losses and process inputs) equivalent to a full-power output of only 19.6 GW(e) if we assume the 62 percent capacity factor used in this study, or 17.3 GW(e) if we assume the $\sim$ 55 percent capacity factor now prevailing in the USA. These two assumed values of capacity factor would make estimated current investment in the US nuclear program correspond respectively to 117 percent and 133 percent of current output from the program—both in the deficit region. Creagan nowhere refers to the percentage of program output that must be devoted to investment, nor to the wholly general dynamic analysis of exponential programs presented in this study, nor to the numerous conservatisms in the assumed P_o/P_i values—three central themes that any fair summary of this study must treat.

Thus Creagan has used odd or incorrect data and conventions to calculate a number that is not very interesting for policy, namely an instantaneous cumulative energy balance for an ensemble of reactors. The purpose of this study, instead, is to use accepted conventions and empirically justifiable, demonstrably conservative data to compare the output of a program with the ongoing investment in it as a function of time. On this basis, the US nuclear program is probably still in the energy deficit region both instantaneously (see above) and cumulatively, and the magnitude of the cumulative deficit can be roughly estimated from the data which Creagan cites. He states that 76 GW(e) of capacity is under construction; if we assume that two-fifths of the energy investment in the construction and initial fuelling of this capacity has already been made, and if we assume the power ratio of 3.3 which Creagan uses in this section of his paper,[†] then the investment to date in plant now under construction is about 210 TWh = 210 × 10^9 kWh. Adding this to the given estimate[†] of

---

[†] Creagan is attempting to use the author's data to support his own conclusion, so they are used here too. Elsewhere in his paper he calculates some larger investment inputs than are derived here, but also assumes 1:1 conversion of electrical investment, thus obtaining an investment energy per 1 GW(e) LWR of 5.2 TWh, compared with 7 TWh calculated in this paper. The faster payback times derived by Creagan arise from this odd convention (see criticism 3) and from his assumption of 80 percent capacity factor.

300 TWh for past investment in plant now operating gives a total investment to date of 510 TWh. Creagan cites a cumulative gross output to date of 380 TWh, from which distribution losses of 43 TWh and process inputs which he estimates at approximately 6.3 percent of gross output, or about 24 TWh, must be successively subtracted, yielding an output of about 310 TWh. This suggests that the cumulative energy deficit of the US nuclear program so far is about 200 TWh. This is the amount of energy which Creagan's 37 GW(e) of operational capacity could produce in 1.2 years at 62 percent capacity factor (with due deductions for distribution losses and process inputs), assuming that no further investment energy were required meanwhile and that the assumed power ratio is not, as the second section of Chapter Twelve claims, overly optimistic. Note, however, that any such deficit calculation is necessary indicative and imprecise, not quantitatively exact (see criticism 9 in this Epilogue). The aim of this calculation is only to show that the data which Creagan claims show an energy profit for the US nuclear program in fact show the opposite.

6. Davis,[k] who was apparently making a general statement rather than directly criticizing this paper, has claimed that *a nuclear plant (specifically, a large LWR) pays back its energy investment in 2.3 months of continuous full-power operation, or in about four to five months of actual initial operation at attainable capacity factors.*

This is a straightforward numerical disagreement, summarized by Table E–1 which gives comparable energy requirements as computed by the author, Davis,[k] and Creagan.[j] All entries are normalized to 1 GW(e) of capacity and to an average capacity factor of 62 percent for ease of comparison.

If due allowance is made for the difference of convention affecting the initial fuel charge, the author's values, based on those of Chapman and Mortimer,[b] appear to be uniformly lower than those of Creagan. This suggests that the claim of conservatism made and explained in Chapter Twelve is not purely theoretical. Indeed, for both initial and reload fuel from high grade ore, the author's values are also lower than those of Davis. Serious discrepancies are evident, however, in Davis's values both for reactor construction and for fuel derived from Chattanooga Shale. Insufficient data are available to assess the source of these discrepancies, though they may well be due to an overly narrow choice of system boundary or to deficiencies in the kWh/kg data reportedly used by Davis.[k] The details of Davis's methodology are unclear and probably do not rest on much experience of energy analysis. In any case, Davis's statement[k] that he used

Table E–1. FOE, Bechtel, and Westinghouse Computations of PWR Energy Inputs

	Price/Chapman-Mortimer[b]		Davis[k]		Creagan[j]	
reactor construction	4055	GWh	673	GWh	4080	GWh
initial fuel charge	2915 (896†)	GWh	909	GWh	1098	GWh
annual reload fuel charge	216	GWh/yr	282	GWh/yr	341	GWh/yr

The above values assume high grade uranium ores, stated by the author and by Creagan to be 0.3 percent U; with Chattanooga Shale, assumed to be 0.007 percent U by these authors and 0.006 percent U by Davis, the *additional* energy requirements beyond those noted above would be:

initial fuel charge	5060 (3992†)	GWh	291	GWh	8896	GWh
annual reload fuel charge	939	GWh/yr	79	GWh/yr	2107	GWh/yr

The parenthetical values marked † are calculated according to the convention used by Creagan and apparently by Davis, whereby electrical investment inputs are assumed to be derived entirely from nuclear electrical output at 1:1 conversion, rather than from fossil fuels at 4:1 conversion as is actually the case at present. The author thinks this convention inappropriate in the current stage of the nuclear program, but shows it for ease of comparison. No such alternative need be shown for annual fuel charge, as the author already assumes 1:1 conversion for electrical process inputs.

"the most pessimistic assumptions" seems highly implausible and his conclusions for the static case are clearly in error by a substantial factor.

This error would be even more important if Davis were doing a dynamic rather than a static analysis, since his low construction value would greatly reduce the effect of investment on the dynamic output of a program. Like Creagan, however (see criticism 5), Davis has not performed a dynamic analysis, but only a static analysis for an ensemble of plants, and his conclusions must be interpreted accordingly.

Some further light is shed on the conservatism of the Chapman–Mortimer P_o/P_i values by an Électricité de France statement[n] (responding to a *France-Soir* inquiry, 26 Feb 1975) that "si l'on ajoute à l'énergie (nécessaire pour la construction et le fonctionnement d'une centrale) toutes les autres énergies consommées pour la construction et la marche de cette centrale, on arrive à un total d'énergie nécessaire à 11 percent de l'énergie produite par la centrale". This 11 percent is merely E_i/E_o, so E_o/E_i would be $1/0.11 = 9.1$ for a large PWR, compared with the Chapman–Mortimer value[b] of 16.5 (assum-

ing five year construction time and 25 year lifetime, roughly comparable to the ÉdF assumptions[n]). The corresponding P_o/P_i would then
be 1.82, compared with the Chapman–Mortimer value[b] of 3.30, and
the percentage of output to be offset against investment, with a
doubling time T_D = 4.3 years, would be not the Chapman–Mortimer
44 percent but rather 80 percent. If T_D = 3.5 years—a more realistic
value for the proposed French program (though it is closer to a ramp
shape than an exponential)—the corresponding values would be 62
percent and 113 percent.

Further details of the Électricité de France computations[n] can be
found in a comparatively detailed paper[o] whose conclusions, normalized to 1000 MW(e) capacity and 62 percent average capacity factor,
are shown in Table E–2. These data suggest considerable conservatism in the Chapman–Mortimer data.[b] Interestingly, the EdF analysis,[o] which appears to neglect distribution losses, computes all
energy inputs from economic data, thus avoiding problems of energy
conversion conventions. A French government review[p] of some
conflicting data is much less clear and detailed, though it appears to
appreciate better than the ÉdF authors the dynamic problems of
rapid growth. (The present study's Chapter Ten is kindly described[p]
as a demonstration "De façon plus génerale, . . . par le calcul mathé-
matique, de façon parfaitement logique".)

Finally, at the June 1975 energy analysis workshop (Lindingö,
Sweden) of the International Federation of Institutes for Advanced
Study, preliminary results were presented from independent Swedish, French, and West German studies of the gross energy requirement (GER) to build a 1–GW(e) PWR. The results, derived from
detailed fiscal input–output studies, are broadly consistent with the
Chapman–Mortimer estimates[b] and appear to provide fuller coverage
of indirect inputs than does the relatively disaggregated study of
Rombough and Koen.[r] Details of the three European studies are to
be published in the professional literature in 1975–6. Process anal-

Table E–2. FOE and Électricité de France Computations of PWR Energy
Inputs

	Price/Chapman–Mortimer[b]	*Électricité de France*
reactor construction	4055 GWh	4250 GWh
initial fuel charge	2915 (896[†]) GWh	2392 GWh
investment in fuel cycle facilities	0 GWh (Chapter 12, section 2, subsection 1, ¶ 2)	1100 GWh
annual reload fuel charge	216 GWh/yr	1068 GWh/yr

yses to check the appropriateness of the input–output sectoral averages for the nuclear case are now underway in the United States.

7. Leach[l] raises several points quite different from those previously discussed; as an experienced practitioner conversant with the IFIAS conventions, he has no difficulty with free energy versus enthalpy distinctions and has tried to clear up[m] some of the confusion introduced by Wright and Syrett.[d] Leach states,[m] however, that *the Chapman–Mortimer energy ratios[b] (for high grade uranium ore) of 10–16.5 for nuclear power stations should be compared with an "exactly equivalent" ratio of 0.25 for present fossil-fuelled power stations.*

This comparison is useful and valid for one specific purpose: determining the fossil fuel content of a kWh(e) of output from a nuclear or fossil-fuelled power station. But the form of the comparison mixes two concepts which should be kept separate, namely, "energy ratio" and "energy conversion efficiency". The energy ratio of a nuclear power station as computed by Chapman and Mortimer,[b] by the author, and by Leach[l,m] shows how much useful energy must be supplied from useful energy stocks (such as, but not limited to, fossil fuels) in order to convert an otherwise useless commodity (uranium) to a useful form (electricity). This comparison neglects[a] the potential energy of the nuclear fuel—most of which is not recovered by modern power reactors. In contrast, the 0.25 "energy ratio" (Leach's usage[m]) of a fossil-fuelled power station is really just a conversion efficiency of one useful form of energy to another, taking into account both the energy released by burning the fuel and the energy required to prepare and use the fuel.

For the sake of definitional clarity, let us digress for a moment to treat this distinction more fully. The reason that the energy content of uranium consumed in a reactor is ignored in computing a true energy ratio is not that uranium is an otherwise useless commodity, but that it is a direct fuel. The heat content of fuels directly consumed to produce output is used in calculating energy conversion efficiency, *not* energy ratio. Remember that the energy ratio of a power station or other energy conversion device is

$$\frac{E_o}{E_i} = \frac{\text{gross useful energy output} - \text{distribution and similar losses} - \text{process inputs}}{\text{investment inputs}}$$

But what are "process inputs"? If the "useful output" of a steam power station is electricity, and if "process inputs" included the heat content of fuel consumed (whether fossil or nuclear), then their difference and hence the energy ratio of the station on an enthalpic basis would have to be *negative*. But since energy ratios are ordinarily used to compute dynamic variables such as the percentage of output that must be offset against investment during a growth phase, it makes more sense to exclude from "process inputs" the heat content of fuels directly consumed to operate the power station and to include only the energy required to prepare, supply, and use those fuels. That is the convention used by Chapman[a, b] and in this study. It complements, not replaces, traditional definitions of energy conversion efficiency, and should not be confused with them by referring to an energy conversion efficiency[†] as an "energy ratio".

In short, energy and power ratios as defined by Chapman and by the author reflect the energy required to permit an energy conversion, not the efficiency with which useful energy output is produced from the sum of that energy plus the energy converted. Interchangeable use[m] of these two concepts blurs two useful distinctions: one between total energy stocks and total nonnuclear energy stocks, and another between the energy content of fuels and the energy required to supply fuels. So long as one is computing only the fossil fuel content of a kWh(e) from various sources, as Leach is doing,[m] these distinctions are irrelevant. But for broader purposes they are very relevant, as the following hypothetical example will show.

Suppose that one is asking whether a unit of electricity delivered to final consumers by a nuclear or by a fossil-fuelled power station, net of investment inputs to new stations, will add less total heat to the earth–atmosphere system; and suppose that one wishes the gross electrical capacity to double every four years during some particular period, which need not be long. For simplicity, we shall ignore the process inputs to both stations, and this simplification will not greatly affect the results. A nuclear station with $P_o/P_i = 3.3$, producing one kWh of gross useful (electrical) output, will also produce two

---

[†] Leach's definition of conversion efficiency is not the traditional one—heat value of useful output ÷ heat value of fuel consumed—but a more useful one—heat value of useful output ÷ energy requirement of energy (ERE). This latter quantity, defined under the IFIAS conventions,[i] is the heat content of the fuel consumed plus the heat content of all the energy needed to extract, prepare, supply, and use that fuel: it thus measures gross depletion of energy stocks in order to produce the useful output, less a credit for any unconsumed stocks recoverable along with the output. The conversion efficiency so defined is comparable with energy ratio, as defined above, only in the special case where (1) distribution of inputs and outputs over time does not matter, *and* (2) the fuel consumed in the system for which a conversion efficiency is being calculated is not of a type consumed as a direct fuel in the system for which an energy ratio is being calculated, *and* (3) one is interested only in the depletion of that particular fuel, not of the direct fuel consumed by the system for which an energy ratio is being calculated.

kWh of waste heat; 0.1 kWh will be lost as heat during distribution to consumers; and all of the 0.45 kWh of output required to operate the industrial processes used to build and fuel the new nuclear stations will also end as low temperature heat, most of it soon. The net useful output to consumers is thus $1 - 0.1 - 0.45 = 0.45$ kWh, and the total heat released is $2 + 0.1 + 0.45 = 2.55$ kWh, or 5.67 times as much. (The gross heat released by the nuclear fuel is of course $0.45 + 2.55 = 3.0$ kWh, but that is not relevant to the question being asked here.) Now, one kWh of gross useful output from a coal-fired power station will also entail two kWh of waste heat release at the power station and 0.1 kWh of distribution losses; but how much of the gross output will be needed for investment in new stations? In referring to Figure 10-11 to find this proportion, we must not use a coal to electricity conversion efficiency; we must instead use a power ratio that ignores process inputs that are merely coal burned under the station's boilers, but that reflects the energy stocks needed to build a coal-fired station. Since such a station is somewhat cheaper than a nuclear one and (more important) does not require an initial fuel charge equivalent to some 14 million metric tons of coal to be assembled before the station can operate, its P_o/P_i is larger than for a nuclear station; Chapman estimates it to be about 8 (see Chapter Twelve). For $T_D = 4$ yr, the percentage of output going to investment would thus be about 20 percent, or 0.2 kWh in our example—less than half as much as in the nuclear case. Thus for a net output of $1 - 0.1 - 0.2 = 0.70$ kWh, our coal-fired station would entail only $2 + 0.1 + 0.2 = 2.30$ kWh of total heat release, a ratio of 3.29, which is only 0.58 as much as in the nuclear case. There is nothing unique or tricky about this example; we have merely chosen a question where the coal investment needed to build the station is relevant and its coal consumption during operation is not. The question asked determines the convention that is appropriate. Hence the importance of clear definitions.

It does matter very much to the dynamics of energy programs that nuclear stations have a large investment input and a process input composed of a small amount of fossil fuel plus a large amount of potential energy in uranium, whereas coal-fired power stations have a significantly smaller investment input (with no large initial fuel charge) followed by large process inputs of coal as fuel. This difference means that thermal nuclear reactors are probably a considerably more efficient way of converting coal to electricity than are coal-fired power stations, and are also an inefficient way ($\sim$ 1 percent) of converting the potential energy of uranium to electricity. But it does not mean that astronomical proportions of the output of a coal-fired power station during a growth phase must be devoted to investment in similar new stations (which would be the case if a power ratio were the same as a conversion efficiency), and it says nothing about whether any kind of power station is an energy-efficient way of using energy resources of all kinds to perform social tasks of all kinds. That is a question largely outside the province of dynamic energy analysis, and indeed of the methods proposed by its critics.

8. Leach points out[1] that *one must not assume nuclear growth to be "indefinitely sustained", particularly since various absurdities would arise such as having more nuclear generation than total energy supply or demand. Practical nuclear growth would be only fast and sustained enough to meet certain policy goals, such as meeting energy demand or substituting for oil, and would then be curtailed.*

This comment has given rise to some confusion, mainly because its details are ambiguously formulated[1] (and must therefore be clarified below at some length). At the outset, however, it is worth setting out several points on which Leach, Chapman, and the author are in complete agreement:

a. Indefinitely sustained growth is impossible, and none of their papers assumes it. (See, e.g., Chapter Thirteen, ¶ 6.) Chapman and the author point out (see particularly the Preface and Chapter Fourteen of this study) that they are considering only those transient effects which arise before growth abates, as it inevitably will, or as a delayed consequence of initial rapid growth. (The transient effects of course depend on the pattern both of the initial growth and of its abatement.)
b. Significant transient problems can nevertheless arise with rapid growth that is only temporary. For example, this study suggests that nuclear growth that is rapid and sustained enough to provide substantial and timely substitution for oil will also have severe net energy problems, or, conversely, that growth that is slow or brief enough to avoid these problems cannot achieve the kind of oil substitution for which it was intended.
c. In general, long term cumulative net energy profits—which depend only on the energy ratio of the nuclear stations built—can be obtained soonest if nuclear growth is as rapid and brief as possible; but this policy also maximizes transient problems, both initial and recurrent.
d. Nuclear growth at any rate and for any period raises important social, technical, and economic questions which are outside the scope of energy analysis (see also criticism 9).

It is only beyond this point that Chapman and the author diverge from Leach[l] in a way that demands careful exposition to avoid further misunderstanding.

Leach agrees that a nuclear program that grows too quickly can always consume more energy than it produces, so long as it keeps on growing. The obvious remedy would be to slow or stop the growth, sit back, repay the energy deficit, and enjoy the energy profits. There would be strong incentives to do this in practice if one understood why it were necessary (an understanding that might not be available from economic signals). Alternatively, owing to practical constraints of economics and logistics, which are the other side of the coin of net energy constraints, such abatement of excessively rapid growth may be involuntary or superfluous. There is no disagreement so far. But Leach tries to argue that rapid nuclear growth *must* stop, and indeed "the faster the nuclear growth, the sooner it must slow down"[m], *because* otherwise more nuclear energy will be produced than there is demand for. This notion is of course correct in the sense that if nuclear output, *net* of investment in new plant, is greater than people are willing to buy, and if their demand cannot be further stimulated, it will be obvious to everyone that there is no point in having more reactors. Unfortunately, Leach appears to argue[l] that *gross* nuclear output, *not* net of investment energy, is theoretically constrained from "crashing through the ceiling" of end use energy demand by society in general (*excluding* those activities engendered by the nuclear program itself). But in fact these two parameters are not necessarily related, because the net nuclear output sold to the general public (exclusive of the nuclear enterprise) can be small, zero, or negative if nuclear growth is fast enough. That is the subject of this study. If the rate of nuclear growth is such that gross nuclear output exactly equals nuclear investment input, then the nuclear program is a sideshow of no current social relevance, neither supplying nor consuming societal energy stocks (except uranium). If the growth is faster than that, then not only can gross nuclear output crash through the ceiling of energy demand by society (exclusive of the nuclear enterprise), but that demand can simultaneously be sucked down through the floor as the usual societal energy supplies are siphoned off to operate the steel mills, cement works, and other facilities suffering from a perceived energy shortage that seems to require the construction of still more reactors, whose relationship to the energy shortages may not be perceived. Leach's scenarios[l] do not show such effects because he has chosen a nuclear growth rate that produces some (not much) net energy during the growth phase rather than requiring a growing net energy subsidy.

Thus when Leach says[1] that "Even if [nuclear programs] ... grew very much faster than historical rates, [they] ... would replace to a major extent both non-nuclear electric stations and usage of 'direct' coal, oil and gas fuels", he is potentially correct in the long run, but only after any excess of nuclear investment over gross nuclear output were no longer increasing fossil fuel demand by supplementing normal fossil fuel demand from outside the nuclear enterprise. Until that happened, net output from the nuclear program would be negative and could not replace anything, save in a fictitious bookkeeping sense.

To make this point absolutely clear, two illustrative scenarios analogous to Leach's but less ambiguously labelled are sketched in Figure E–1. Both are intended to show qualitative behaviour only; they are indicative schematics, and must not be construed as predictions, simulations of any actual programs, or exact calculations of anything. Both scenarios assume $P_o/P_i = 3.3$, but the first assumes a doubling time T_D of five years, so that the percentage of output to be offset against investment is 35 percent, while the second assumes $T_D = 2.5$ year, so that the corresponding percentage is 120 percent, just into the deficit region.

Figure E–1. Two Hypothetical and Purely Illustrative Nuclear Growth Scenarios

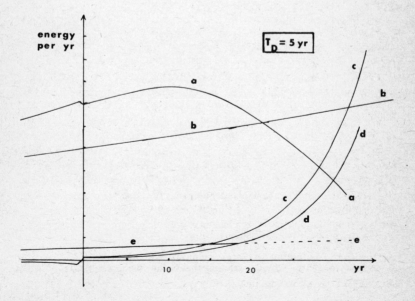

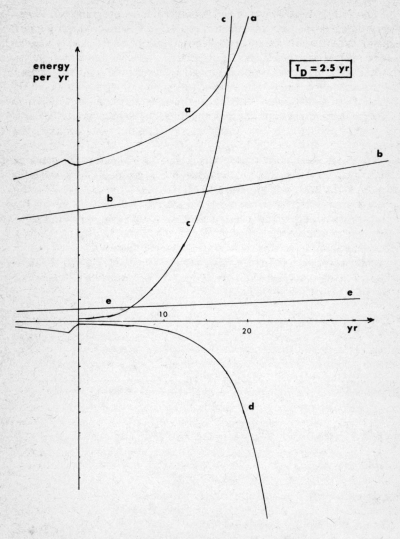

Two hypothetical and purely illustrative scenarios for programs of nuclear power stations with power ratio $P_o/P_i = 3.30$. The curves are labelled thus:

A gross consumption of fossil fuel
B end use energy demand (excluding that of the nuclear enterprise)
C gross nuclear output minus process inputs
D gross nuclear output minus process and investment inputs
E end use electricity demand (excluding that of the nuclear enterprise)

See text for other assumptions.

The first scenario shows a fossil fuel saving similar to that shown by Leach. At the start, gross consumption of fossil fuels (A) (which Leach calls "gross primary energy") and energy at the point of end use (B) are as shown by Leach,[l] and are growing at 1.4 percent/year and 1.0 percent/year respectively. (Recall that these numbers, like all those assumed in these scenarios, are purely illustrative and need not be an exact version of any real data.) At time t = −6 yr, an exponential program of nuclear construction begins, and the first nuclear capacity, assumed (after Leach) to have a magnitude of 1.7 units, is commissioned at time t = 0. From this point onwards the process inputs required to produce the nuclear outputs have been directly debited against them (C); in this context "process inputs" are taken to include distribution losses. The investment inputs—35 percent of gross outputs—are directly debited against gross outputs to produce net outputs (D) as shown. The nuclear growth can then continue until the gross nuclear output *minus both* process *and* investment inputs (a curve labelled D) has saturated its market among end uses of energy—the time and level of saturation need not concern us—and this may occur before or after gross nuclear output exceeds the specified level of end use demand. (At or somewhat before the time of saturation, nuclear investment will cease—if demand cannot be further stimulated—and nuclear output before and after investment will suddenly become the same but will find relatively little demand, owing to the sudden quiescence of the energy-consuming nuclear construction. Investment must later restart, however, in order to replace aging reactors, thus producing recurrent oscillations in the construction rate.) But long before all this, at times fully shown by the graph, nuclear output will increasingly supplement fossil fuel supplies and thus will allow gross fossil fuel consumption to decrease, gradually approaching a level equal to end use energy demand by society (exclusive of the nuclear enterprise), minus nuclear output net of investment and process inputs to the nuclear program, plus fossil fuel conversion losses (both static and dynamic) incurred in meeting end use demands that are not met by nuclear power after it has saturated its available end use market. This market will presumably exceed traditional demand for electricity (E), owing to vigorous and widespread efforts at electrification.

Consider now an initially similar scenario—equally illustrative and imprecise—in which more rapid nuclear growth is attempted in order to achieve the fossil fuel savings sooner. In this scenario, as shown by Figure 10–8(c) of this paper, the gross nuclear output minus both process and investment inputs (D), is increasingly negative, and gross fossil fuel consumption (A), after an initial rise for nuclear investment before the first nuclear stations are commissioned, starts to rise faster, driven by growth in both end use demand (B) and nuclear deficit. (In practice, it could rise even faster than shown because of the higher energy requirements of more marginal fossil fuel technologies to which such an economy would soon be driven.) *Of course the nuclear growth will eventually abate,* either through practical constraints or because society starts to listen to its energy analysts (not its economists)—*but not because of the kind of theoretical "ceiling" that Leach proposes.*

These sketches of the general behaviour of two hypothetical systems show, first, that it is not gross nuclear output, nor gross output minus process inputs, but rather gross output minus process and investment inputs that is constrained to stay within the ceiling of end use demand for nonnuclear purposes; and second, that whether prompt fossil fuel savings result from the nuclear program depends on the rate of nuclear growth. Neither scenario shows the interesting region where aging first-generation reactors must be replaced by investing energy derived either from new (and presumably scarce) fossil fuel supplies or from cutting a rather large notch into societal demand for nuclear electricity.

The author hopes that these two illustrations have helped to clear up the ambiguities introduced by Leach's labelling of his graphs. If he wishes his graph of nuclear output to mean gross output, not net of investment, then he must debit the investment energy explicitly to gross fossil fuel consumption and include it in end use energy demand;[†] but if he wishes to meet nuclear investment demands from gross nuclear output in order to show a large saving of fossil fuels, he must plot nuclear output as net of investment, not gross. Some compromise between these methods would also be possible, but the nuclear investment energy must be explicitly debited somewhere, and the conclusions should be presented in a form that does not depend on fortuitous choice of nuclear growth rate.

That said, however, the present analysis differs from Leach's mainly in emphasis, not in technical conclusions: Leach stresses long term energy statics whereas this study stresses transient energy dynamics, and the technical differences between the studies are less than might appear. This difference of approach is discussed in the Preface to this study, the original draft of which was prepared (in consultation with Leach) for the joint press conference at which Leach and the author both released their respective papers on 18 Dec 1974.

[†] In a personal communication (30 April 1975), Leach explains that this was his intention and that nuclear investment should be part of end use energy demand, though the correction is small at the slow growth rates he considered.

9. A final comment is in order on the purposes to which this study and similar analyses have been, and should be, put. Energy analysis is a tool for examining many of the energy implications of policy, just as economic analysis is a tool for examining many of the fiscal implications of policy. Conclusions about energy, like conclusions about money, are not in themselves policy conclusions, but can contribute to them through the exercise of welfare judgments. With energy, as with money, just because a policy is wasteful (or conserving), it is not necessarily a bad (or good) policy. The value of the analysis lies in giving policymakers a fuller understanding of particular kinds of consequences of particular policies than they had before.

Two general observations on methodology seem worthwhile. First, computational conventions other than those adopted here could be devised. The present conventions seem a sensible way of addressing the questions being asked. Provided always that the results are interpreted in the light of the appropriateness of the conventions used, it would be possible to use others. The important thing is that the conventions all be made explicit, as has been done in this paper. Second, the use of enthalpy rather than free energy as the basis of the present analysis does not mean that free energy analysis is not useful and appropriate for other purposes. Indeed, it is important to develop free energy analysis (a very difficult task) to help to examine mismatches of energy quality between sources and uses. Better thermodynamic matching of energy quality supplied with energy quality needed is undoubtedly an important potential source of energy savings, and deserves far more attention using common sense at least as much as complex computations.

Energy analysis is subject to numerous quantitative uncertainties, most of which will be evident to any careful reader of this paper, and some of which are not likely to be resolved by future research, though many can and will be. The numerical results in this paper are not, and cannot possibly be, definitive or precise. Indeed, it is because many of the parameters that determine energy dynamics are uncertain, disputed, or constantly changing—including the power ratios of various reactors (perhaps of mixed types) and the proposed rate of nuclear construction—that this paper has taken a wholly general approach to the dynamics of energy inputs and outputs in exponential programs. This generality should help the reader to develop a sound qualitative intuition for the sorts of transient problems that rapid growth can produce, and should offer a sufficient methodological basis to calculate, in an indicative way, the probable magnitudes of the energy flows relevant to policy: particularly the relative magnitudes, which are the most resistant to major inaccuracy.

Arguments based on energy analysis have a specific and limited place in the taxonomy of nuclear issues.[q] Nuclear power has many costs and benefits which society is called upon to assess and compare. Many of the costs are large and extremely important; some seem to many analysts to be unacceptably large no matter what the benefits may be. But if costs and benefits are to be formally balanced, then whatever the benefits are claimed to be, considerations arising from energy analysis are bound to reduce them, thus increasing the ratio of costs to benefits, or, as Chapter Fourteen puts it, making the nonenergetic arguments about nuclear power appear in a new light. Thus net energy problems are not, and should not be considered, a principal cost charged against nuclear power but rather a factor serving to reduce the benefits against which the formidable nonenergetic costs are to be balanced.

NOTES

a Chapman, P F, *New Scient 64*:866 (19 Dec 1974).

b Chapman, P F and Mortimer, N D, "Energy Inputs and Outputs for Nuclear Power Stations", ERG 005, Energy Research Group, Open University, Milton Keynes, Bucks., England, Sept 1974, revised Dec 1974.

c Kenward, M, *New Scient 65*:51 (9 Jan 1975).

d Wright, J and Syrett, J, *New Scient 65*:66 (9 Jan 1975).

e Bethe, H, letter to J Harding, 21 Feb 1975.

f Eden, R, personal communication to A B Lovins, 22 Jan 1975.

g Chapman, P F, *New Scient 65*:230 (23 Jan 1975).

h Slesser, M, *New Scient 65*:97 (9 Jan 1975).

i Slesser, M, "Energy analysis: conventions and methodology", IFIAS (Nobel House, Sturegatan 14, S–102 46 Stockholm, Sweden), 1974, $10, and *Nature 254*:170 (20 Mar 1975). For some similar thermodynamic material, see Gyftopoulos, E P *et al.*, *Potential Fuel Effectiveness in Industry*, Ballinger for The Energy Policy Project (Cambridge, Massachusetts, 1974).

j Creagan, R J (manager, R&D Planning), "Comments on 'Dynamic Energy Analysis and Nuclear Power'" and "Net Output of Energy from Nuclear Sources", 18 Dec 1974 and Oct 1974 respectively, Westinghouse Power Systems Planning (Westinghouse Electric Corp., 700 Braddock Ave, E Pittsburgh, PA 15112, USA).

k *Nucleon Wk 16*, 10, 7 (6 March 1975), reporting a contemporary speech by K Davis (a vice president of Bechtel Corp.) at the New Orleans Conference, Atomic Industrial Forum.

l Leach, G, "Nuclear Energy Balance in a World with Ceilings", International Institute for Environment and Development (27 Mortimer St, London W1, England), 18 Dec 1974.

m Leach, G, *New Scient 65*:160 (16 Jan 1975).

n Groupe Diogène (Groupe d'Etudes sur l'Homme, la Nature et l'Expansion, Université Cl. Bernard, 69621 Villeurbanne, France), "Le Bilan Énergétique du Programme Électro-Nucléaire Français", Les Amis de la Terre (16 rue de l'Université, 75007 Paris), March 1975.

o Électricité de France, "Énergie Consommée et Énergie Fournie par une Centrale Nucléaire", March 1975.

p Division de l'Équipement, des Transport et de l'Énergie, Direction de la Prévision, Ministère des Finances, "Note pour le Directeur du Cabinet" (38/C45, 2 Apr 1975) and "Le Bilan Énergétique de l'Industrie Électro-nucléaire" (39/C45, 2 Apr 1975).

q von Hippel, F *et al.*, "The Net Energy from Nuclear Reactors," *Professional Bulletin*, Federation of American Scientists, p 5, Apr 1975.

r Rombough, C T and Koen, B V, *Nucl Techn 26*:5 (1975).

Index

About the Authors

Amory Bloch Lovins resigned a Junior Research Fellowship of Merton College, Oxford in 1971 to become British Representative of Friends of the Earth Inc, a US nonprofit conservation group. A consultant physicist (mainly in the USA) since 1965, he now concentrates on energy and resource strategy. His current or recent clients, none of whom is responsible for his views, include the OECD, several UN agencies, the International Federation of Institutes for Advanced Study, the MIT Workshop on Alternative Energy Strategies, and other organizations in several countries. He is active in international energy affairs, has testified before parliamentary and congressional committees, has broadcast extensively, and has published four earlier books, several monographs, and numerous technical papers, articles, and reviews.

John H Price took his PhD in solid-state physics from Monash University (Australia) in 1971, then worked for a time with the Australian Commonwealth Scientific and Industrial Research Organization. From March 1974 to May 1975 he was an energy consultant to Friends of the Earth Ltd in London. He has published a number of technical papers.